# NEW STUDIES IN INDIAN AND COMPARATIVE PHILOSOPHY

# NEW STUDIES IN INDIAN AND COMPARATIVE PHILOSOPHY

R. RAJ SINGH
BROCK UNIVERSITY, CANADA

JACQUELINE KUMAR
QUEEN'S UNIVERSITY, CANADA

COMMON GROUND

First published in 2025
as part of **New Directions in the Humanities Book Imprint**
**Common Ground Research Networks**

University of Illinois Research Park
2001 South First St, Suite 201 L
Champaign, IL 61820 USA

Library of Congress Cataloging-in-Publication Data

Names: Singh, R. Raj, 1948- author. | Kumar, Jacqueline, author.
Title: New studies in Indian and comparative philosophy / R. Raj Singh,
  Brock University, Canada ; Jacqueline Kumar, Queen's University, Canada.

Description: Champaign, IL : Common Ground Research Networks, 2025. |
  "First published in 2025 as part of the New Directions in the Humanities
  Book Imprint"--Title page verso. | Includes bibliographical references.
  | Summary: "This book presents groundbreaking research on critical
  themes in Indian philosophy, challenging traditional interpretations
  often shaped by entrenched scholarly biases. It offers fresh
  perspectives on pivotal topics and includes comparative analyses of
  Western philosophers such as Schopenhauer and Simone Weil, who were
  deeply influenced by Indian philosophical thought. Their engagements
  with Indian philosophy are critically assessed, following a detailed
  exploration of their enduring interest and contributions to the field"--
  Provided by publisher.
Identifiers: LCCN 2024057294 (print) | LCCN 2024057295 (ebook) | ISBN
  9781966214069 (HBK) | ISBN 9781966214076 (PBK) | ISBN 9781966214083
  (pdf)
Subjects: LCSH: Philosophy, Indic--History. | Philosophy, Comparative. |
  East and West.
Classification: LCC B131 .S5494 2025  (print) | LCC B131  (ebook) | DDC
  181/.409--dc23/eng/20241213
LC record available at https://lccn.loc.gov/2024057294
LC ebook record available at https://lccn.loc.gov/2024057295

Cover Design: Phillip Kalantzis Cope
Cover Image: Shutterstock

# TABLE OF CONTENTS

# PREFACE

The field called comparative philosophy assumes that a single, homogeneous world philosophy can be envisioned, and a synthesis of eastern and western thought can be accomplished, if we acknowledge that philosophy is a universal undertaking and has happened in all lands. This book offers some studies of comparative philosophy, particularly reflecting on the work of some contemporary European thinkers who seem to be deeply interested in philosophies of India. At the same time, this book offers some new interpretations of Indian thought-systems. We also have here a bunch of specific studies in Indian philosophy which strive to rise above the traditional rationality-based investigations in favor of more living and devotion (*karma* and *bhakti*) based interpretations of Indian thought. The enterprise of comparative studies sheds a new light and enables more fulsome interpretation of the thinker's standpoint as the concepts designed by a thinker are exposed more comprehensively. A case in point is Schopenhauer's concepts of the will to live compared with Vedantic concept of *maya* (illusionary world-liness) or Buddhist concept of *trishna* (craving) or Heidegger's Being compared with Gandhi's *satya* (Truth).

In Part I, we have included seven chapters that explore from newer perspectives the philosophical contributions of some prominent Indian thinkers, namely, Gandhi, Kabir, Sri Aurobindo as well as essays on themes of *bhakti* and *yoga*. The first three chapters on Gandhi expose his stature as an original philosopher with an original ontology rather than his popular image as a political leader. The essay on Kabir outlines his meditation on the meaning of death and his view of an authentic life. Chapter 5 seeks to show that *bhakti* (devotion) remains an important ingredient of Buddhist worldview and bhakti is not strictly a Hindu notion. In Chapter 6, the themes of empathy and yoga are highlighted. Sri Aurobindo's concept of integral yoga and technology is studied in Chapter 7.

In Part II, seven chapters on the theme of comparative philosophy are compiled. In the first three chapters, the connections of Schopenhauer's philosophy with Indian philosophies are studied, along with a comparison of his aesthetic theories with those of Tagore. Chapter 11 compares Heidegger's ontological investigations with those of Gandhi. Chapter 12 delves into the themes of death and authentic life through a comparison of Plato's *Phaedo* with the Katha Upanishad. The last two chapters, Chapters 13 and 14, trace Simone Weil's connections with Hindu and Buddhist thought and show how her readings of Indian philosophies impacted on her work as well as her short but deeply authentic life.

R. Raj Singh
Jacqueline Kumar

# ACKNOWLEDGMENTS

A previous version of Chapter 8 appeared in Robert L. Wicks, ed. *The Oxford Handbook of Schopenhauer*, Oxford University Press (New York: 2020). A version of Chapter 10 previously appeared in Ken-ichi Sasaki, ed. *Asian Aesthetics,* Kyoto, Japan: Kyoto University Press, 2010. A version of Chapter 12 was previously published in *Asian Philosophy*, 4 (1994): 9–16.

# PART I

## Studies in Indian Philosophy

# CHAPTER 1

# Gandhi as Philosopher

*R. Raj Singh*

It is not commonly acknowledged that Gandhi was a philosopher of first rank. His contribution to the body of philosophical thought, scarcely measured hitherto, is most original, fundamental and promises to inspire philosophers of the future. Numerous accounts of Gandhian thought by scholars from history, political science, and journalism have invariably focused on Gandhi's thoughts on so-called practical problems of his life and times. Gandhi's contribution to philosophy has scarcely been analyzed. His simple equation between *satya* (truth) and *ahimsa* (nonviolence) is not merely an idealistic remedy for the social and political problems set into motion by materialism and greed of our times. It is also an original philosophical insight into the grounds of Being. It is an original contribution to the science of Being qua Being. His contemplations are certainly enriching and unique interpretations of eastern thought. This thought also amounts to a philosophical dialogue between Eastern and Western ways of thinking and is therefore a significant contribution to philosophy as such.

Among thousands of books written about Gandhi and his message to the world, there is hardly any that deals strictly speaking with Gandhi, the philosopher. Of course, Gandhi had much more to offer by way of intellectual stimulation through the written word than what may be called, strictly, philosophy. He wrote about all sorts of social, political, religious, and moral issues, both perennial and timely in nature. The bulk of his writings consist of journal articles and correspondence in which he responded to important moral questions, current affairs as well as personal problems and dilemmas of his correspondents. He did so to establish an amazing heart-to-heart contact with his countrymen and foreign friends. The pivotal concepts of truth and nonviolence were the goal and inspiration of all his analyses and conclusions. The body of his written work consists of a few books published in his lifetime, numerous journal articles, and speeches and correspondence published in over ninety volumes by the Government of India.

The collected works, being chronological rather than thematic, are not suitable for a thematic study of Gandhian thought. However, various anthologies in various sizes, themes, and forms are available for the study of Gandhian thought along with numerous pen-portraits of his life. A selection of anthologies and biographies including Gandhi's very revealing autobiography often suffice as an introduction to his philosophical worldview. Thus, Gandhi's philosophical insights are mostly strewn among his numerous journal articles and letters.

Gandhian studies are for the most part devoted to this thinker's contributions to the practical issues of 20th-century India, with some references to his international stature. Within the academic literature, works by political scientists, historians and scholars of religious studies analyze Gandhi's thoughts on various practical issues of his times along with some standard theoretical expositions of his concepts of *ahimsa, satya, satyagraha, sarvodaya*, etc. Of course, Gandhi's remarkable life and the sum-total of his actions, especially his outstanding service to his nation and his countrymen, has been scrutinized and documented in a vast body of second literature. However, to the scholarly custodians of Gandhian studies and purveyors of the Gandhi industry, the very notion of Gandhi as a philosopher is an anathema. An extensive analysis of Gandhi's theoretical contemplations is taken as an affront to Gandhi's practical achievements in political and religious spheres. In other words, between his theory and practice, most people who know something about Gandhi are impressed by his practical and succinct adages. Since a bulk of them have based their view of Gandhi through movies, documentaries and hearsay, and have not read any of Gandhi's writings, they maintain a positive or negative judgment of his historical persona, based on their own current value orientations. Thus, many young people, especially those enrolled in institutes of technology and science courses in the universities, regard Gandhi as a backward-looking unmodern leader, who did not realize the glorious possibilities of science and technology. The Hindu nationalists still hold grudges against Gandhi for being too soft on Muslim radicals and Pakistan. Many would regard him as a wily politician who employed original tactics to checkmate his political rivals. Although by and large, Gandhi is less popular in the land of his birth than in the world in general, many Indians do recognize the father of their nation as a saintly thinker and a far-sighted leader, who occupies his proud place among a long line of spiritual masters of the ancient land.

In this chapter, an attempt will be made to expose Gandhi's central concept of *satya* (truth) and outline his significant contributions to philosophy. The exposition of Gandhi's fundamental ontology will require another chapter, in which his all-important concept of *ahimsa* will be studied from a philosophical point of view. It will become clearer through our interpretations that we don't have to water down the notion of "philosophy" to impose the title of "philosopher" on Gandhi, a title he himself would not have taken as a compliment in its narrower sense. A brief comparison of Gandhian thought with that of Martin Heidegger will illustrate that Gandhi does fulfill the expectations of being a fundamental ontologist, without having been a practitioner of strictly academic and armchair contemplation. It will also expose an affinity between Heidegger and Gandhi on the issues of ontology, poetic dwelling and technological times.

## Gandhian Ontology

An authentic thinker needs to have a single and fundamental object of thought. This object is both the inspiration and final aim of all his thoughtful pursuits. "To think is to confine yourself to a single thought,"[1] says Heidegger, who is convinced that "thought's courage stems from the bidding of Being"[2] According to Heidegger, this single point of departure, this rootedness in Being, is the innermost energy of the craft of philosophizing, which begins from a wonder about Being and turns into a preoccupation with and an investigation of Being. In so far as philosophy does not dismiss but envisions and employs the broadest possible perspectives on all that is and all that ought to be, it may be deemed to be rooted in fundamental ontology. To spell out the ontological grounds of philosophy and reiterate its all-encompassing approach has been a major theme of Heidegger's thought.

A philosophical study of Gandhi's writings shows us that his thoughtful understanding of Being (*satya*) as nonviolence (*ahimsa*) is a major contribution to the field of ontology and as a thinker he not only confined himself to a single thought but also carried out the bidding of Being in his work. Thus, being preoccupied primarily with the meaning of Being and in spelling out the basic tendencies of modernity and technological times Heidegger has a lot in common with Gandhi.

However, any comparison between Gandhi and Heidegger and their respective notions of Being may arouse immediate objections. Heidegger is a Western philosopher preoccupied primarily with a critique of the march of Western

---

[1] Martin Heidegger, "The Thinker as Poet," in *Poetry, Language, Thought,* trans. Albert Hofstadter (New York, Harper Perennial Modern Classics, 1975), 4.

[2] Ibid., p. 5.

metaphysics and has almost nothing to say about the eastern philosophical traditions to which Gandhi belongs. Gandhi is clearly a people's philosopher whereas Heidegger may be called the philosopher's philosopher. Heidegger, if the reports about his naïve romance with Nazism are true, was a failure as a political thinker whereas Gandhi successfully led a largely nonviolent political struggle to win independence of India and acquired in the estimation of many, the rank of a philosopher-king. Heidegger meditated on Being in Germany's black-forest, Gandhi did so in the public arena. Some will call Heidegger an armchair philosopher and Gandhi a man of action (*karma yogi*). Others will call Gandhi a social reformer and Heidegger a sophisticated academician. It will also be pointed out that Gandhi openly equates his notion of Being with God whereas Heidegger is avowedly a secular thinker.

These relatively superficial differences between two of the foremost thinkers of the 20th century cannot be denied. The object of our study is not to prove that Gandhi and Heidegger are similar in all respects. One of the benefits of comparative philosophy is that it enables us to comprehend and appreciate the otherwise hidden implications of the works of the thinkers or themes under investigation. When one examines the thought-system of a thinker from the vantage point of the conceptualizations of another, exploring and responding to the selfsame problems, a new light is shed on the work of both. Thus, the object of our study is to expose the affinity between the standpoints of Gandhi and Heidegger on issues of ontology and technology. We will assess Gandhi's status as an original philosopher by outlining his remarkable contribution to the field of ontology in comparison with Heidegger's ontological project. It will also offer a new elucidation of Heidegger's later thought on technology and the loss of poetic dwelling in our times.

Despite the above-mentioned formal differences between the two thinkers, reflection on the meaning of Being remains the basic project of their thought systems. Thinking and acting in the bidding of Being constituted the core of their philosophical explorations. What Heidegger calls Being and temporal and existential implications of which he traces in his works, cannot be essentially different from what Gandhi calls *satya* and regards it as a coin the other side of which he expresses as *ahimsa* (nonviolence). Both these thinkers point toward a forgetfulness of Being that characterizes our times and toward the pitfalls of a thoughtless faith in and applications of technology. Since Heidegger addresses primarily the academic readers and Gandhi speaks to innocent masses, there is a difference in their terminologies and the styles of writing. But both express creatively and powerfully the conclusions of their thought quests.

Heidegger's remarkable contribution lies in his valuable reminders to contemporary Western philosophy that thinking about Being must remain part and parcel of the activity called philosophizing. Even though Heidegger remains open to other possible frameworks for the meaning of Being,[3] and calls his own efforts in ontology merely preparatory, provisional and incomplete,[4] he confines himself to an exposition of the temporal horizon of the meaning of Being in accordance with the traditional Greek understanding of Being lodged in a temporal span. Gandhi, however, offers an entirely new basis for a fundamental understanding of Being to contemporary ontology. This new point of departure for ontological contemplation is what he calls *ahimsa*, the inner meaning of *satya* (Truth), that is, *sat* (Being).[5] Gandhi's originality in the field of ontology lies in proposing an alternative notion of Being to its age-old philosophical understanding rooted in temporality, and thereby proposing a new challenge to "thinking about Being" with its infinite possibilities and prospects for "thought." Furthermore, although Gandhi borrows the concepts of *satya* and *ahimsa* from his own tradition of Indian philosophy, acknowledging these as "as old as the hills,"[6] what remains his original contribution is as follows: (1) the uplifting of *ahimsa* in its traditional characterization as an ethical virtue to its new exposition as an ontological ground; (2) the application of *ahimsa* as a fundamental ideal to the practical problems of human existence as well as to the problems of modernity and technicity. Thus, Gandhi's ontological insight is not only an original contribution to Indian philosophy but also a thought-provoking enrichment of the philosophy of Being, which is beyond the Eastern and Western categories. When Gandhi repeatedly affirms in his works that "*ahimsa* is the law of our Being," "*ahimsa* is the other side of the coin of *satya*" and "Truth is God,"[7] he imparts in very simple words his insight that nonviolence is nothing shorter than the meaning of Being. *Ahimsa* has always been advanced as an ethical virtue and has been a central thematic concept in Indian philosophies and religions from ancient times. Buddhism emphasized it as *karuna* (compassion), as the essence of the eightfold path, and as the central theme of the *Mahayana* movement. It is an important exhortation

---

[3.] Martin Heidegger, *What Is Called Thinking*, trans. F. E. Wrick and J. G. Gray (New York: Harper & Row, 1968), 3.

[4.] Martin Heidegger, *Being and Time*, trans. J. Macquarrie and E. Robinson (New York: Harper & Row, 1962), 21–24.

[5.] M. K. Gandhi, *All Men Are Brothers*, ed. Krishna Kriplani (New York: Continuum, 1987), 74 (*Yeravada Mandir*, 1935).

[6.] Ibid., p. 1 (*Harijan*, March 28, 1936).

[7.] Ibid., p. 74 (*Yeravada Mandir*, 1935). All emphases within quoted text are from the original.

in the edicts of Emperor Asoka, who voluntarily renounced war in the 3rd century BC. The Jain religion considers *ahimsa* as the supreme dharma (moral law) in its well-known aphorism (*ahimsa paramo dharma*). Within his own philosophical tradition Gandhi is by no means the author of the concept of *ahimsa*.

Gandhi's contribution to human thought lies in his exposition of *ahimsa* as an ontological principle in which human beings participate by nature in order to be essentially human. He labors to explain various perspectives that *ahimsa* is not merely an ethical value, and violence and nonviolence are not two equally open alternatives of conduct. Violence is but a violation for it violates the core of Being; it is inhuman because human beings basically and constantly think, create, and participate in Being. Our creative endeavors within the world are carried on in *ahimsa*, the *dharma* (the law) of our Being. Gandhi's other contributions are well known. His exemplary living of *ahimsa* and his application of it to the 20th-century social and political predicaments. Like Heidegger, he exposes the exploitative and earth destroying consequences of blind applications of technology in service of human greed for wealth and power. Gandhi does not endeavor to reverse the clock of technicity but only informs us that the possibilities of living the life of *ahimsa* are still open and still real.

## Gandhi's Concept of Being as "Satya"

Gandhi uses the term *satya* or Truth for the ultimate reality, calling it his "pole star all along during life's journey."[8] That means his preoccupation with what he calls "Truth" was a lifelong quest. That Gandhi approaches this notion of the Real intimately but philosophically, that is devotedly but undogmatically is evident from the title he chose for his autobiography, namely, "the story of my experiments with Truth." Gandhi's choice of the name *satya* or Truth for the Being of beings is based on several considerations. Firstly, it is a concept well known even to the most innocent villager, that is, it is not a term understood only by scholars and intellectuals. Secondly, it is not a sectarian term, confined merely to a particular religious or cultural tradition. Thus, Gandhi refrains from using the traditional Vedantin (Hindu) term *brahman* for Being. Thirdly, Truth is something to which both the believers and non-believers in God can relate.

---

[8.] M. K. Gandhi, *The Essential Writings of Mahatma Gandhi,* ed. Raghavan Iyer (Delhi, Oxford University Press, 1993), 229 (*Young India,* December 10, 1925).

Fourthly, Truth is a notion in which theory and practice, value and conduct find their immediate confluence; Truth seems to carry its commandment for truthful conduct with it. That Gandhi means *sat* by *satya* is clearly stated by him:

> The word *satya* comes from *sat*, which means "to be," "to exist." Only God is ever the same through all time…I have been but striving to serve that truth.[9]

> The word *satya* is derived from *sat*, which means that which is. *Satya* means a state of Being. Nothing is or exists in reality except truth. That is why *sat* or *satya* is the right name for God. In fact it is more correct to say that Truth is God than to say God is Truth.[10]

The equation of Truth with God is a hallmark of Gandhi's philosophical and religious thought. While it is indicative of his tendency to simplify his message for his audience and readers, his conclusions are based on lifelong "experiments with truth" and original thinking. In his simple equations such as "Truth is God," "*satya* and *ahimsa* are two sides of the same coin," "*ahimsa* is love," "*ahimsa* is justice all around," he presents the crux of his philosophical achievement in the language of people in a universal idiom. Without losing his soul as an Indian philosopher, he can communicate to readers around the world about perennial moral and existential issues of fundamental importance.

When Gandhi says, "Truth is God," both Truth and God are given connotations that are far from being commonplace. The equation of truth with God is not only indicative of Gandhi's own *bhakti*, an affirmation of a devotional pursuit of truth, by means of *ahimsa*, but also an attempt to depersonalize and desectarianize God. It is a God that is not a person but indistinguishable from *dharma*, the moral order, the law. It is a God that the Buddha installed rather than unseated. It is a God that is nothing but Truth. If called by its essential name Truth, it appeals to Hindus and non-Hindus, Christians and Muslims, Indians and Westerners, theists and atheists, alike. It can be reached by method of a life of *ahimsa*, the law of the being of a human being, by its devoted pursuit (*bhakti*) through service of fellow humans and all things that live. For Gandhi, *bhakti* is essentially service. Truth is the "religion," not to be confused with "religions." We will discuss Gandhi's

---

[9.] Ibid., p. 225 (*Navajivan*, November 20, 1921).

[10.] Ibid., p. 231 (Letter to Narandas Gandhi, July 23, 1932).

concept of God in a separate section but let us review briefly his all-important equation of Truth with *ahimsa* and its ontological implications.

It is Gandhi's equation of *satya* with *ahimsa* that is an original contribution to philosophy. For no other thinker has designated *ahimsa* as the very meaning of *sat*. Gandhi has opened up a new dimension for a thinker's thinking about Being:

> *Ahimsa* and Truth are so intertwined that it is practically impossible to disentangle and separate them. They are like two sides of a coin, or rather a smooth unstumped metallic disc.[11]

> Are non-violence and Truth twins. The answer is emphatic "No." Non-violence is embedded in Truth and vice-versa.[12]

Gandhi's elevation of *ahimsa* to the level of Being makes it much more than mere non-injury. It is given a positive meaning and posed as a challenge to thinking. Thus, it is not easy for anyone to tell *ahimsa* apart from *ahimsa* simplistically.

> Non-violence is not an easy thing to understand, still less to practice, weak as we are.[13]

> I have never claimed to present the complete science of non-violence. It does not lend itself to such treatment.[14]

Although Gandhi clearly advocates impassioned thought on that silent but beckoning reality of *ahimsa*, and the application of caution, doubt, and restraint in defining it, as well as readiness to revise one's view of truth in the light of new facts, he goes beyond a mere armchair meditation on *ahimsa*. He endeavored to apply his ontological insights to guide his contemporary men and women toward nonviolent living and toward a predominantly nonviolent society, often teaching by the example of conduct and through concrete social and political projects.

Gandhi's integrated worldview developed out of what he called his "experiments with truth." "To think is to confine oneself to a single thought,"[15] says

---

[11.] Gandhi, *All Men Are Brothers*, p. 74 (*Yeravada Mandir*, 1935).

[12.] Ibid., p. 76 (*Harijan*, July, 1947).

[13.] Ibid., p. 89 (*Young India*, February 7, 1929).

[14.] Ibid., p. 79 (*Harijan*, February 22, 1942).

[15.] Heidegger, "The Thinker as Poet," p. 4.

Heidegger. What he means is that a thinker must weave his thinking around a single fundamental object of thought which is an inspiration and final goal at the same time. *Satya*, that is *ahimsa*, was Gandhi's single tireless pursuit. It was the inspiration and aspiration of his thought. Reflecting on the meaning of Being as nonviolence gave him numerous cues for personal reform and social transformation. Being as nonviolence remains for him an inexhaustible object of thought which he, as a believer, equates with God. In his emphasis on *ahimsa* as a fundamental attribute of Being, Gandhi has introduced a new dimension in the philosophy of Being. "To be is to be in non-violence" is an insight that will continue to intrigue philosophers and social reformers for a long, long time.

## Gandhi's Quest for Satya

Gandhi's quest to fathom the implications of Truth was lifelong and personal. For him, pursuit of *dharma* (moral order) by an individual as well as the society boiled down to "following the Truth," and he often did not distinguish between Truth, truthful conduct and truth-telling. Nevertheless, the enigma of what he calls the absolute truth which he equates with God, is philosophically pursued by him at various stages of his career. In his brief account of his childhood in the autobiography, Gandhi mentions how deeply a play based on the legend of King Harishchandra moved him as a child of seven:

> This play—Harishchandra—captured my heart. I could never be tired of seeing it. But how often should I be permitted to go? It haunted me and I must have acted Harishchandra to myself times without number. "Why should not all be truthful like Harishchandra?" was the question I asked myself day and night. To follow Truth and to go through all the ordeals Harishchandra went through was the one ideal it inspired in me. I literally believed in the story of Harishchandra. The thought of it all often made me weep.[16]

A perusal of Gandhi's career documented copiously within the numerous biographical sketches that constitute the bulk of secondary literature on him, shows that he developed his concept of truth through ceaseless philosophical reflection as well

---

[16.] M. K. Gandhi, *The Story of My Experiments with Truth—An Autobiography* (Ahmedabad: Navajivan Publishing House, 1948), 7.

as through his lived experiences of his remarkable life. Although he was much impressed by Christian thought as well as by his careful readings of Western classics, particularly by the writings of Ruskin and Tolstoy, he is fundamentally driven by a Vedanta worldview of which he offers a most universal, nonsectarian, secular, and philosophical version. Thus, within his elucidations of the concept of Truth, the echoes of the Vedic notions of *brahman, atman, dharma*, and *maya* can be heard.

In his youthful years in South Africa, Gandhi realized early in his career that he needed to communicate his ideas in a universal and secular terminology that would be easily understood by Hindus, Muslims, and Christians, Indian and Western readers alike. Thus, he developed a talent for expressing deeply philosophical insights in simple, concise but powerful language. His deep study of the Hindu and Vedic texts is indicated by an article[17] that he wrote in 1905 in response to a certain convocation address delivered by Lord Curzon, viceroy of India, at Calcutta University. This article published in one of the first journals edited by Gandhi, namely, *Indian Opinion*, reacts to Lord Curzon's assertion that "the highest ideal of truth is to a large extent a Western conception" and that "undoubtedly truth took a high place in the moral codes of the West before it was similarly honoured in the East, where craftiness and diplomatic wile have always been held in much repute."

In response to this thoughtless verdict that the concept of Truth and its importance as the cornerstone of ethics is a purely Western gift to the East in modern times, Gandhi politely asks for Curzon to withdraw his "baseless and offensive imputations." He commends some selected texts from Indian scriptures, beginning with some quotes from *Sama Veda, Mundaka Upanishad*, and *Taittiriya Upanishad* as well as from the Mahabharata epic and from some modern texts of Sikhism and Kabir, indicating that the importance of the pursuit of Truth was always emphasized in Indian scriptures and philosophical texts. It is interesting that Gandhi recognized the high value given to Truth in Sikhism wherein the founder of the Sikh faith Guru Nanak addresses God with the name "Sach" (satya) frequently in his hymns. This is followed by Gandhi who also maintains that the essence of God is Truth in assertions such as, "I thought earlier that 'God is Truth' but now have come to the conclusion that in fact, 'Truth is God,'" that is, Truth is the most outstanding attribute of God. Here are some scriptural quotes offered by Gandhi to Lord Curzon for his consideration:

[17] M. K. Gandhi, "Oriental Ideal of Truth," *Indian Opinion*, April 1, 1905, in *Moral and Political Writings of Mahatma Gandhi* (Delhi, Oxford University Press, 1973), 150–154.

(1)  Cross the path so difficult to cross. Conquer wrath with peace; untruth with Truth. (Sama Veda, Arka parva).

(2)  Truth alone prevails and not untruth. Truth is the pathway which learned men tread. (Mundaka Upanishad, III.1.6)

(3)  There is nothing greater than truth, and Truth should be esteemed the most sacred of all things. (Ramayana)

(4)  No act of devotion can equal Truth; no crime is so heinous as falsehood; in the heart where Truth resides, there is God's abode. (Kabir)

This letter was published in Gandhi's journal Indian Opinion in 1905. This indicates that Gandhi's involvement with the concept of truth was already underway in his South Africa days. Although Gandhi mentions that street drama "Harishchandra" impressed him so much in his boyhood days. Thus, this "pole star" of life's journey had appeared in Gandhi's earliest days and began to shape his philosophical progress which turned into an original contemplation of Being in his mature career.

# CHAPTER 2

# Gandhi and the Grounds of Nonviolence

*R. Raj Singh*

Our times seem to unfold violence in its traditional as well as unforeseen modes. It raises its head so frequently and in so many forms that many accept it as a reality that can only be dealt with, not done away with. Most people disapprove of it morally, but many accept it ontologically by believing that it is here to stay not only as an instinctual drive but also as a potent safeguard and as an effective deterrent.

What is this bewildering phenomenon called violence? It is disapproved as an end yet approved as a means to combat itself. Many are appalled by it, but for many it is fascinating and entertaining. In psychological life it is sheer agony. In social life, it is a clash of interests. In politics, it is the exploitation of the multitudes. In religious spheres, it appears in the form of sectarianism and fanaticism. In family life, it demeans the most fundamental of all relationships.

If philosophy is to explain and enrich our life, it must reflect about violence. Does violence have a deeper structure? One of the approaches toward an adequate definition of violence can be to trace its relations with nonviolence. If violence and nonviolence are mere contraries, to define one is to have defined the other as well. If the presence of violence is not merely the absence of nonviolence and vice versa, then we have to describe the nature of both individually. The attempts to define violence philosophically, rare as they are, have seldom explored the nature and role of nonviolence as a first step toward understanding what violence is. But one such attempt, remarkable in its scope and application, was made by Gandhi.

In this chapter, we will deal with the problem of the definition of nonviolence and that of recognizing its role in this age of technology. We will particularly expose Gandhi's concepts of *ahimsa* (nonviolence) and *satyagraha* (truth insistence) to show how in this thinker's scheme of things forces of violence can be identified and resisted in today's world. Gandhi's ideas provide not only a conceptual apparatus to think about what our world has become but also show a way out of our self-destructive tendencies.

As an example of the analyses which bypass the issue of nonviolence and probe the nature of violence directly but philosophically, let us first consider a definition proposed by Newton Garver. In his article "What Violence Is,"[1] Garver informs us that violence is not merely a philosophical force but a violation of a person. When persons are violated with respect to their bodies it is physical violence, whereas the violation of their ability to make their own decisions may be called psychological violence. These two kinds of violence have their personal and institutionalized forms, according to Garver. Examples of physical violence are muggings, rape, murder, riots, terrorism, war, and those of psychological violence are personal threats, character assassination, slavery, racism, sexism, etc. The merit of Garver's account does not lie in the distinction of the psychological from the physical—for all these violent physical acts also have their psychological repercussions—but in his recognition that violence is a violation of human rights. These rights are stated by Garver as follows: "(1) the right to determine what one's body does and what is done to one's body; (2) the right to make one's own decisions and to deal with the consequences of one's actions."

The implications of the violation of the rights defined by Garver can be understood in their wider context. At the most general level such violations may include any and every act of injustice. It is implicit in Garver's account that violence, both visible and invisible, has a deeper structure. To understand the roots of violence philosophically one may ask: what is it the violation of? Can it be called the violation of nonviolence?

When then is nonviolence? According to Gandhi whose whole life was devoted to the investigation and practice of this concept, it is the law of our species; "it is a great force which is active every moment of our lives; It is felt in our every action and thought."[2] The first thing that Gandhi wishes us to appreciate is that nonviolence or *ahimsa* is not to be equated with violence or *himsa* as two alternatives in our active life. *Ahimsa* is lived experience for the most part. It is eventless, unspectacular, and unnoticed but, nevertheless, present in all we think and do. History being a record of spectacular events tends to highlight violence, but the history of civilization has been one of progressive *ahimsa* and diminishing violence. *Ahimsa* is the central concept in Gandhi's thought. His personal and

---

[1] Newton Garver, "*What Violence Is*" in *Philosophical Issues*, ed. James Rachels and Frank Tillman (New York: Harper and Row, 1972), 223–228. First published in The Nation, 209 (1968): 817–822.

[2] M. K. Gandhi, *Moral and Political Writings of Mahatma Gandhi*, ed. Raghavan Iyer. Vol. 2 (London: Oxford University Press, 1986), 238.

social experiments, his writings, speeches, and his exemplary conduct were all geared toward explaining the role of *ahimsa* in human life. Yet he does not give us a succinct definition of it apart from saying that it is the only means toward self-realization.

In *Beyond Good and Evil,* Nietzsche remarks that "everywhere the destinations of moral value were at first applied to 'men,' and were only derivatively and at a later period applied to 'actions,' it is a gross mistake, therefore, when historians of morals start with questions like, 'why have sympathetic actions being praised?' "[3] What Nietzsche means is that distinguished lives and noble character were there to be witnessed before people started to wonder about questions such as "what is virtue?" Hence, lived moral thinking impresses us more than the unlived moral speculation. Gandhi was a thinker who could justly claim: "my life is my message."

Accordingly, as we consider the philosophical grounds of Gandhi's message, we must also consider what kind of a man he was and what kind of life he sketched for a nonviolent social worker. His writings consisting of books, journal articles, speeches, diaries, and letters have been published in ninety volumes.[4] They contain the results of his experiments, the conclusions of over sixty years of thinking about the nonviolent life of contemporary man. Gandhi says that he has written nothing for writing's sake nor for the sake of knowledge but for the sake of causes dear to him. Hence, if odd statements are lifted out of his writings without context and without an appreciation of his general quest, they must seem inconsistent and full of platitudes. However, a consistent philosophical ground does show itself in Gandhi's life and work. He was not a scholar or a philosopher of the kind we have in the universities. He was not an otherworldly Eastern mystic either. He was a practical thinker who applied himself to problems concrete human beings are facing today. In the words of Tagore, he was a lover of man, not of ideas.

Why should one hold on to *ahimsa* and not let it be violated by violence? For the sake of *satya*, Gandhi said. *Satya* is the Sanskrit word for Truth, of which the root word is *Sat* (Being). Gandhi takes *Satya* in the sense of *Sat*, although he translated it as Truth. One has to cultivate nonviolence because it is the other side of Being. "*Ahimsa* and *satya* are like two sides of a coin or rather of an

---

[3] Friedrich Nietzsche, *Beyond Good and Evil*, trans. Helen Zimmern (London: George Allen & Unwin, 1967), 228.

[4] Publications Division, Government of India has published Gandhi's complete works in ninety volumes under the title *The Collected Works of Mahatma Gandhi.*

unstamped metallic disc."[5] "*Ahimsa* is Satya" means that one is not embracing
nonviolence because one wants to be "human," that is, one-self. Why is *ahimsa*
the meaning of Being? Because violence is essentially Being destructive. It does
not destroy merely things but bonds among things; it violates the existence itself.
Not destruction but creation or "emergence and persistence" is the meaning of
Being. Man, who is a builder by nature and receiver of Being, has *ahimsa* as
the law of his species.

Why does Gandhi translate *Satya* as Truth and not as Being? He wants the
goal of all our goals to be named Truth because it has a direct connection with
one's conduct. It is a concept that is not confined to a particular religion and is
one that is relevant for atheists and theists alike. To borrow the Vedantic terminology, *Satya* is understood at a *parmarthika* (ontological) level but named
at *vyavaharika* (practical) level as Truth by Gandhi. Truth for him is what *Tou
Agathon* is for Plato. As Heidegger asserts in his "Plato's Doctrine of Truth," to
think of *Agathon* in merely moral terms and in terms of a value is inconsistent
with its original Greek meaning as "the most phenomenal of beings."[6] In the
same way *Satya* and *ahimsa* are not merely moral but ontological concepts of
Gandhi. "There is an unalterable Law governing everything and every being
that exists or lives...Nothing is or exists except Truth." Gandhi's Truth Has
all the characteristics of *Samkara's Brahman*, that is, *Sat.chit.ananda* (Being,
consciousness, bliss) except that he does not call it *Brahman*.

While opposing sectarianism Gandhi did not work for the demise of religion.
By repeatedly asserting "God is Truth" and "Truth is God," he wanted to direct
people's living faiths toward nonviolent conduct and social progress. Religion that
is to be kept alive is not the "formal religion or customary religion but that religion
that underlines all religions."[7] By the assertion "God is Truth" he meant God is
not a personal being but a supreme idea, principle, or law which is to be upheld
in nonviolent conduct and love. By maintaining "Truth is God" Gandhi wants to
convey that the Truth that he is referring to is not epistemological but ontological.
It is not merely "correctness," but that which gives all existence the warrant to be.

Is Gandhi's concept of *ahimsa* original or is he simply recirculating an ethical concept of Indian thought? Of course, the notion appears in ancient Hindu,

[5] M. K. Gandhi, *All Men Are Brothers*, ed. Krishna Kriplani (New York: Continuum, 1987), 96.

[6] Martin Heidegger, "Plato's Doctrine of Truth," trans. John Barlow in *Philosophy* in *The Twentieth Century*, ed. William Barrett and Henty Aiken, Vol. 3 (New York: Random House, 1962), 263.

[7] M. K. Gandhi, From *Yeravada Mandir* (Ahmedabad: Navajivan Mudranalaya, 1945), 1.

Buddhist, and Jain scriptures, but Gandhi's originality lies in ascribing an onto-logical meaning to it as well as in applying it to contemporary social, economic, and political situations.

*Ahimsa* is not passivity according to Gandhi. It is not merely avoidance or shunning of violence but actively offering resistance to it. The practice of *ahimsa* engages us in acts of love and compassion for living beings as well as in an ongoing struggle with the forces of violence within us and around us. Thought of *ahimsa* exhorts us to cultivate Being; thus, "non-participation" is not equivalent to "being" nonviolent. "*Ahimsa* is nothing if not a well-balanced and exquisite consideration for one's neighbor."[8] Not to hurt life is no doubt part of *ahimsa*, but it is its least expression. Gandhi acknowledges that perfect *ahimsa* in the sense of nonviolation of life is impossible. Our acts of breathing, eating, and physical movement involve annihilation of life in some form. However, the cultivation of being in human life means the reduction of the cycle of violence as far as possible. Gandhi even condoned euthanasia if all other avenues were exhausted.

> Trouble with our votaries of ahimsa is that they have made non-killing a blind fetish and put the greatest obstacles in the way of the spread of true ahimsa in our midst. There may be far more violence in the slow torture of men and animals, starvation, and exploitation to which they are subjected out of selfish greed, the wanton humiliation and oppression of the weak and the killing of their self-respect that we witness all around us today, then in mere benevolent taking of life.[9]

It was in response to "the wanton humiliation and oppression of the weak and the killing of their self-respect" that Gandhi formulated the concept of *Sarvo-daya* (emancipation for all). In the name of *ahimsa,* one should neither cause nor tolerate indignities and fear. Honor and resistance are more important than noninjury. *Ahimsa,* Gandhi repeatedly asserted, is a method of the truly brave, that is, those who are "ready to die but unwilling to kill."[10] *Ahimsa* is most potent when it is practiced in thought, word, and deed. For one who wishes to work for emancipation, *ahimsa* is to be a living creed not just a policy. *Satyagraha* is to be carried out by these few soldiers of nonviolence.

---

[8.] Gandhi, *All Men Are Brothers*, p. 51.

[9.] Gandhi, *Moral and Political Writings of Mahatma Gandhi*, p. 227.

[10.] Ibid., p. 272.

What is *satyagraha?* Literally, it means insistence on *satya*. It is a dual instance, that in the sense of self-discipline and that in the sense of striving to achieve justice. One insists on adopting the right means and on achieving what is one's and one's neighbor's due. The root word *agaraha* in *satyagraha* means both pleading and insisting. One begins by pleading to an informing the wrong doer about what is wrong and insists on his change of heart. It is a pleading turning into demanding. In *satyagraha* what is to be overcome is the "us" and "they" dichotomy; one is to despise the wrong not the wrongdoer. This overcoming of adversaryhood and hate is nonviolence of thought. Nonviolence of word means refraining from harsh language, slogans and verbal warfare. Nonviolence of deed means readiness to pay in the coin of suffering but not causing physical damage to property or bodily harm to anybody.

For the *satyagraha* self-discipline, that is, nonviolent living is most important. His or her chief qualification is readiness to die. Gandhi had no illusions about the enormity of the task of ridding our life of violence. Justice for all, peaceful coexistence, abolition of hunger and war are not the ideals that will be easily realized. He found it strange that some reformers were hoping to secure disarmament and peace by holding symposia and public information campaigns. Mere boycotts of war effort will not end war. Noncooperation with violence has to be total and to be strengthened with the coin of suffering. *Satyagraha* is not a game of numbers. Gandhi purposely restricted the number of activists in his movements. What is required is a significant commitment to serve, patience, perseverance, faith, and fearlessness. Gandhi did not want his followers to imitate him in renunciation, fasting, and austere lifestyle but encouraged them to carry on self-reform at their own pace, for the first battle with violence is to be fought in the life of the self. However, he did define some ideals that those desirous of practicing nonviolence should focus on in their personal lives. Some of those ideals are *Brahmacharya*, nonstealing, nonpossession, control of the palate, etc.

According to Gandhi, *Brahmacharya* or "Brahman-conduct" is the direction of all one's energies toward service and practice of self-control. Nonpossession is a refusal to own what one does not really need or a reduction of one's possessions as far as possible. To let *ahimsa* abide in us the palate requires our particular attention for it is the seat of taste and of speech. One has to eat to live and to survive; a sumptuous meal should make one guilty for it is not available to all. Acquiring things that one does not really need while these are needed by others is stealing. Economic exploitation that is built in most economies of the world is also stealing. We are all thieves in this sense and ought to reduce the cycle of theft as far as possible. Nations too are in possession of stolen wealth. Thinking along such lines and practice of social duty and all our actions will enable us to live more nonviolently.

Gandhi realized that pure *ahimsa* does not dawn upon us in a makeshift way. It might fail as an expedient or as a policy, but it succeeds as a way of life. It requires an attempt equal to the force of violence it is supposed to encounter. Gandhi's ideas are relevant for both so-called developed and developing nations today. These ideas grant us a perspective to identify the actions and policies that are constantly encouraging the forces of violence. At the same time, Gandhi reflects on how nonviolence can be preserved and cultivated in today's world. Some of the visible catalysts of violence or economic and political exploitation, technology, mass production, centralization, the status of women, sectarianism, racism, current state of international relations, etc.

The problems associated with the impact of technology were studied as the relation between man and the machine by Gandhi. He realized that technology has the nature of being all-encompassing. It eliminates the spiritual worldviews, centralizes power structures and standardizes all measures of reality. Heidegger refers in *An Introduction to Metaphysics* to a darkening of the world or emasculation of the spirit in our times. According to him, the essential episodes of this darkening are: "the fight of the gods, the destruction of the earth, the standardization of man, the pre-eminence of the mediocre."[11] Gandhi too is concerned about these very impacts of technology and industrialism. Technology as "one way of revealing Being (which) is overwhelming men and beings and all other ways of revealing" as Heidegger explains in *The Question Concerning Technology*"[12] It is what is most alarming about technology for Gandhi as well. He exhorted India to remain being India and not lose its soul in imitating the West, not because he loved India as his own, but because man must continue to be diverse and must not let himself be standardized. Gandhi thought that because technology is here to stay we must study what it does to human relations. The return to the machineless age is neither possible nor desirable, but the violent impacts of technology and industrialism can be reduced through a nonviolent restructuring of society.

---

[11] Martin Heidegger, *An Introduction to Metaphysics*, trans. Ralph Manheim (New Haven: Yale University Press, 1959), 45.

[12] Martin Heidegger, *The Question Concerning Technology*, trans. William Lovitt (New York: Harper and Row, 1977), 3–35.

Gandhi can find his *satyagraha* to India for several reasons none of which is chauvinistic. He wanted at least one *satyagraha* to succeed, so that people of the world, impressed with this example, will believe in the efficiency of nonviolent means to redress social and political wrongs. He knew that the tide of technology and industrialism would sweep away the alternative worldviews. He said that "if the village perishes India will perish too. India will be no more India. Her own mission in the world will get lost."[13] Gandhi thought that *ahimsa* must be seen to be believed and nonmaterialistic people from the villages could show it in their innocent life. Moreover, to one's service, which is the positive meaning of *ahimsa*, one's neighbors have the first claim. If service is to be our way of life and not merely an occasional active patronage, it is more consistently carried out in the vicinity of one's home. True service, Gandhi said, is like the payment of a debt, not mere charity.

> I must refuse to insult the naked by giving them clothes instead of work they sorely need. I will not commit the sin of being their patron, but on the learning that I have had assisted in impoverishing them. I would give them neither cast-off clothing, but the best of my food and clothes and associate myself with them in work.[14]

Gandhi maintained that unrestricted technology and urbanization constituted the greatest threat to the diverse cultures of the world. Gods of India were sure to take flight just as the Greek gods, as man's goals became entirely this worldly. It is essential therefore that the parts of the world which have not yet fallen prey to "the development model" must resist it, modify it, and not demean what they themselves have to offer to the world. This does not mean that Gandhi idealized poverty. He had his own plan for the renewal of the village which had been taking a beating from colonialism.

Gandhi's ideas on what is violent and how to resist it were dismissed by many as the longings of a visionary both in the land of his birth and elsewhere. His austere lifestyle and the self-discipline he required from the *Satyagrahis* gave many the impression that his program was too radical and unreal and constituted a denial of what had been achieved through modernity and technology. All such impressions are rooted in a mistaken view of Gandhi. Economics, ecologists, humanists, and democrats are finding out that the acts of violence against the

---

[13.] Gandhi, *All Men Are Brothers*, p. 116.

[14.] Ibid., p. 122.

have-nots and against nature cannot go on forever. What Gandhi suggests does not deny modernity; rather, he is devoted to resolving modern problems and bringing the much needed hope. He asked all nations to introduce economies of restraint based on voluntary reduction of wants and acknowledge that all excess are acts of stealing.

According to Gandhi, unrestricted industrialization and mass production are wasteful and lead to economic inequality. The gulf between ethics and economics widens in proportion to the size of the industries a nation has. "Today Machinery merely helps a few to ride on the back of millions. The impetus behind it all is not the philanthropy to save labor, but greed."[15] Gandhi visualizes nonviolent societies in which the self-employed producers—farmers and artisans engaged in the production of local requirements—will be predominant. He believed that any system that curtails the economic self-realization of the small-scale producer is against human nature. Some large-scale industry producing electricity, steel, machine and tools, ships, etc. may exist, but only the small units of production should be the backbone of a nonviolent economy. Unadulterated capitalism and communism are both violent systems based on a rigid assumption of human selfishness. The real choice is not between capitalism and socialism, but between centralization and decentralization, Gandhi said. The problem is to cultivate a milieu in which people's ethics and economics go hand in hand.

State is the epitome of violence. "It can never be weaned from violence to which it owes its existence"[16] maintained Gandhi. If man can be and must be his own governor, the state should have a minimum role to play. "I look upon an increase in the power of the state with greatest fear because while apparently doing good by minimizing exploitation, it does the greatest harm by destroying individuality which lies at the root of all progress."[17] Increase in the volume of legislation, the codification a family relationships (rights of the child, the rights of the grandparents) which is taking place in the West today is based on the assumption that unless the state intervenes, everything will go wrong. To assume, in the Hobbesian manner, that people are basically selfish and have to be governed is to repudiate the existence of the moral fiber of humanity. In Gandhi's worldview, small communities should govern themselves. The

---

[15] Ibid., p. 115.

[16] Ibid., p. 132.

[17] Ibid.

principle of people caring for their neighbor should extend itself culminating in a world government. The village should be the core of political power, and the least power should be available at the national level. Decentralization is most consistent with nonviolence. "*Swaraj* will be a sorry affair if people look up to it for the regulation of every detail of life."[18]

But until the *Swaraj* (moral self-government) comes, what can we do to correct the wrongs of economic violence? Gandhi's answer:

> All exploitation is based on cooperation, willing or forced, of the exploited...there will be no exploitation if people refused to obey the exploiter. But self comes in and we hug the chains that bind us. This must cease. What is needed is not the extinction of the landlords and capitalists, but a transformation of the existing relationship between them and the masses in something pure and healthier.[19]

The rich are to be left in possession of their wealth but persuaded to use only a part of it on their personal needs, and act as trustees on the remainder to be used for society. The idea of trusteeship provides a way out of the dilemma our world faces as it vacillates between socialism and capitalism: "make people free and they become unequal; Make them equal and they lose freedom." If the rich continue ignoring the idea of trusteeship and continue exploiting the poor, the means of nonviolent noncooperation are to be employed. As the poor realize that the rich accumulate wealth with their cooperation, they will be strong enough to withdraw their cooperation to get their due. However, Gandhi wanted that *satyagraha* should be used sparingly, with calm deliberation and always for a social cause. Using it for selfish motives, such as in disputes for higher wages, is bound to bring grief and failure.

To conclude, nonviolence is not merely the absence of violence but self-realization of men in the Gandhian worldview. The human being is truly human when innocently engaged in or actively cultivating nonviolence. Gandhi calls nonviolence the other side of *Satya* or *Being*. To cultivate nonviolence is to insist on and sustain the participation of the spirit in worldly life. It is also the precondition of human relations; one cannot be an authentic social being without it. Decentralization, self-government, haves acting as trustees for the have-nots,

---

[18] Ibid.

[19] Ibid., p. 124.

small-scale industry, self-employment or the practical measures of nonviolence which will reduce violence the world over. Conversely, Gandhism diagnoses centralization, too much government, disparities between the rich and the poor, unchecked large-scale industrialization, and the greed for material life as the real sources of violence. The visible increase in violence in our times has revealed the impotence of the systems based on violence. The failure of communism to provide a free play to individual aspirations, the failure of capitalism to usher in *laissez-faire* economies, the failure of the materialistic concept of development and so on point toward the fact that only a nonviolent way of life will be a human way of life.

Philosophically, nonviolence is one of the fundamental meanings of Being. Being is essentially understood by us as presence. It is a presence that frees itself from violence in its emergence and lawful persistence. Even though violence is close at hand, the state of nonviolence is fundamental, ever-present and all-pervasive. Violence is but a violation, a disturbance, an error.

CHAPTER 3

# Gandhi on War and Peace

*R. Raj Singh*

Contemporary historians continue to detail the discordance between the unparalleled upswing in technology, prosperity, and standards of living of the 20th century and the colossal and equally unparalleled slaughters of masses of humanity in this very century. These bloodsheds were combined with a complete disregard of the laws of war not only in the two major world wars but also in several minor conflicts of this last century. Niall Ferguson, in his recently published book *The War of the World*, recounts the horrors of violence in our times and why the 20th century was so spectacularly bloody. It was not so.

> Just as a result of tens of millions of combatants and civilians slaughtered during the two world wars but also the many other conflicts...in which a million people perished. What was more, these struggles brought with them ever-greater levels of atrociousness and barbarity, so that the "descent" was also a downward spiral toward beastly cruelties and genocides, a falling away from liberal enlightenment "laws of war" and a complete disregard for the Hague conventions: mankind descending into animals.[1]

Ferguson identifies three major reasons for the repeated explosions of violent conflicts of the 20th century. These are "ethnic conflict, economic volatility and empires in decline."[2]

Interestingly, Gandhi struggled with all of these three versions of violence throughout his public life. Economic volatility and its most painful outcome, namely, poverty as well as inequalities between the rich and poor, were Gandhi's

---

[1] Paul Kennedy, " 'The Worst of Times?,' a Review of Niall Ferguson's *The War of the World* (Penguin, 2006)," *New York Review of Books* 53, no. 17 (November 2006).

[2] Ibid.

chief concerns. Sarvodaya (welfare of all) and trusteeship by the rich were his original ideas for a nonviolent social order. With respect to the fading away of empires and their bloody aftermaths, Gandhi struggled hard to prevent the partition of India, but failed to convince his own party readers, who were too eager to secure the independence as soon as possible. In any case, Gandhi was striving with all his might to make at least one freedom struggle based on nonviolent resistance (*satyagraha*) spectacularly successful, so that other nations, subdued by foreign rule, will be inspired to believe in nonviolent remedies for international conflict management. In any case, independence of India did have a domino effect on the impending demise of other empires, most of which left behind further violence, conflicts, and problems that made the 20th century, the most violent century ever.

Gandhi correctly identified ethnic conflict as a major catalyst for violence in the world. He philosophized about this problem extensively in his writings in addition to his grass root political activism to promote interreligious and inter-racial harmony. He emphasized that interreligious discord is ultimately based on a superficial understanding of major religions as fundamentally different from each other and having different concepts and worldviews. In fact, he strongly believed that, at bottom, religion or dharma is a singular and not a plural. "By religion I do not mean formal religion, or customary religion, but that religion which underlies all religions."[3] Gandhi's contribution to philosophy is composed, in part, of his reflections as an original philosophy of religion:

> After long study and experience, I have come to the conclusion that (1) All religions are true; (2) all religions have some errors in them; (3) all religions are almost as dear to me as my own Hinduism, in as much as all human beings should be as dear to one as one's own close relatives.[4]

> I do not believe in the exclusive divinity of the Vedas. I believe the Bible, the Koran and Zend Avesta, to be as much divinely inspired as the Vedas. My belief in Hindu scriptures does not require me to accept every word and every verse as divinely inspired...I decline to be bound by any interpretation, however learned it may be if it is repugnant to reason or moral sense.[5]

---

[3] M. K. Gandhi, *All Men Are Brothers*, ed. Krishna Kriplani (New York: Continuum, 1987), 54 (Report from Sabarmati, 1928).

[4] Ibid., p. 56 (*Young India*, October 6, 1921).

[5] Ibid.

According to Gandhi, that single common ground of all religions is the moral law, that is, *dharma* and is executed by a God whose essence is the moral law or *satya*. In a world where religious exclusivity has produced a clash of civilizations labeled as Christian/secular Western versus radical Islamic. In such sweeping cultural divides, common humanity remains unappreciated and underemphasized. Human beings continue to be compartmentalized simplistically and given abstract and assumed identities. An individual's multiple identities based on his or her vocation, accomplishments, talents, interests, professional memberships, and personal beliefs are bypassed and dismissed while he or she is given a single dominant identity such as Western, Arab, Islamic, Chinese, etc. Amartya Sen in his new book *Identity and Violence* explains this cultural labeling of people, as follows:

> Communitarian thinking has been in ascendancy over the last few decades in contemporary social, political and moral theorizing, and the dominant and compelling role of social identity in governing behavior as well as knowledge has been widely investigated and championed. In some versions of communitarian thinking, it is presumed…that one's identity with one's community must be the dominant identity a person has…This approach has had the effect of rejecting the feasibility of assessing…normative judgments of behavior and institutions across cultures and societies, and it has sometimes been used to undermine the possibility of serious cross-cultural exchange and understanding.[6]

Gandhi's philosophical reflections revolving around the twin concepts of *ahimsa* (nonviolence) and *satya* (truth) enable us to think about war and peace in an original and fundamental manner. What we call peace is a state that can be described as that of nonviolence, an unspectacular normalcy which abides unless disturbed by violence. Nonviolence or *ahimsa* is a central problem in Gandhian thought and throughout his creative life Gandhi attempted to clarify the philosophical meaning of nonviolence and traced its role in the building of human society as well as its implications for the contemporary human condition. Since nonviolence pervades all aspects of human life, being as Gandhi calls it "the law of our Being," it also sustains what is known as world peace or peace among nations or absence of war. Thus, Gandhian thought offers us some original but basic insights on the subject of world peace.

---

[6.] Amartya Sen, *Identity and Violence* (New York: Penguin Books, 2006), 33–34.

Gandhi's reflections on the issue of world peace are for the most part nar-rowly understood in the welter of the secondary literature on Gandhian thought. The problem of world peace has mostly been studied by way of analyses of Gandhi's various comments and rejoinders on the international affairs of his times. The works of this type are preoccupied with unraveling the often puz-zling and seemingly inconsistent standpoints of Gandhi toward the war effort of the Allies in World War I and World War II. The firm belief in the efficacy of *satyagraha*, even in major conflicts such as World War II, was found to be unconvincing. How could *satyagraha* deal with someone like Hitler? Gand-hi's response was dismissed as too impractical. Although these analyses do provide some factual information about how Gandhi responded to the current events of this day, their authors often miss how Gandhi stood with respect to the fundamentals of world peace. His response to some of the well-meaning but ineffective crusaders of peace in the Western countries was: "All activity for stopping war must prove fruitless so long as the causes of war are not understood and radically dealt with."[7]

In order to trace the fundamental "causes of war" as exposed by Gandhi, causes that are, according to him, neither fully understood nor radically dealt with by the nations of the world, we must consider his original insights on the meaning of nonviolence. For as Gandhi said "the attainment of freedom, whether for a man, a nation or the world, must be in exact proportion to the attainment of nonviolence by each."[8] These considerations are necessary if we are to assure ourselves of a reasonable understanding of the philosophical enigmatic concept of *ahimsa*. Nonviolence must be addressed as a philosophical problem before we trace its social and political implications. The widely pervasive specific but narrow definitions of violence and nonviolence make Gandhi's conceptual corrections all the more relevant. One can explore in the web of Gandhi's reflec-tions concerning nonviolence, several attempts to positively identify this unseen but ever present force as well as attempts to remove widespread negative and narrower notions of it.

Gandhi repeatedly calls *ahimsa* "the law of our Being," as well as the other side of the coin of *satya*, which is his chosen name for Being as such. Both of these characterizations of nonviolence amount to a simple but philosophically

---

[7.] M. K. Gandhi, "A Complex Problem," *Young India*, May 9, 1929, in *Moral and Political Writings of Mahatma Gandhi*, Vol. 2, ed. Raghavan Iyer (Oxford: Clarendon Press, 1986), 472.

[8.] Gandhi, *Moral and Political Writings of Mahatma Gandhi*, p. 460 ("War or Peace," *Young India*, May 20, 1926).

seminal insight that nonviolence is the meaning, that is, the framework of Being as such. This means that nonviolence is not merely an ethical choice but an ontological reality, that is, the manner in which all things abide. Human being in virtue of its special relation to Being as such and being an intutor, builder, cultivator, and preserver in the commerce of Being, has a special relation to nonviolence according to Gandhi, for it is the way human being remains human.

Gandhi by his own admission uses the term *satya* (truth) in the sense of *sat* (Being).[9] He calls it truth in the popular sense since truth is considered worthy by all, believers and unbelievers, Hindus and non-Hindus alike. As a believer himself, he regards *satya* as the chief attribute of God, indeed as God himself. At first he said "God is Truth" but later "Truth is God."[10] That is, truth is not just one of the attributes of God but "the" attribute or essence of God. Now *ahimsa* as the framework of Being has a higher and more pervasive status than that of violence. Violence is a violation of the ongoing natural, unspectacular state of being human, which also means being at peace. Violence is a disruption in being ourselves. Thus, nonviolence and violence are not equally available and equally possible means of human action. However, in our misunderstanding and over-simplification of the meaning of nonviolence, we take it as the contrary of or mere absence of violence which is itself misunderstood and over-simplified as merely "physical violence" (i.e., destruction and bloodshed). Historians and journalists perpetuate this obvious, narrow, and privative understanding of non-violence as they are apt to be impressed more by the visible scars of violence than by that invisible but all abiding and onward moving albeit subtle presence of nonviolence.

In Western philosophical heritage from Parmenides to modern times, a meta-physics of presence has attributed a temporal meaning to Being. As explained by Heidegger from ancient Greek times, Being has always been understood in terms of time.[11] In his chief work entitled *Being and Time*, Heidegger provision-ally accepts this Greek meaning of Being. However, he reflects in his *What Is Called Thinking*[12] that time is not the only horizon of Being; other meanings can

---

[9.] Ibid., p. 157 ("What Is Truth," *Navjivan*, November 20, 1921).

[10.] Ibid., p. 164 (Speech at Meeting in Lausanne, December 8, 1931).

[11.] Martin Heidegger, *Being and Time*, trans. J. Macquarrie and E. Robinson (New York: Harper & Row, 1962), 45.

[12.] Martin Heidegger, *What Is Called Thinking*, trans. F. E. Wrick and J. G. Gray (New York: Harper & Row, 1968).

possibly challenge our thinking. It seems to me that Gandhi is the thinker who, as his most original contribution to ontology, proposes this alternative meaning of Being, and thereby challenges world philosophy to begin tracing the varied implications of the insight that "to be means to be non-violent." For Gandhi reminds us again and again in his writings that fuller implications and potentials of nonviolence have yet to be thought of and realized.[13]

How does this ontological meaning of nonviolence affect the specific problem of world peace? First of all, Gandhi grounds this particular problem in the wider problem of the meaning of Being. That is, he ontologizes the problem of world peace by pointing out that nothing short of nonviolence all round or the good of all (*sarvodaya*) will assure an enduring world peace. World peace cannot be attained merely by holding symposia and/or by founding international bodies. This widening of the problem of world peace into the problem of nonviolence does not mean that Gandhi is turning it into a fuzzy and impossible ideal. Not just abiding in nonviolence but to promote nonviolence is part and parcel of being human. Man is a builder and cultivator of Being. The march of civilization has been a slow but sure progress of nonviolence. Gandhi wants us to study the problem by considering its widest possible roots, yet he regards nonviolence as both promotable and achievable:

> The first condition of non-violence is justice all round in every department of life. Perhaps it is too much to expect of human nature. I do not however think so. No one should dogmatize about the capacity of human nature for degradation of exaltation.[14]

Gandhi also used to say: "I positively refuse to judge man from the scanty material furnished to us by history." In order to promote a nonviolent world order, we have to recognize the obvious as well as the subtle forces of violence, which give rise to bloodshed, destruction and war. Gandhi strives to clarify that violence is not just physical injury and bloodshed. In reality, violence exists in human society in the form of inequality, injustice, exploitation, greed and unbridled material-ism. Unless the rage of this broader violence subsides neither nonviolent world order nor world peace can be realized. Gandhi believes that it is well within our

---

[13.] Gandhi, *All Men Are Brothers*, p. 79 (*Harijan*, February 22, 1942).

[14.] Ibid., p. 77 (April, 1940, quoted by D. G. Tendulkar in *Mahatma*, Vol. 5).

means to reduce the power of the abovementioned forces of violence. The task is difficult but not impossible:

> Not to believe in the possibility of permanent peace is to disbelieve in the godliness of human nature. Methods hitherto adopted have failed because rock-bottom sincerity on the part of those who have striven has been lacking.[15]

Reluctance to deal with fundamental catalysts of violence characterizes this lack of sincerity. While leaders of powerful nations readily declare themselves as advocates of peace, there is neither a real movement toward the acknowledgment of the factors of violence nor self-sacrificing action to resist the breeding grounds of violence.

> If the recognized leaders of mankind who have control over the engines of destruction were wholly to renounce their use, with full knowledge of its implications, permanent peace can be obtained. This is clearly impossible without the great powers of the earth renouncing their imperialistic design. This again seems impossible without great nations ceasing to believe in soul-destroying competition and to desire to multiply wants and therefore, increase their material possessions.[16]

Thus the root cause of war, according to Gandhi, is the thoughtless multiplications of wants, not heeding to the truth that a voluntary restriction of wants is what civilization consists of.[17] Gandhi identifies the unequal economic status of nations combined with exploitative industrial power structures leading to what he calls the "soul-destroying competition" as the chief catalyst of war.

Another factor in the current international situation is the phenomenon of technology, treated in Gandhian thought as man–machine relation. Obviously, inequality among nations is accentuated by the degrees to which the have and have-not nations possess technology.

> What is the cause of present chaos? It is exploitation, I will not say, of the weaker nations by the stronger, but of sister nations by sister nations...My fundamental

---

[15.] Ibid., p. 111 (*Harijan*, May 16, 1936).

[16.] Ibid.

[17.] Ibid., p. 98 (*Yeravda Mandir*, 1935).

objection to machinery rests on the fact that it is machinery that has enabled nations to exploit others.[18]

Gandhi's other chief concern is whether technology will jeopardize full employment and whether it is bound to alter the Eastern way of life particularly the relatively autonomous status of the village:

> I would say that if the village perishes, India will perish too. India will be no more India. Her own mission in the world will get lost...[However], provided that village industry is maintained, there will be no objection to villagers using even the modern machines and tools. Only they should not be used as a means of exploitation of others.[19]

Being preoccupied primarily with the contemplation of Being and in identifying the basic tendencies of modernity and technological times, Gandhi has a lot in common with Heidegger.[20] Both these thinkers bemoan the forgetfulness of Being (called *satya* by Gandhi) that assails our age and point toward the pitfalls of a thoughtless faith in applications of technology combined with blind transfers of technology. Their chief concerns are what Heidegger calls the standardization of earth,[21] a view of nature as a "standing reserve" for industrialism as well as a treatment of technology as the superior most brand of knowledge. These thinkers view with alarm the steamroller of Westernization in the garb of the so-called technology transfers, leading to the destruction of what Heidegger calls poetic dwelling of man and Gandhi the Eastern way of life.

Neither Gandhi nor Heidegger should, however, be interpreted as backward-looking enemies of technology. They both realize that the lock of technicity and industrialism cannot and should not be reversed. It is the blind faith in technology and downgrading of "atechnical" graces of human life that concerns them. It is the universal application of Western-technical model as the concept of development that, according to them, constitutes thoughtlessness. The fine graces and

---

[18] Ibid., p. 114 (*Young India*, October 22, 1931).

[19] Ibid., p. 116 (*Harijan*, August 29, 1936).

[20] R. Raj Singh, "Gandhi and His Original Ontological Contemplation," in *Mahatma Gandhi: 125 Years*, ed. B. R. Nanda (London: Wiley Eastern, 1995). See also R. Raj Singh, "Non-Violence, Gandhi and Our Times," *The International Journal of Applied Philosophy* 5 (1990): 35–41.

[21] Martin Heidegger, *The Question Concerning Technology*, trans. W. Lovitt (New York: Harper & Row, 1977), 3–35.

higher potentials of humanity cannot be realized by mere technical advancement. The alternatives to the Western-technical model should remain alive and well. Equality does not mean standardization. Thus, according to Gandhi, diversity, decentralization and trusteeship of have-nots by the haves are the concepts that will promote nonviolent national and international orders. Standardization, centralization and the exploitation of the East by the West will keep us engaged in violence and having to deal with war.

Commitment to peace requires a "rock bottom sincerity" which has hitherto been lacking. In the acts of war, millions lose their lives. An untold number of young people are persuaded to die for their nations. But to secure permanent peace, we are hardly willing to pay sacrifice ourselves. According to Gandhi, a satyagrahi is one who is never ready to kill but is ever ready to die. Gandhi showed it many times in his life that he was ready to die for his cause. The viceroy Lord Linlithgow described Gandhi's fasts unto death as a "political blackmail (himsa) for which there can be no moral justification."[22] To this Gandhi replied: "it is on my part meant to be an appeal to the Highest Tribunal for justice which I have failed to secure from you."[23] It is foolhardy to believe that a process that reaps blood and gore and millions of souls can be ended by mere talk. Gandhi's words are instructive. "Just as one must learn the art of killing in the training for violence, so one must learn the art of dying in the training for non-violence."[24] He called it a self-evident proposition that "the desire to kill is in inverse proportion to the desire to die."[25] In a world of mass confusion and wanton materialism things of lasting value have to be purchased with suffering, if satyagraha is to replace war as a method of conflict resolution. Gandhi's reaction to the explosion of atom bomb over Hiroshima and Nagasaki is indicative of his basic attitude to war and peace:

> So far as I can see, the atomic bomb has deadened the finest feeling that has sustained mankind for ages. There used to be the so-called laws of war which made it tolerable. Now we know the naked truth. War knows no law except that of might. The atom bomb brought an empty victory to the allied arms but it

---

[22] M. K. Gandhi and Lord Linlithgo, "Gandhi's Correspondence with Lord Linlithgo," in *The Gandhi Reader*, ed. Homer A. Jack (New York: Grove Press, 1956), 369.

[23] Ibid., 370.

[24] Gandhi, *All Men Are Brothers*, p. 77 (*Harijan*, September 1, 1940).

[25] Ibid., p. 88 (*Young India*, January 21, 1930).

resulted for the time being in destroying the soul of Japan. What has happened to the soul of the destroying nation is yet too early to see.

Mankind has to get out of violence only through non-violence. Hatred can be over-come only by love. Counter-hatred only increases the surface as well as the depth of hatred.[26]

CHAPTER 4

# Kabir on Death and Authentic Life

*R. Raj Singh*

Kabir (1398–1518) was one of the foremost thinker poets of medieval India whose poetic reflections have come to have a deep impact on Indian thought and folklore. Kabir's contemporary poet Pipa who was also a disciple of Ramanand, compares Kabir's songs to the shade of a bo-tree (*kalap-vruksh*) which removes the pains of worldly life and makes one transcend what is commonly said and commonly conceived. Pipa was the king of Gagron state and Kabir a humble weaver from Benares.[1] Kabir's work offers a sharp critique of the organized, ritualistic, priest-dominated Hindu and Islamic faiths of the day, along with socially accepted customs, dogmas, and rigid caste-based divisions which encouraged contempt for the lower castes. But Kabir was not just a critic. He offers a thoughtful and cohesive alternative, a simple method to achieve a relationship with a nondualistic, attributeless, and everlasting Being to be realized through the way of love-laden *bhakti* (devotion). Many contemporary and later *bhakti* saints have mentioned Kabir's contribution very respectfully in their works. These include Tukaram and Mahipati from Maharashtra, Nivaran Sahib from Gujrat, and Sankaradev from Assam, as well as the already mentioned Pipa, who was a fellow disciple of Kabir's Guru Ramanand.[2]

## Historical Sources of Kabir's Life and Works

There is hardly any way to establish the factual details of the lives of *bhakti* saints who were the pioneers of the devotional movement (13th–18th centuries) of North India which seems to be inspired by an earlier *bhakti* movement of South India that was underway since the 4th century contributions of the poets called Alvars.

---

[1] Purushotam Agarwal, *Kabir: Sakhi Aur Sabad* (New Delhi: National Book Trust, 2015), 7, 12.

[2] Ibid.

None of the saint-poets have left behind any autobiographies. They were much rather concerned with exposing their soulful experiences and their very own knowledge of the self (*atman jnana*). This self-knowledge of theirs is found in various hints sprinkled in their poetic works rather than in the form of any detailed works in prose. These same tendencies are characteristically present in Kabir's compositions. Instead of relying on the hagiographies and legends produced by the Kabir sectarians and unreliable religious historians, it is better to pay attention to the autobiographical information contained in Kabir's own works. For example, it is abundantly clear from Kabir's songs and couplets that he was a weaver by caste and spent most of his life in the holy city of Benares. Some scholars pay a lot of credence to an introductory text written by Anantdas in mid-16th century as well as the mention made by Hariram Vyas in 1555 of Kabir being a disciple of Ramanand. Both these testimonies were given within 100 years since Kabir's demise. In an anthology of various *bhakti* saints' writings produced in 1582 by Nabhadas, fifteen songs of Kabir were included, which certify Kabir's recognition as a prominent *bhakti* saint poet in the 16th century and beyond. Abdul Fazal, a Muslim historian comments in his work *Ain-e-Akbari* (1595) that "Kabir's words are very popular among the people...his path is open to all and his thought is high and pure and he appeals to both Hindus and Muslims." Fazal also writes that Kabir was quite famous in the reign of Sikander Lodi (1489–1515) and that Kabir did not agree with the tired old religious practices of the people.[3]

The first guru of the Sikhs, Guru Nanak visited Hindu pilgrim destinations including Benaras from 1507 to 1515. If we accept that Kabir died in 1494, Guru Nanak's visit happened ten or fifteen years after. It is quite evident that Guru Nanak met with the earliest disciples of Kabir who had already produced anthologies of Kabir's works, for Kabir himself never wrote anything. Guru Nanak who had collected the hymns of many prominent *bhakti* saints during his travels, also took a huge body of Kabir's works in his possession. These works of *bhakti* saints in the form of mostly hymns and couplets remained the prize possessions of the first guru of the Sikhs, who passed them on to the fifth guru Arjan who compiled the *Adi Granth* in 1604. This anthology, which became scriptural cannon of Sikhism called the *Adi Granth*, contains 224 songs (*sahads*) and couplets (*slokas*) and three other minor works of Kabir. Thus, *Adi Granth* contains the most authentic and substantive as well as an unadulterated version of Kabir's works. There have been no changes to this body of work which Guru

---

[3] B. J. Singh, *Sant Kabir* (Amritsar, India: Waris Shah Foundation, 2006), 45.

Nanak took in his possession sometime between 1507 and 1515. That the next four Sikh gurus inherited this collection is indicated by their occasional responses and analyses of Kabir's *sahads* and *slokas* (song and couplets) in their own writing.

## Kabir's Life: Some Reliable Facts

If we consider some hints given in Kabir's authentic writings, it is quite evident that he was a weaver by caste and profession and spent most of his life in the holy city of Benares. "O Kabir my caste is the laughing stock for all; Bless this caste though, it let me know the lord."[4] Many scholars maintain that he was a Muslim by birth because of his parents Neeru and Neema were Muslims weavers. There are others who believe that he was a Hindu. If we look at his writings, we must acknowledge that Kabir's worldview is entirely Hindu and he possessed the deepest and most original knowledge of the concepts of the Hindu tradition. This is clear from a simple glance on his basic writings. We may safely conclude that he must have adopted Hinduism by his own free will even if the story of him being brought up in a Muslim family is true. His work offers scathing critiques of the simplistic and hypocritical beliefs and rituals that were being practiced by Hindus in his times along with occasional criticisms of Muslim rituals and dogmas. While he seems to reject all organized religion and priesthood, his quest was to expose the true spirit of Hinduism and of religion (*dharma*) which prevails over and above so-called religions (i.e., the various competing religious systems or established religions). Human being's most fundamental connection with attributeless Being within us that abides as the ground of all entities (*nirguna brahman*) was primary objective of Kabir's analyses. Thus, he is also recognized as the foremost exponent and practitioner of *nirguna-bhakti* (devotion to the attributeless deity).

Another major fact of Kabir's life is that he became the disciple of Ramanand who was a prominent guru in Benares and master of many other outstanding *bhakti* saints, namely, Ravidas, Dhanna, Pipa, Sain, etc. The way Kabir came to be a disciple of Saint Ramanand is described in an interesting story. The Guru was initially reluctant to allow Kabir as a follower because Kabir happened to be a Muslim weaver, an untouchable according to Hindu orthodoxy. But Kabir devised a plan to win over Saint Ramanand. Ramanand used to go to the banks of the holy river Ganga at the crack of dawn. Kabir lay down in the dark steps

---

[4] Guru Arjan Dev Ji, *Adi Granth* (Composed in 1694), 1368.

leading to the river. Ramanand stumbled upon the body of Kabir accidently and exclaimed, "You belong to Rama, say Rama, Rama." These profound words were taken to heart by Kabir whose life changed that day onward. The true guru who is supposed to show one the value of God's name acts as a mediator between man and God. Ramanand must have been an open-minded saint, for some of his other disciples like Ravidas were also from the lower castes. It is also accepted that Kabir had a happy married life with his supportive wife named Loee. They had a son and a daughter named Kamal and Kamali. Many medieval sources indicate that in his advanced years Kabir left Benares for Maghar. It was a popular belief that those who die in Benares are guaranteed to attain salvation (*mukti*), whereas those who expire in Maghar return to a lower life-form of a donkey. Perhaps Kabir wanted to disapprove this superstition or he realized that his inner knowledge assured him a part of immorality anyway, he made a statement by his final move to Maghar. He says in a *sabad* "after my whole life was lost in the city of Shiva, came the time of death, and I took off to Maghar."[5]

There is no doubt that Kabir earned his honest living working as a weaver. He made a statement through his way of life that to live a life of *dharma* one is not obligated to abandon either the household or the work done with both hands. His wife Loee and son Kamal are mentioned in his couplets:

Says Kabir, hear O Loee[6]

He refers to his son as follows "lineage of Kabir is stained as son Kamal came quitting the name of Hari, and brought home the goods."[7] It is obvious that having spent a long time in the holy city of Benares, Kabir was fully schooled in the fine details of the Hindu tradition. It is quite evident from his writings that the spirit of Vedic insight and devotionalism was his chosen faith. Although he offers an occasional critique of the Muslim dogmatism and practices of meat-eating, he also reflects sometimes on to the true spirit of Islam. His remarks on the Muslim faith are sporadic and of the nature of a superficial bird's eye view. But when it comes to the grounds of the Hindu faith, he speaks like an insider and offers a remarkable insight and attention to detail that is combined with an original philosophical appraisal. His critiques of idol worship, polytheism, worship

---

[5.] Ibid., p. 326.

[6.] Ibid., Rag Asa, 48.

[7.] Dev Ji, *Adi Granth*, 1370.

of personal gods, belief in God in human form (*avataras*), puritanism, and adherence to the rigid caste system are so logical and convincing. At the same time he does not offer mere critiques but also suggests a thoughtful alternative worldview based on other lofty ground principles of Hinduism such as the path of *bhakti* (devotion), the existence of the soul (*atman*) and attributeless divine being (*brahman*), the superiority of nonviolence, the theory of *karma* and rebirth etc. His transcendence from the simplistic understanding of competing religious bodies the quest of true "religion beyond religions" is what makes him an original thinker. He explains the higher meaning of guru-*bhakti*, the rejection of the bonds of *maya* (illusionary worldliness), the role of the word of the guru and mind's higher potentials open to everyone. His exposition of the futility of the pursuit of gold and sexual indulgence and his references to the mystical concepts such as tenth gateway (*dasan-dwar*) beyond which lies no ocean of *samsara*, offer an appraisal of religious phenomena in a remarkably original fashion.

## Kabir's Work

Kabir's poems and couplets (*sahads* and *slokas*) were compiled by many of his disciples and devotees shortly after his demise. It is acknowledged that Kabir himself wrote nothing in his lifetime.

It is easy to surmise that his devotees had memorized his powerful words and compiled them in various anthologies. His simple but deeply meaningful compositions seem to come from a poetic genius and make a direct appeal to the hearts of simple folk who made their living by the sweat of their brow. These were not meant for priests and scholars although Kabir's analyses of the religious issues and the Vedantic tradition impressed upon all sections of the society.

The sources of Kabir's poetry and collections of his work are numerous. Hazari Prasad Dwivedi identifies over six dozen anthologies.[8] Many of these collections contain spiritual materials and additions made by Kabir sectarians and devotees. The authenticity of those medieval and modern collections is questionable. Such literature also contains commentaries and expositions (*tikas*) of the principal collection titled *Bijak* revered by the Kabir sects. In addition to *Bijak,* two other anthologies are recognized by Kabir scholars, namely, *Kabir Granthavali* and *Adi Granth.*

---

[8.] Hazari Prasad Dwivedi, *Kabir* (New Delhi: Sahitya Sarovar, 1942), 29.

Although the devotees of the Kabir-panth (Kabir sect) recognized *Bijak* as the most ancient collection that was written by Dharamdas in Kabir's lifetime. However, many scholars doubt that Dharamdas was a contemporary of Kabir and maintain that *Bijak* was composed at a much later date. This is evidenced by a comparative analysis of *Bijak* with the *Granthavali,* the language of the latter being more ancient. The contents of *Granthavali* and *Adi Granth* have a great deal of similarity. Out of 227 hymns (*sahads*) and 240 couplets (*slokas*) of the *Adi Granth,* 65 *sabads* and 106 *sakhis* are also found in the *Granthavali,* whereas there is a lesser similarity of content between *Adi Granth* and *Bijak.* Shyam Sunder Das published a collection of Kabir's poems under the title *Kabir Granthavali* in 1928 based on some ancient manuscripts the earliest of which is claimed to be dated 1561 and second one dated 1881 with an enlarged but similar content. The date of the earlier manuscript seems to have been altered with a different handwriting. In any case, the several versions of *Bijak* and *Granthavali* have been altered and added on to by different editors in the past four centuries and the authenticity of the manuscripts and the dates of their origin being a matter of scholarly controversies, the only authentic and unadulterated source of Kabir's work is the *Adi Granth.* Not a word of which has been altered, nor anything is added on it since 1604, when it was compiled by Guru Arjan, the fifth guru of the Sikhs. During his visit of Benares, Guru Nanak in ca. 1510 secured one of the earliest versions of Kabir's works; this copy was unaltered and later in 1604 made part of the sacred scripture of Sikhism. Thus, *Adi Granth* is the most reliable source of Kabir's work. Accordingly, we will analyze a selection of Kabir's poems from the *Adi Granth,* to expose his worldview and his original contemplation regarding death.

In addition to these important written sources, namely, *Bijak, Granthavali,* and *Adi Granth,* we must acknowledge the important role played by the oral tradition of the recitation of his *sakhis* (couplets) and *sahads* (songs). These poems full of devotion, and wisdom (*jnana*) have always been sung by the bards from all parts of North India in both Hindi-speaking and non-Hindi-speaking regions. In the various dialects and styles of Hindi, the language that Kabir spoke, his songs appear in many innovative versions. Even in non-Hindi-speaking region like Gujrat, Maharashtra, Orissa, Assam, and Punjab, slightly modified versions of his songs come alive. In our day and age, popular Kabir devotional singers like Prahlad Singh Tipanya, Bheru Singh Chouhan, Kaluram Bamaniya, and Mooralala Marwada have posted their popular videos on YouTube.

With the advent of the *bhakti* movement in northern regions of India, religious insights were delivered by the oral traditions of devotional singing in the various vernacular languages spoken by the people. Textual materials in classical Sanskrit language were mostly read by the priestly castes of *brahmins,* whereas people belonging to the farming and working classes memorized and sang hymns written by saintly *bhakti* poets like Surdas, Kabir, Ravidas, and Mira. Such saint-poets transmitted the essence of Hindu worldview in powerful poetic and musical compositions which answered to the religious passions among millions of common folks. The northern *bhakti* movement spread like a wildfire and brought about a renaissance in Hinduism from 13th to 17th centuries. Scriptural studies, ritualism, and dominance of priestly castes was deemphasized and rejected and loving devotion of the lord and direct connection between *bhakta* (devotee) and *Bhagvan* (the blessed lord) was practiced and celebrated.

The *bhakti* saints had some followers and disciples during their lifetimes, but their songs were sung by wondering ascetics who moved from one part of the country to another spreading the word of these devotional masters. The minstrels formed groups of devotional singers who often met in the places of pilgrimage or religious assemblies and recited the hymns of *bhakti* saints. Ever since the demise of Kabir an oral tradition of the recitation of his *sahads* has flourished within the Hindu speaking northern states and groups of devotional singers emerged in different places and have always recited Kabir's songs in their own dialects and styles. The modern-day Kabir singers who often post their videos have inherited different versions of Kabir's songs from their forefathers. The oral tradition has preserved a part of Kabir's literature that is not found in the written anthologies of *Bijak* and *Granthavali.* The existence of such an oral reservoir, freely modified and altered to suit the regional dialects and musical styles, indicates that Kabir's songs often bearing critiques of false practices of established religion was not dependent on the written documents to appeal to the hearts of the innocent masses. It comes to them in a form that is not defended by the written word. Kabir makes a direct appeal through music and song of the hearts of his listeners and sends a message that exposes man's connection to the attributeless Being (*Brahman*).

In most of his songs, the last lines contain his signature call to his reader or listener, that is, "*suno bhai sadho*" (listen O' brother ascetics) "*Kahat Kabir suno bhai santo*" (says Kabir, listen O Saints). While it seems that he regards all his listeners as saints or ascetics of some sort, this is only a literal meaning. But in such a curious way of addressing his readers in the last lines of his songs, which has become his trademark, he has a deeper expectation from the listening readers. Says Kabir to the saints and *sadhas* (something in a nutshell) that only those who are ready to live like a true sadhu (ascetics who overcome *maya* or "illusionary worldliness") or those who are attempting to live a saintly life, will get to the bottom of this wisdom (*jnana*) contained in the hymn. Just reading or listening is not good enough. Knowing and living of love (*jnana and bhakti*) must go hand in hand.

## Kabir's Couplets of Wisdom

The two lined couplets of Kabir, also known as *slokas* or *sakhis* or *dohas* have become part of the folklore of the northern states of India, not all of which are Hindi speaking. While all the written anthologies such as *Adi Granth, Grantha-vali,* and *Bijak* include many of these nuggets of wisdom, these *dohas* are also preserved in the oral traditions associated with Kabir in different styles and dialects. The anthologies contain different sets of the two-liners but also have some in common which authenticates the authorship of Kabir. However, many couplets recited by different hymn singers from different regions of North India have obviously modified the original versions found in the classical anthologies.

Here we will consider a selection of Kabir's couplets preserved in an unaltered form in the *Adi Granth,* especially those which particularly expound on the theme of death and authenticity. In *sloka* number 5, Kabir reflects as follows:

> A rare one is he, O' Kabir who dies while living
> Fearlessly he recalls the glory of One who abides in all directions.[9]

Of course, the poetic merit of the couplet is much diminished in translation. But Kabir's message is unmistakable. He says that there are very few individuals are to be found in our world, who are practicing voluntary renunciation of the illusionary worldliness (*maya*). One who gives up *maya* is a true practitioner of death, a death contemplator, one who has embraced death while living a distinctive life—a life that is deemed to be comparable to death by the worldly minded people who are steeped in *maya*. Such practitioners of death obtain fearfulness while they recognize and revel in the glory of divine presence that Kabir too witnesses in whichever direction he turns. The couplet imparts the insight that to witness the omnipresent divinity, one ought to be dead to the preoccupations of *maya* in which common humanity is entirely absorbed at all times. Only after giving up of worldliness voluntarily, one can realize and witness *brahman*. Thus, a program of living authentically is a prerequisite to realize and know (*jnana*)

---

[9] Dev Ji, *Adi Granth,* p. 5

*brahman,* the divine Being abiding in all entities in all directions. Thus, we can see that in two lines, Kabir has outlined the essence of the Hindu worldview. Say no *maya* as far as possible to obtain the glimpses of Brahman, which transcribes in a nutshell the essential wisdom of the *Upanishads* and the *Bhagavad-Gita.*

Not only *maya* is to be abandoned but also something more formidable, namely, egoism. The authentic life ought to be a life of humility. This ego (*aham*), the sense of me and mineness (*mamta*), is harder to relinquish but it is worth the effort, as Kabir says: "Let that die away O Kabir, on whose demise there is ease ; they will call it good, none will take offence."[10] Kabir is referring to human ego (*aham or haume*) which must not be allowed to have an upper hand in an authentic life. When ego departs, one is at ease and admired by all. No one takes offense if you diminish your ego and embrace humility. The death that is to be practiced in life is the death of the ego. Renunciation of excessive worldliness and ever emergent ego (*maya* and *aham*) are the chief ingredients of death contemplation. Here is a classic *sloka* of Kabir that expresses the philosophical meaning of death in a nutshell:

> Kabir, the death that the world is afraid of brings me joy
> Only by dying, one gains that supreme bliss.[11]

The death that often arouses fear in the thoughts of a worldly minded individual laden with attachment (*moha*) to family and materialism, in fact brings joy to a saintly person like Kabir. For Kabir realizes that one becomes a candidate for knowing the supreme bliss of *brahman*, only after dying, that is, after a renunciation of the world of *maya,* combined with avoiding the traps of *moha* (too much love of near and dear ones). Renunciation of *maya*, *moha*, and *mamta* (mineness) or of strong bonds with those you call your own ("my wife," "my son," "my family," "my tribe," etc.) is a prerequisite for being a true philosopher who can possibly accomplish a blissful knowledge of the Being of all Beings. The vision of philosophical truth and of Being as such comes to those who are adept in the art of dying that is, giving up what people call the (high) life:

> O Kabir, there is death after death in the world, but no one knows how to die
> One who dies such a death, shall not die again.[12]

---

[10] Ibid., p. 9.

[11] Ibid., p. 22.

[12] Ibid., p. 29.

There is case after case of death in the world, the fact of death repeats itself all the time. But far few are those who know how to die. Only the rare one practices dying while living. One who is steeped in *maya* clings to his near and dear ones and to his possessions is dying the death all the time, being fearful of losing his family and his various possessions. Every time one is afraid of dying and parting from one's possessions and relatives, one is receiving a jolt of death. But one who voluntarily detaches oneself from a clinging to relatives and possessions, is more prepared to look actual death in the eye and will be free from the daily onslaught of the fear of losing this or that. Acknowledging the presence of the divine Being the constant recitation and remembrance of his name (*Rama-nama*) also enables one to achieve detachment from *maya* and overcome the fear of death. The cases of death that one frequently comes across also arouses philosophical wonder in us:

> The bones burn like wood, hair like grass
> Seeing this world burning, Kabir is saddened.[13]

Referring to the Hindu custom of burning the body, Kabir contrasts the usual love of the body with its final destiny of being burnt at the funeral pier. The scene of the bones burning like wood and hair like dry grass, point to the absurdity of our usual obsession with the body and matters of the body. Fulfilling the basic needs of the body such as sustenance, clothing, shelter, and sleep is deemed as a genuine need that must be fulfilled before the devotion to God can begin. But obsession with the body combined with various indulgences such as dressing and caressing of the body defy the truth that the body is neither timeless nor the entirely of one's self. Looking at the bodies being burnt on daily basis on the banks of the holy river Ganga in his native city of Benares, Kabir obviously had additional reasons to contemplate the meaning of death. His conclusion is that the commonplace death rituals made him indifferent to the love of the world, prompting him to be disenchanted toward *maya* to which everyone clung with the assumption that body was all in all and its incessant cravings were to be fulfilled. Thus, the word "disenchanted" (*udas*) is very meaningful. *Udas* also means "sad" or indifferent when we are saddened by the promises of *maya* and its disappointing final outcomes symbolized by the funeral pier, we are prompted toward *bhakti* of the spirit that is beyond attributes (*Brahman*) and we are inspired to turn away from excessive worldliness rooted on the body and matters of the

---

[13.] Ibid., p. 36.

body or crass materialism that prevails in the world. It also arouses indifference in us toward the antics of the worldly minded people. In another couplet that has become an adage, Kabir says:

> Do it now what is to be done tomorrow, do it right now instead of later
> Nothing shall happen when death is upon you.[14]

Certainty of death and uncertainty of its timing is a double- edged truth that offers a life lesson of death. The most valuable things are not to be postponed but must done soon enough without dithering. According to Kabir, the most vital thing is to get into the flow of *bhakti* and strive to get in touch with the divine Being. The recitation of Rama-nama (name of Rama) that enables one to transcend the world of *maya* does not warrant postponement: why not invoke sweet remembrance of the divine Being right now. Why not let the forgetfulness (suspension) of the worldliness transport you to a contact with the divine. Often, the worldly preoccupations and urgencies cheat us out of the philosophical as well as the divine possibilities. As Kabir says in a *sabad* popular in the oral tradition: "three moments have deceived me out of the wealth I should have accumulated for the passage beyond." That is, the flow of three moments (past, present, and future) slide past us with deception, robbing us of the possibilities of authenticity. Life is easily lost in inauthentic motions, going through mundane tasks, while possibility of being truly human is lost from moment to moment. Thus, "do it now... do it right away" is Kabir's advice. Whatever is most important, and nothing is more important than philosophizing on the nature of Being and meditating on the love of the lord. Nothing is more important than Knowledge of Being and love (*Jnana and Bhakti*). A huge insight of Kabir in two lines.

## An Appraisal of Kabir's Selected *Sabads* (Songs)

A wide range of spiritual and religious issues are raised in Kabir's numerous songs found in the classical anthologies of *Granthavali*, namely, *Bijak* and *Adi Granth*. In these songs, the basic religious instinct and longing is creatively outlined and commonplace oversimplifications and mistaken beliefs prevailing in the medieval Hindu world are analyzed and denounced, beliefs such as *avatar-*

---

[14.] Ibid., p. 138.

*vada* (i.e., theories of God appearing in human form), for example, Krsna in the *Mahabharata* and Rama in the epic Ramayana. He also disapproves of the firmly embedded systems of social stratification in Hindu society, namely, the caste system, which treats even a spirituality elevated saint like Kabir as a low caste weaver. Of course, Kabir's work shows all the spiritual tendencies of a *bhakti* saint that were part of the northern *bhakti* movement that took India by storm in a religious renaissance from the 13th to 17th centuries. All these *bhakti* saints rejected ritualism and showed their religious fervor in poetry, song, and music. They all wrote their work in vernacular and regional languages rather than in classical Sanskrit. Ordinary folks from the villages and townships could understand and sing their songs in their own spoken languages, giving rise to a strong oral tradition of migrating bands and hymn singers who spread the message of the *bhakti* saints in all directions. However, some *bhakti* saints did embrace the theory of *avatara* (God in human form) and worshipped the deity of Krsna or Rama. But Kabir belonged to the *nirguna* (attributeless) *Brahman* tradition and considers it impossible that God can appear in human form. His God is *Brahman* who dwells in all beings, as the Being of all entities. Most of all this divine entity dwells within us and can be known within us through *jnana* (knowledge of the ground of all things). Thus, looking for God in the temples and in the rituals of the priests and pilgrimages are entirely futile. Kabir addresses this divine spirit within man mostly as *Rama* or sometimes as Hari (Krsna), the same synonymous of God prevalent among all Hindus. But his *Rama* does not mean the avatara in the Ramayana, nor does his *Hari* mean Krsna of the Mahabharata, the epic saga. Kabir's *Rama* is attributeless *Brahman* within us and to relate to this inner and outer spirit is the supreme goal of human life. Kabir firmly denounces religious antics of the priests and the priestly caste of the Hindus as well as the practices and rituals of the Muslim priests (mullahs), especially the mullah's torture of animals in the rituals of meat purification (*halal*). Being a follower of the true spirit of Hinduism, Kabir was a strict vegetarian and condemned hunting animals and even of destroying plant life or gathering of leaves and flowers for temple rituals.

We know that the death of the other, especially the demise of a near and dear one leaves a deep impact on us which only time is supposed to heal. Some thinkers like Heidegger maintain that death is strictly speaking one's own and it is not something that can be either experienced for the purposes of retelling or something that can be shared. However, regarding the all-too-common mourning after someone's death, Kabir offers the following reflections:

Why mourn the death of the other
You could do so if you yourself were to live on
I would not die the way the world would die
For I have known the wellspring of life (1)

Why douse this body with many perfumes
If the supreme bliss is forgotten thereby (2)

There is one well and five striving to draw water
The rope is broken but the foolish mind craves water (3)

Says Kabir when true thought emerges
There is neither the well nor the seekers of water. (4).[15]

When we know full well that we ourselves are going to depart from life one of these days, it is not logical to engage in excessive mourning for the departed ones. Kabir says with confidence that he would not die the same way as the world is passing on, for he has met with the everlasting source of life, one who is the originator of life. Those who contemplate the everlasting Being *and* have received its glimpses, do not die in the same manner as the worldly minded meet their end. One who has given up *maya* as far as possible and has had the experience of contemplation of the divine, the prerequisite of which is voluntary renunciation of worldliness, would be ready for the biological death in a way that a creature of *maya* will never be. One who gives up *maya* and the one who clings to *maya* experience different kinds of death, even though death is the same for all mortals. For the contemplator the process of death has already cast its positive shadow upon his life, and he is no stranger to the art of dying. For the worldly minded person death is a calamity and an unwelcome destiny, for the only shadows that the awareness of morality has cast on his life has been comprised of dread and inauthenticity, that produces a fear and dismissal of death as the opposite pole of life. Thus, Kabir says that being a contemplator he is sure that he is not going to die the same ways as the multitudes who will be dragged out of existence.

Kabir remarks in the second stanza that it is foolish for the dandy to wear fine clothes and to apply perfumes on this body. The process of enjoying these worldly experiences is bound to make one forget that time is better spent in

---

[15.] Ibid., Rag Gauri, p. 12.

contemplating the divine and awaiting the supreme bliss of its grace in the form of a brief glimpse of union with *Brahman*.

In the third stanza Kabir refers to a well around which there are five seekers of water. The rope that is used to pull a bucket of water happens to be broken but the mind that is devoid of true knowledge (*matti-hari*) is still making futile exertions to draw water. Kabir is using the metaphor of well for the love of the body, and five classical moral errors of craving (*kama*), anger (*krodha*), greed (*lobha*), attachment (*moha*), and pride (*ahamkara*) which are making futile efforts to obtain happiness symbolized by water. When the mind (*buddhi*) strives through the methods of sexuality, anger, greed, attachment and pride to achieve gratification of sensual pleasure, it is as if the proper means, symbolized by the rope are broken (or absent) and improper means of five moral errors (*avgunas*) are being deployed. For the happiness or bliss (*ananda*) cannot be secured though the five ever present moral errors or moral lapses.

In the fourth and final stanza Kabir concludes that it is only when the buddhi (mind) is uplifted to a higher (thoughtful) level and rises above the five errors, that the well disappears as well as those cravings of the mind to obtain sensual gratifications from the dark well of the body.

Thus, the song suggests that too much lamentation on the demise of a near and dear one does not make sense because we too are destined to follow the departed one to the abode of *Yama* (the god of death). The better and more thoughtful thing to do is to prepare for one's own death by embracing death in this very life by voluntarily giving up these futile strivings for gratification through morally degrading methods of *kama, khroda, lobha, moha,* and *ahamkara*. That is why a special kind of death is in store for Kabir, whereas the worldlings will simply die off or will be taken out by the biological death. Those who arrange their life as "being-toward" death, as Heidegger puts it, are different from those who are inauthentically dismissing death from out of their lives and regard it as something which will inevitably appear at the end of their life and should never be invoked within their life. Kabir is a theist, and he expresses his death contemplation which was alive and well and underway in his life. In his contemplation or thoughtful recitation of the name of the Lord he has had a vision of the great reservoir of everlasting life that is *Brahman*. Thus, his life is free from the fear of death and there is a certain readiness and practice of death within his life. The same readiness or rehearsal of death that distinguished the life and death of Socrates.

Thus, Kabir uses the classical concepts of Hindu thought such as five moral traps (*agunas*), love of the body and matters bodily (*deha-adhyasa*) to bring home a simple spiritual message to the simple folk in their own language. The fear of death should be overcome through the constant contemplation of the name of the Lord, the giver of everything who will enable you to suspend the life of *maya* and come alive in the life of *atman* (soul), the vision of *brahman* within oneself. A similar thought is expressed in another song of Kabir:

> The death that puts the whole world in dread
> That death is exposed in the guru's word (1)
>
> Now how will I die when my mind is reconciled with death
> They go through death after death, who haven't known Rama (pause)
>
> All are clamouring about death and dying
> But only the one who dies steadily, is free and immortal (2)
>
> Says Kabir the mind is joyful
> Gone are the doubts leaving behind supreme bliss (3)[16]

In this song, Kabir says that obviously death is portrayed as a dreadful prospect by the whole world. However, the true meaning of death is highlighted in the guru's word (*sahad*) of the Sat guru (True Guru or Everlasting Guru) who has left behind his exposition of spiritual enigmas in his written word (*sahad*), which is a revealed word and not just a poem.

Kabir emphasizes that those who have made room for death within life, who have reconciled with death by taking up dying as a way of life, will not die an ordinary death. They have adapted to the life lessons of death by accepting it as a way of life. Most others, however, are going through death after death because they haven't known, that is, lived out the knowledge of Rama, or *Brahman*. Dying death after death is used in two senses. Fear of death is a sort of experience of death that the worldly -minded person takes as a possible as well as certain loss of all the goods and relations that one possesses. This image of the loss of everything produces an ongoing scepter of death. The second meaning has to do with Hindu mythology. Being in the cycle of s*amsara* is also equal to undergoing death after death. Having to be born again and again in samsara, is also having to die again and again.

In the second stanza, Kabir says that people are referring to death and dying all the time without considering its meaning and implications. Only the one who dies

---

[16] Ibid, Rag *Gauri*, p. 20.

"steadily," that is, goes through living in the shade of death within his own life does not consider death as an event at the end of life but as present all through the design of his life. Such a one is the only one who has experienced immortality of a sort, for such a one is free of the fear of death having welcomed the presence of death in his life.

Thus, having welcomed death within one's life, being resolved to practice the death of *maya* steadily in one's life, one's mind dwells in joyfulness (*Ananda*), says Kabir in the third and final stanza. It is also a state where the doubt that *maya* can possibly deliver happiness disappears leaving behind supreme bliss (*param-Ananda*) *This param-Ananda* serves as a glimpse of immortality in mortal life as well as moments of union with *Brahman*. Thus, the dividends of death contemplation are explained in terms of Kabir's original exposition of the meditative pathway of the recitation of the name of the lord (Rama) the prerequisites of which are the practice of the death of *maya* and egoism. This is the way of true *bhakti* according to Kabir, which essentially requires death contemplation.

This detachment from *maya* or worldliness is not meant to be absolute. Absolute detachment from the world and worldliness is impossible while one is alive in the flesh. In one of his songs[17] Kabir explains the state of mind and lifestyle of a detached individual who is adept in undergoing the death of *maya*.

> In life this one dies and then comes alive
> And thus, dwells in emptiness (*Sunya*)
>
> within defilements he remains spotless (Niranjan)
> and does not obtain again the ocean of *samsara* (1)

Such an adept practitioner of death and contemplation voluntarily dies, that is, says no to *maya* and such dying comes alive to the life of *atman*. This authentic practitioner achieves a stunned state of *sunya* (emptiness) of the mind and dwells more and more therein unperturbed by the usual and frequent thoughts of worldly matters, as well as temptations brought about by the five evils, namely, *kama* (cravings), *kroadha* (anger), *lobha* (greed), *moha* (attachment), and *ahamkara* (egoism). The state of *Sunya*, is an original concept in Buddhism. Kabir was in contact with *Natha yogis*, a band of ascetics quite popular in Kabir's times. These yogis like Guru Gorakh Nath were influenced by Buddhist notions of meditation, samadhi (deep contemplation) and *Sunya*, etc.

---

[17] Dev Ji, *Adi Granth*, 46.

Another character of such an authentic contemplator is that he or she can remain undefiled and spotless in a world full of defilements and temptations of *maya*. In *anjana* he can remain *niranjana*. Anjana is the word used for darkness of the pursuits of *maya* or excessive worldliness, the net result or ultimate consequence of which is darkness of suffering. Being in the world means living in midst of seemingly sweet but essentially bitter consequences of our worldly activities. The word *anjana* is also used for black mascara applied to the eyes. The point is to live a life of detachment as far as possible in our life of worldly necessities and ambitions. Let us live detached (as far as possible) in a world of attachments, undefiled (*niranjana*) amid defilements (*anjana*) of *maya*. If we can do so, we will not have to come back to or be reborn in this ocean of *samsara* (*bhav-jal*), Kabir says this in a nutshell consistent with Hindu mythology of the reincarnation of the atman (soul) not yet ready for salvation (*moksha*) and caught up in the ocean of *samsara*.

To remain spotless (niranjana) in a world of defilement and taint does not mean an absolute break with the world. The yogis and ascetics (*sadhus*) who claimed to abandon the world of *maya* altogether were false claimants who do not understand what true *bhakti* (devotion) means. It was part of Kabir's mission to expose such false claims of the priests and yogis. He had a very down to earth approach to how being in the world is to be purified and modified to make room for the *bhakti* (devotional love) of the lord. His theism was cleansed of the notions of personal God with well-defined attributes, and of *avatara* or God appearing in human form. It also stayed clear of the polytheism and mythology although he shows a penetrating knowledge of all sorts of beliefs of the Hindus in his critical analyses of such notions in his work. He exposes an original possibility of *bhakti* toward an attribute less- lord within us and belonging to *nirguna brahman* in a simple, direct and love-laden way in his work. To achieve this union with the lord a rejection of *maya* is necessary but not an absolute or complete rejection. An extreme asceticism is not required. Just simple and authentic life of contemplation as well as complete devotion in the form of a continuing recitation of the name of the lord (*Rama-nama*). In order to perform this *bhakti,* some material needs have to be met, for *bhakti* cannot be done on empty stomach and need not be done in the forest away from the family. In a very special song, Kabir prays for some basics so that he can do what is most valuable for him to do, that is to invoke the name of the lord in a sweet silent thought:

> Cannot do bhakti while hungry
> Take please your rosary away... (1)

Madhava, I can't be hesitant on this issue
If you don't provide, I must ask for it

I ask for two (four pounds) of flour
A (pound) of ghee (butter) and some salt
Two pounds of dal (lentils) I request
That will enable me to live through the day (2)

I ask for a cot with four legs
A pillow and a mattress
To cover I want a comforter
To worship you with love (3)

I am not being greedy
Your name is all I care for
Says Kabir my mind is fully involved with you
And this involvement makes me know you lord Hari (4)[18]

Kabir is being very realistic in his conversation with the deity. The idea of return-
ing the rosary is very meaningful. One may pretend to do *bhakti* with the outward
display of turning the heads of rosary (*mala*). But real *bhakti,* that is, the constant
recitation of lord's name cannot be done in a state of hunger and deprivation. If God
does not grant those basic provisions, there is no harm in praying for them in order
that real *bhakti* be performed without interruption. Thus, Kabir asks for four pounds
of flour for the rotis, one pound of ghee or clarified butter and some salt as well as
too pounds of lentils. These are essentials to live on and for having two meals a
day. These pleadings to God indicate that Kabir practiced a simple way of a strict
vegetarian like the other Hindus living in Benares. He condemns the meat-eating
and especially the torturous killing of animals (*halal*) in the name of religion, a
common practice among some Muslim followers who were told that there is no
bar on meat-eating for them. Of course, not all the poor Muslim population could
afford to eat meat on regular basis. Most of them lived just like their fellow Hindus
and particularly shunned beef-eating so as not to disrespect the Hindu neighbors.

The third stanza makes a further request for a functioning cot that has its four
legs intact, along with a mattress, a comforter, and a pillow, so that this disciple
(*jan*) of God can continue with the noble task of *bhakti* immersed in love. It is to

---

[18.] Ibid., Rag Sorath, p. 11

be noted that real contemplation of the divine also requires adequate sleep, and to sleep one needs bed, mattress, and pillow. Kabir also remarks that he is not being greedy as some extreme homeless ascetics (*yogis*) might think, because Kabir is distinguished only due to his practice of God's name. Kabir concludes that his mind is only focused on one-pointed involvement, a single-minded contemplation. And this involvement has blessed him with a special knowledge (*jnana*) of lord Hari. It is mentioned in the *Upanishads* that the knowledge of Brahman (*vidya*) is so different from the knowledge of things in the world (*avidya*). Kabir is expressing the wisdom of the *Upanishads*, for example, *Katha Upanishad* in simple words and powerfully poetic style for the simple folk without any pretense of priestly status and scholarship of the Vedas. But the inner insight of the Vedas is very well captured in many of his special songs.

The authentic life is defined by Kabir as a life with the presence of death in it. A life that pursues only the indulgent life with no practice of death is neither real nor complete. An authentic life seems to halt the materialistic cravings to make room for a philosophical reassessment of human life which is a contemplative reappraisal of an individual resolve to live a higher life. In a *sabad* (song) from Raga Sorath, he says:

> That without which one does not quite live, that
> by which one obtains the success of one's toils
> that which is called a true life
> Is unachievable without dying (1)
>
> Now about that true life it is pointless to offer many descriptions
> When one has oneself weighed it against the transitoriness of all things (pause)
> One who has rubbed on the slate of life to obtain oneness of soul and oversoul
> And witnessed the essence of the world without the use of eyes
> The son has produced the father and created a city within to cease his wonderings (2)
>
> . . .
>
> One who knows how to die while alive
> Gains the saintly eternal peace
> Kabir too has gained that wealth
> By his devotion to the Lord Hari, with renunciation of mine-ness (4)[19]

---

[19.] Ibid., Rag Sorath, p. 6.

Without the experience of authenticity, one has been merely sliding through a vegetative life and has failed to experience the true life, which only the practice of dying reveals, says Kabir in his thoughtful *sabad*. That inner and deeper meaning of life is obtained as the crown of one's spiritual toils which involve an ongoing practice of death, that is, a constant rejection or renunciation of what is falsely branded as high life available only to the rich and lucky ones. But all these material pursuits are chimeras of *maya* which rob one of the possibilities of true life (*sad-jivana*), that is, a life full of the endowments of the eternal which are unavailable in the transitory life. The root word for *sad* is *sat* or *satya*, which means the everlasting Being. Thus, *sad-jivana* is life in the shade of the eternal, wherein one mediates on the eternal lord rather than chasing transitional attractions of *maya*.

In the second stanza, which has the word "pause" at the end of the second line, means that these two lines contains the theme of the entire *sabad*. Kabir says here in a nutshell that about the true life (*sad-jivana*) it is needless and pointless to put forward various descriptions because it is something known only to those who have experienced it personally and found it as something that contrasts with the usual transitory appearance and disappearance of the worldly phenomena. This living of authentic life is not something strictly definable through one or the other description. But the quality of this higher life is something to be personally experienced by those authentic practitioners.

In the next stanza Kabir implies that one who has rubbed on the slate of life and made valiant spiritual efforts for the union of his *atman* (soul) and *Brahman* (the divine Being), and has had no need of using his eyes, with which one spectates the world. Such a one has visualized the essence of the world with an inward look on his *atman* which contains the presence of the divine Being inside him. The son (*jiva* or human entity) has created a wondrous city within and reproduced the father. This divine father often remains unnoticed but comes alive due to the spiritual toils of the authentic practitioner.

Kabir sums up in the fourth stanza that one who knows how to die while living, one who is adept in the art of dying or rejecting (with a voluntary resolve the life of *maya*), gains eternal peace, that is, the reward of a saintly life. Kabir maintains that he too has obtained this true wealth by fully dedicating himself to the Lord Hari and by giving up his egoism and self-love. We should keep in mind that Hari is the popular name of God that Kabir often uses for the attributeless *brahman*. He also uses the name Rama for God in the same sense.

This is a powerful song of Kabir that gives us a glimpse of his unique way of death contemplation blended with *bhakti*. The art of dying while living offers a unique spiritual experience that is unavailable to those mired in excessive worldliness. It is not just an experience of knowing the soul by moving away, as far as possible, from worldliness, as described by Socrates in Plato's *Phaedo,* but it is also a poetic experience of *bhakti* (devotion), which is part and parcel of the human heart. Thus, the effort to get nearer and nearer to God by voluntarily getting away from worldliness and offering one's highest love to the lord is an essential part of Kabir's contemplation. We notice that he shunned the theological and scholarly games of the Hindu priesthood and scriptural studies and offered a simple pathway to the innocent masses who responded by making his poetry their own, by making it a part of folklore and by heeding his call for living the nonritualistic and simple religious life.

In the *Adi Granth*, the *slokas* (couplets) and the *sabads* (songs) are compiled in separate sections. The *sabads* are classified into different *Ragas* (melodies) and various *Ragas* serve as the chapters under which the works of the Sikh gurus as well those of the twenty-two *bhakti* saints are compiled. Among the *bhakti* saints, Kabir's work is given the maximum coverage (in *sabads and slokas*). This prominence given to Kabir indicates that Kabir's approach to God as *nirguna brahman*, his dismissals of polytheism, his denial of belief in avatars (God in human form) as well as ritualism was deemed to be very compatible with Sikhism.

In the middle of the *sabad* collection of *Raga Maru*, a special *sloka* is included by the editor of the *Adi Grantha,* namely, Guru Arjuna, the fifth guru. It is as if this couplet was deemed to be too special to let it be part of the odd *slokas* in this anthology. This short couplet offers a wonderful summation of human life as a struggle for moral upliftment:

> A drum in the sky beats on, marking the ardent in the heart
> The warrior has occupied the field and is eager for skirmish (1)
> The gallant is to be recognized as one who battles for the poor
> Even cut down to pieces, this one, but flees never the field (2)

"A drum in the sky beats, marking those ardent in the heart" is an acute description of the man's connection with the divine Being. It is popular belief among the Hindu mystics that while human body has nine obvious openings or doors, it also has a tenth doorway (*dasam-dwar*) lodged in the brain behind the middle of the forehead. The spiritually accomplished person can open this doorway to infinity and gets attuned to the ceaseless music emanating from *brahman* (*anhad-nada*). The drum that beats in the sky, hits on target the mind, and through the mind, the heart of the warrior. The warrior has assumed his or her place in the field, that is, the arena of human life to do battle or skirmish with immoral temptations of *maya,* especially with the five moral pitfalls, namely, *kama, khroda, lobha, moha,* and *ahamkara* (craving, anger, greed, attachment, and pride).

One may also call that one a true gallant who battles for the poor and the down-trodden. In this moral struggle to fight on behalf of the poor and humble fellow humans, the true warrior allows himself to be cut down but never abandons the field of action. This *sloka* of Kabir outlines that human entity's life is a battle, first, to defeat the moral enemies (*kama*, etc.) and then to resist the forces that keep the poor in poverty.

As part of the critique of the false rituals and show offish practices of the Hindu priests (*Brahmins*) and the innocent masses duped by them, Kabir paints a picture of the inauthentic life which steers away from death and contemplation. He emphasizes in the form of the meditation on the lord's name (*Rama-nama*), which according to his understanding of God as *nirguna brahman* (attributeless Being) is the simplest method of relationship to the divine Being. At the same time, its prerequisites make the recitation of the lord's name a difficult path. The prerequisites of staying away from *maya* and ridding oneself of egoism make this spiritual living a formidable commitment. Staying away from *maya* and egoism, as far as possible, means acknowledging and accepting death within life. This pathway is open to all humans, not just the Hindus:

> First the Lord's light appeared and then all emerged including all (people) good or bad
> People, don't be deceived
> The creator is the creation; within people abides the lord completely present everywhere[20]

This is the simple but profound summation of the Vedantic (Hindu) view of reality that finds no difference between the creator and his creation.

Kabir who exhorts the inauthentic man to recognize how his entire life has been wasted; the wastage of one's authentic potentials is all too common. All

---

[20] Ibid., Rag Prabhati, p. 43.

our achievements are based on the work of some special moments in a sea of wasted moments. *Maya* and egoism spare no one:

> True religion you have forsaken O crazy man
> True life abandoned
> Having filled your stomach, you are sleeping like a beast
> And have lost the purpose of human birth
> Never been in the company of saints, busy always in false pursuits
> Living like a dog, a pig, you are wandering, coming and going
> You think of yourself in higher proportions and others as punctuation marks
> But those who always chase mind's cravings
> Are known to live in hell. (2)
> O you lustful, angry, crafty, deceiving useless man
> You spend all your time denouncing others, being forgetful of God
> Says, Kabir, you contemplate nothing, O foolish muddled peasant
> You haven't known the name of *Rama,* how will you cross over this *samsara*

In this portrait of the everyman, Kabir has shown the omnipresence of inauthenticity, which makes us forgetful and dismissive of death. The life of restraint is seldom followed by the multitudes who choose to forsake their *Deen* (religion/moral path). In the service of their stomach, preoccupied with eating and drinking and sleeping take away most of their time. The nobility of human birth is lost in their lifestyle. Kabir mentions in the second stanza that such inauthentic individuals prefer the company of revelers like themselves and do not seek out the assembly of saintly persons. They are always busy in worldly pursuits, which are ultimately false. Such people are very proud of their so-called practical pursuits. But having never examined what is truly meaningful they wander about like dogs and pigs in the same locality never venturing out to a higher plane of divinity. Such worldly minded people are often full of themselves, constantly fanning their ego and asserting a self-styled greatness. They always apply smaller measure for others who, in their eyes are as insignificant as little punctuation marks in a script. If there is hell then such persons who are constantly answering to the mind's cravings, must be headed for that hell.

Most people who have not controlled the five moral degradations (*kama* etc.) are chided by Kabir for being lustful (*kama*), angry (*khrodha*), crafty (*chaturi*), clever, deceptive, and useless. Why do they spend all their time taking pleasure in denouncing others. That is why most people love gossip and politics, perfect pastimes for finding faults in others. It reminds us that Heidegger includes "idle talk" as an important preoccupation of inauthenticity. Someone on his or her way to discover their relationship to the divine will have no time for castigating and denouncing others who are but foolish victims of *maya.* The authentic person will be able to forget and forgive these childish antics of suffering masses and will move on to a contemplative life. But you remain largely uncontemplative, foolish, and muddled about your aims, if you have not known the wonderful gift of the name of the lord. The recitation of the lord's name (*Rama-nama*) brings a higher sort of knowledge not of the world and its things but a Knowledge (*jnana*) that is the foremost blessing of being human, the knowledge of Being (lord) that is attributeless, limitless and not affected by *maya,* and purer and higher than *samsara.*

Kabir's critique of false ritualisms and antics of a foolishly materialistic as well as arrogant worldling are too numerous in the body of his work. We could only touch upon a fraction of his literary output which is full of logic as well as wisdom. His couplets and songs do not merely offer criticisms of pretentious religious people and their extreme dogmas, but they also bring forward a resolution to the problem of authentic living. The method of the recitation of the lord's name is supposed to bring one to a higher plane (*akhara*) where mystery of Being does not end but begins, and where thought awaits the gifts of contemplation. It is a state where all dogmas have disappeared, and a two-way *bhakti* love keeps us glued to knowledge (*jnana*). At the same time, Kabir's insight on the connection between death and contemplative life is quite an original contribution to the philosophy of death.

# CHAPTER 5

# Bhakti and Buddhism

*R. Raj Singh*

*Bhakti*, at a fundamental level, is so essentially a "human" experience, that it cannot be confined to a particular tradition. Since this term is a part of Sanskrit vocabulary and obviously originated and gained currency in certain Vedic religious outlooks and practices, it is often narrowly understood and defined as "Hindu devotion." Thus, expositions of *bhakti* of Socrates or *bhakti* of Plotinus would be treated as philosophically exotic and culturally hybrid speculations. Even within Indian religious and philosophical traditions, *bhakti* remains poorly understood both historically and philosophically. It is commonly believed that *bhakti* suddenly appeared as one of the three Yogas in the *Bhagavad-Gita*. Even in the various interpretations of the Gita Bhakti is often narrowly understood as an expression of theism, merely as the *bhakta's* devotion for his or her *Bhagavan,* a relationship with the divine Being, and thus absent in *nastika* (nontheistic, non-Vedic) religions like Buddhism and Jainism.

However, a simple etymological probe will indicate that *bhakti* has more anthropocentric an existential connotation rather than being originally and primarily indicative of human–God relationship. *Bhakti* was always meant to introduce the human factor into philosophical abstractions and religious enigmas. The status of *bhakti* as a perennial tendency of Indian thought is missed when its pervasiveness is overlooked by the cultural historians preoccupied primarily with its periodic and varied eruptions. The philosophical role of *bhakti* is missed when it is taken as an alternative to *Jnana* (knowledge) rather than "living *jnana*." A succinct meaning of *bhakti*, as pin-pointed by a later classic *Narada Bhakti Sutra* (10th century) is *parama-prema* (higher attainment of love). As "loving devotion" and a basic involvement of the human soul with things it finds valuable and fulfilling, *bhakti* is not a sole possession of Indian philosophies and religions. As a basic longing of the human heart, it is universal. However, Indian traditions offer a remarkable fusion of *bhakti* and *jnana,* as well as some rigorous investigations into and experimentations with the nature of *bhakti*. A study of Indian world-views from the pivotal point of *bhakti* reveals original and fascinating insights into human nature and human potential.

The aim of this paper is to show that *bhakti* was already in vogue in religious circles when the Buddha appeared on the Indian religious scene. This ancient form of *bhakti* was not only a catalyst in the formation of the Buddha's new worldview, but *bhakti* continues to pervade the dharma of the Buddha in its early doctrinal period as well as in *Mahayana* developments. In order to identify the pervasiveness but subtle presence of *bhakti* in the earliest statements of the *Buddha-dharma,* both *bhakti,* and dharma need to be precisely defined in terms of their essential as well as relevant philosophical meanings and implications. This means that we will retrace the broader and original meaning of *bhakti* in order to study its role in the formation and elucidation of the Buddha's dharma. However, as we shall see that "dharma" carry several special meanings within Buddhism, and thus in this short essay we cannot possibly enumerate all the various ways of *bhakti* visible in Buddhist ethics, religious practices, movements and doctrinal developments. Thus, we will confine ourselves to Buddha-dharma in the sense of "the basic teachings of the Buddha" and will remain focused on the pre-Mahayana period. When we glean through the records of early Buddhism, we notice that even though the ancient Buddhist *sutras* do not show any debt to the *Bhagavad-Gita* and did not produce *bhakti* classics such as the *Bhaga-vat-purana, Narada Bhakti Sutra,* and *Shandilya Bhakti Sutra, bhakti* not only shaped the existential focus of Buddhism but remained part and parcel of that tradition. Nicol Macnicol in his *Indian Theism*[1] published in 1914, has a chapter titled "Theism within Buddhism" which gives an account of the presence *bhakti* within early and *Mahayana* Buddhism. More recently, B. G. Gokhale (1981) has explored the aspects of *bhakti* in the first five centuries of Buddhism in his article "Bhakti in Early Buddhism."[2] Both these scholars have contributed toward correcting the view that *bhakti* is exclusively a Hindu practice and shown with attention to detail the presence of *bhakti* in Buddhism with citations from *nikayas* and *Mahayana* documents. However, Macnicol is obviously equating *bhakti* with theism, and Gokhale is too sure about the meaning of *bhakti* as faith (*Sradha*). Gokhale says,

---

[1] Nicol Macnicol, *Indian Theism* (Delhi: Munshilal Banarsidas, 1915).

[2] B. G. Gokhale, "Bhakti in Early Buddhism," in *Tradition and Modernity in Bhakti Movements*, ed. J. Lele (Leiden: E. J. Brill, 1991).

There is no need for us to go into the detailed implications of the philosophical aspects of history of faith and knowledge since we are concerned here with the development of the *bhakti* element in early Buddhism...Nor is there much need for us to discuss at length the origin and development of the *bhakti* element in early Buddhism...Nor is there much need of us to discuss at length the origin and development of the term *bhakti* in Brahmanical literature, (Or)...whether the movement...originated first...in its Vasudeva-Krishna evolutions.

In my view, however, the philosophical implications of the idea of *bhakti*, and understanding of its etymology and an appreciation of its history, are of utmost importance. One has to have a picture of "the thought ferment" of the 6th and 5th centuries BC. India to study the continuing presence of *bhakti* in the Buddhist outlook. Not only *karma* and rebirth but also *bhakti* constitutes what Buddhism shares with Vedanta. Furthermore, one can only "attempt" to define perennial thematic concepts such as *bhakti*. These are never conclusively or exhaustively defined, for to do so will be an oversimplification. Thus, to study the rise of *bhakti* in Buddhism we will proceed toward the times of the Buddha by way of short historical overview of the pre-Buddhist evolution of *bhakti* and its presence in the non-Buddhist and non-Jaina schools and sects of the age in which the Buddha put forward his worldview.

But before we do so, a brief note on the various chief meanings of dharma within Buddhism is in order. The word "dharma" carries various meanings in the early Vedic as well as in early Buddhist traditions. Needless to say, it cannot be defined easily, nor can it be translated casually. The law of lawfulness, the ground, the established order, the moral order, duty, doctrine, religion, the fundamental nature of things, etc. are some of its traditional meanings. It is a word that was well chosen by the Buddha for his doctrine and for his new heterodox religious system as a whole. It is well known that the term "dharma" has been widely employed within Buddhism in three significant ways. Firstly, dharma is understood in the sense of "Buddha-dharma," that is, the teaching or the doctrine of the Buddha. As indicated in the triple refuges sought by the Buddhists, namely, the refuge in the Buddha, in the dharma, and in the *sangha* (community), the truth of the teaching is to be viewed as independent from the personality of the teacher. That the Buddha wished the noble truths to take precedence over himself and the doctrine itself to remain true and everlasting teacher of the *sangha* is testified by the various extant records (*sutras*) of his discourses and made abundantly clear in *mahaparinibbana suttanta*, which reports on the last moments of the life of the Sakyamuni Buddha. The *sutra* is comparable in many ways to Plato's *Phaedo* in so far as it succinctly recapitulates the personal standpoints of the master, the entire life's philosophy of the Buddha in one stroke of death contemplation. That the dharma is one thing and the authority of the Buddha another is clearly stated in this oft-quoted concise statement from the *anguttara-nikaya*:

> Whether the Buddhas arise, O *bikhus*, or whether the Buddhas do not arise it remains a fact and the fixed and necessary constitution of being, that all its constituents or transitory [and, it is repeated, *dukkha* (unsatisfactory) and lacking in *atman* (soul, substance)]. This fact a Buddha discovers and masters, and when he has discovered and mastered it, he announces, teaches and publishes, proclaims, discloses, minutely explains and makes it clear, that all the constituents of Being are transitory...*dukkha*...[and] lacking in *atman*.[3]

The second broad sense in which the term "dharma" is employed within Buddhism is that of proper conduct, moral conduct and duty. Due to the prevalence of the *bhakti* ethos, the proper conduct was meant to have nothing to do with the traditions *varna dharma* (duties of the class to which one belongs), but it means moderate and fitting conduct indicated by the term *samma* in the fourth noble truth. It may also mean code of conduct prescribed for the *bikhus* (monks) and *upasakas* (novices). The third important use of the term dharma within Buddhism is dharma as reality or "the way it is." Dharma is not only understood as reality and as nature of things, but "realities" are also called dharmas. We should keep in mind that "reality" is understood in its dynamic and transitory sense; dharmas are not to be taken as substances but as irreducible ultimates.

Besides these three chief uses of the term dharma several of its other ontological and cosmological meanings are traced within Buddhism in general and Buddhist philosophical schools in particular. However, in the following study of the bond between *bhakti* and *Buddha-dharma*, we will confine ourselves to dharma in the first abovementioned sense. Let us now turn toward the original and ancient meaning of the word *bhakti*.

The verbal root of the term *bhakti* lies in Sanskrit *bhaj*, means "to share," "to partake," "to participate."[4] Since sharing with persons indicated a communication,

---

[3.] M. Dhavamony, *Anguttara-nikaya*, iii.134, in *Buddhism in Translations*, trans. H. C. Waren (Cambridge, MA: Harvard University Press, 1953), Foreword.

[4.] M. Dhavamony, *Love of God according to Saiva Siddhanta* (London: Oxford University Press, 1971), 11–45. Dhavamony offers a comprehensive etymological analysis of the term "bhakti."

*bhaj* was used in the sense of love, and with respect to various aspects of love, such as to possess, to enjoy, to prefer, to adore, to worship, to commit oneself, and to be loyal. *Bhakti* then etymologically conveys the sense of participation and sharing. In the classics of Sanskrit literature composed from the 5th century onward, derivatives of *bhaj* are used to speak about both secular and religious love, about the relationship between man and woman, the reverence toward a guru, worship of gods, man's love of God, and God's love of man. The synonyms of *bhakti* are all synonyms of *prema* (love) such as *priti, sneha, anuraga,* and *anurakti.*[5]

The birth of *bhakti* seems to have taken place in the Vedas. *Rig Veda* contains numerous hymns to several gods, often personifications of the powers of nature or clan gods. If *bhakti* is an attitude of love, devotion, friendship, and reverence, it is certainly present in these human outpourings of communion with the divine. Homage is paid to, mercy is sought from, and power is recognized of major gods such as Varuna, Agni, Indra and several minor deities. Although the term *bhakti* Is not to be found in the *Rig Veda* hymns, the root word *bhaj* is present.[6] The essential tendencies of *bhakti* such as recognition of God's charity, friendliness and deep involvement in human affairs, as well as man's self-surrendering prayer (*nivedana*), symbolic offering (*archana*), and sweet recollections of god's goodness (*smarna*) are all evident. The notion of *sraddha* (faith), the companion concept of *bhakti*, which is a religious prerequisite of all forms of Hinduism, Buddhism, and Jainism, is certainly present in these hymns, and the term itself is used many times.

What is most interesting is that the devotee of the *Rig Veda* constantly addresses gods as father, mother, brother, relation, and honored guest and invokes God's friendship (*sakhya*). This means that religious love was being measured by secular love, or that no distinction was made between *prema* and *bhakti*. The relation with the divine was one of love and love's attendant expectations, offerings, and involvements. This love appears in a sense of *karuna* within Buddhism as *Guru-bhakti* For the Buddha is equally visible.

Next era, that of the Upanishads, is an age of speculation. Here the basic existential questions are spelled out and pursued with a vigor and originality that not only set into motion various philosophical schools but resulted in the birth of Buddhism and Jainism. It was later in this age that the composition of the epics

---

[5.] Ibid., 20.

[6.] *Rig Veda*, 1.156.3; 8.32.14; 9.113.14; 9113.2; 10.151.2; 10.151.2,3,7.

*Mahabharata* and *Ramayana* had begun. *Bhakti* blossoms a second time and appears in many forms in the central Vedic tradition as well as in the heterodox traditions of Buddhism and Jainism. There is concrete historical evidence that theistic cults of *Pancharatra* and *Bhagvatas* were in vogue[7] resisting the impersonalization of *Para-brahman* (ultimate absolute) of the Upanishads. What is remarkable is that *bhakti* penetrates all speculative and spiritual endeavors of the age: the upanishadic thinkers, Jains, Buddhists, the devotees of the *Bhagvata* and *Pancharatra* faith. The culture of *bhakti* pervades even the sects called *nastikas*, that is, those who did not recognize Vedas and their appendages as the supreme authority. These sects have not left any written scriptures or documents of their own, but are referred to in the Vedas, Brahmanas, Aranyakas, and Upanishads, both derogatorily and in terms appreciative of their asceticism, religious drive, and spiritual quests. However, almost all references to them in the Buddhist and Jain *Suttas* are critical and unappreciative. For instance, in *Brahmajala sutta* of the *Digha Nikaya,* sixty-two non-Buddhist are mentioned and are called holding wrong views or *micchaditthi. The sramanas* and *Jatila Brahmanas*, who did not recognize the Vedas, are mentioned in many ancient texts. Buddhism and Jainism were themselves *sramana* sects. The *Vinaya* mentions Alara Kalama and Uddaka Ramaputta with whom Buddha had personal contact. Some of the religious leaders called *titthiyatirathkara* or heretics in ancient Buddhist *sutras* were: Purana, Kassapa, Pakudha Kachayana, Makkhali Gosala, Ajita Kesakambin, and Sanjya Belathiputta. One of the surviving sects was that of the *Ajivikas* which lasted up to the 14th century AD.[8] Although the *Ajivikas, Carvakas*, and other prominent sects were the target of Buddhists, Jains, and the *astika* (*believers in the Vedas*) faiths, they too participated in a common religious ethos, a culture of *Guru-bhakti* had taken place by the time the Buddha and Mahavira appeared. The Rg Vedic tendency to anthropomorphize religious devotion reflects itself in the *Guru-bhakti* upheld in *Svetasvatara-Upanishad.*

The tendency of *bhakti* attitude to uplift *prema* to *parama-prema,* begins to perceive the presence of God in the person of the Guru. This belief is fully in evidence in early Buddhism. It is interesting to notice that the incarnated lord that appears in the *Bhagavad-Gita,* as well as the Buddha, Mahavira, and the deities of the *Pancharatra* faith were called *Bhagvan*, a term indicating the supreme object of *bhakti*.

---

[7] *Rig Veda*, 8.32.14; 9.113.2,4; 10.151.2,3,7.

[8] R. G. Bhandarkar, *Vaisnavism, Saivism and Minor Religious Systems* (Strasbourg: K. J. Trubner, 1913), 2–14. See also: P. Banerjee, *Early Indian Religions* (Delhi: Vikas Publishing, 1973).

When we study the origins of Buddhism and Jainism, we notice that these traditions also embraced the way of *bhakti* from their very inception. Not only did they inherit convictions concerning *karma,* rebirth, and the necessity of final liberation from the Vedic tradition, but also the spiritual ethos of *bhakti. Bhakti*-faith that was always the faith of the masses was essentially opposed to the caste system and was characterized by adoration of the spiritual stalwarts in human form. A proselytizing spirit always pervaded it. The *bhakta,* old and new, were never obsessed with their private salvation but always wanted to share their joyful insights with the masses. Also, the messages of *bhakti* were always transmitted in the common languages and not in Sanskrit. It is likely that all these elements were present in the *Bhagavata Pancharatra* cults as well as social life at the time of the appearance of the Buddha and Mahavira. They simply adopted all the above-mentioned features of the *bhakti*-faith in their new systems. After the attainment of enlightenment, the Buddha had no qualms about sharing his *arya-satyas* (noble truths) with mankind. Buddhism was opposed to the caste system, and its founders and saints have a missionary spirit, and spread their word in the common languages, at least in the first few centuries. The hierarchies of spiritual status among the *tathagatas, arhats* within Buddhism kept alive a modified *Guru-bhakti.* This is not to say that Buddhism does not offer an original ontology. It clearly seems to be reacting to the Vedic assumptions. Buddhism offers an explicitly humanistic and antimetaphysical philosophy. Nonexistential questions were dismissed by it as unfruitful, and the Buddha exercised his majestic silence about the theistic speculation, as we read in the *Majjhima Nikaya,* in the so-called arrow sermon of the Buddha.[9] Buddhism shows the same preoccupation with existential questions and nonmetaphysical orientations that were typical of the *bhakti* traditions.

Thus, *bhakti* as the practice of love, as the existential rather than metaphysical approach, as the fusion of the abstract truth with ideal ways of living, the doctrine (dharma) and its abiding presence in its adept practitioners (*arhats*) comes into and pervades Buddhism well before the arrival of *Mahayana.* It is in this ancient form of *bhakti* that makes Buddhism a living philosophy as well as a philosophical religion. In the dharma of the Buddha, the fusion between *nirguna* (abstract) *saguna* (concrete) *bhakti* takes place. It is visible in the Buddha's last words recorded in the *Mahaparinibbana suttanta:* "decay is inherent in all component things, work out your *nirvana* with diligence." Abstract truth

---

[9] S. R. Goyal, *A Religious History of India,* Vol. I (Meerut: Kusumanjali, 1984), 133–162.

is offered here as an impetus for *the* ultimate project of existence. This fusion between *nirguna* and *saguna* is visible, as Vinoba Bhave[10] explains, in the daily prayer of the Buddhists, seeking refuge in the Buddha (*saguna*) and in the dharma (*nirguna*) and in the community (*saguna*). This *saguna bhakti* shows through the logical analysis of the implications of dependent origination in Nagarjuna's *mula-madhyamika-karikas.* In his works, Nagarjuna does not lose sight of the existential issues at hand and shows his care for the *saguna* as he intersperses his discourses with tributes to his master. The following is but one example:

> In the admonition to katayana, the two theories concerning "existence" and "non-existence" have been refuted by the bhagvat who adept in existence as well as non-existence.[11]

---

[10.] Warren, *Buddhism in Translations*, 117–122 (*Majjhima-nikava*, 63).

[11.] *Mulamadhyamaka-karika*, XV.7, in David J. Kalupahana. Trans. Nagarjuna (Albany, NY: SUNY Press).

CHAPTER 6

# Empathy and Yoga Philosophy

*Jacqueline Kumar*

The term "empathy" is now widely used, whether in descriptions of some-one's personality, their daily interaction with others, or their lack thereof. It is challenging to find a definitive definition of the term, as it has been employed in many different ways and contexts. Generally, empathy is understood as the ability to emotionally comprehend what others are feeling, see things from their perspective, and imagine oneself in their situation. Essentially, it is summarized as placing yourself in someone else's shoes, experiencing feelings similar to theirs. Although simple in concept, this understanding of empathy has sparked serious debate in the literature, as we will explore.

As a word, empathy is relatively new in the English vocabulary, with its first popular reference in a 1955 edition of the *Reader's Digest*.[1] However, the concept dates back to modern philosophy. The works of David Hume and Adam Smith on sympathy underpin our current notion of empathy. Amy Coplan's interprets that "it seems that the process Hume referred to as sympathy is the same or at least very similar to what we call empathy or mirroring/contagion."[2] Since Hume and Smith, many attempts within philosophy and psychology have emphasized the importance of empathy developed alongside each one during the 20th century.

Despite its various uses, empathy has recently faced criticism, contestation, and even rejection. It has been described as potentially dangerous and problem-atic, with some claiming it is "a poor moral guide." Psychologist Paul Bloom in "Against Empathy: The Case for Rational Compassion," and philosopher Jesse Prinz in "Against Empathy" have generated significant debate with their arguments against empathy. They oppose the idea that we need more empathy

---

[1] Susan Lanzoni, "A Short History of Empathy," *The Reader's Digest: The Atlantic*, October 15, 2015.

[2] Amy Coplan and Peter Goldie, *Empathy: Philosophical and Psychological Perspectives* (Oxford: Oxford University Press, 2011), xxi.

and argue that it may not be a morally desirable emotion to cultivate.[3] I oppose this rejection of empathy as a primary source of moral motivation and turn to Indian philosophy and the four yogas that better capture my circle of empathy.

In this chapter, I briefly clarify what empathy means by considering the different stages or components that constitute it. These stages form a process involving feelings, reasoning, and action-oriented disposition, which I call the process of empathy. This process allows us to live a moral life by combining propositional components of morality with affective-intuitive components. I refer to this as the "circle of empathy," a process involving three co-constitutive stages: fellow-feeling, perspective-taking, and an action-oriented disposition.

The necessity to explore the stages of empathy is demonstrated by Western moral philosophy's preoccupation with theoretical questions. While answering whether morality is reducible to emotion or reason is important, these metaethical issues may detract from our lived moral experiences. I argue that a (re)imagined concept of empathy is needed to explain how we ought to act morally.

Indian philosophy offers a concrete moral practice which better captures how empathy functions in the moral life and as a lived experience. Rather than projecting the notion of empathy onto Indian philosophy, this approach will show us that Indian philosophy provides a different set of concepts and ideas useful for analyzing this universal phenomenon. By tying Indian thought to my understanding of empathy, my aim is to ground our discussion in living morally rather than reducing it to theoretical debates on the nature of morality. Further, I hope that Indian philosophy will illuminate the circle of empathy and its three co-constitutive stages (i.e., affective/intuitive, perspective-taking, and action-oriented disposition).

## Empathy and the Four Yogas

When we speak of the moral life, we often overlook the fact that different languages and cultures highlight and characterize relevant concepts in unique ways. In this chapter, I will point out that although the term "empathy" is not explicitly used in the Indian *yogic* tradition, we can find much that illuminates our understanding within the framework of the four yogas: *bhakti* (love/devotion), *karma* (action), jnāna (knowledge), and *rāja* (psychic control). We must be careful not to import

---

[3] Paul Bloom, *Against Empathy: A Case for Rational Compassion* (New York: Harper Collins Publishing, 2016), 28.

philosophical ideas from Western Philosophy when dealing with Indian philosophy. However, examining the four yogas helps us understand that "empathy" is not solely a product of Western thought. Instead of projecting Western notions of empathy onto Indian philosophy, my approach will show that Indian philosophy offers a different set of concepts and ideas useful for analyzing this universal phenomenon. Incorporating different conceptual resources will ground our discussion on the lived experience of the moral life, rather than focusing solely on philosophical debates bound to distinctive traditions about the nature of morality.

I argue that the process of empathy involves three co-constitutive stages: affective/intuitive, perspective-taking, and action-oriented disposition. The circle of empathy encompasses three co-constitutive components or stages: (1) affectivity/intuitive; (2) contagion; and (3) action-oriented disposition.[4]

At the first stage, affectivity, the empathizer senses the emotion of another person, such as distress or delight, and shares in that person's affective state. This stage may also be described as mirroring or mimicking the one in distress or delight. Secondly, the empathizer rationalizes these feelings and places themselves in the other's shoes. This is the "epistemic" stage or cognitive stage, where the empathizer comes to know the other's situation. Thirdly, with the affective and epistemic stages in sync, the empathizer resolves to act when appropriate. This disposition to act is internal to the process of empathy which makes one willing to contribute to the well-being of the other. For example, if $x$ is happy, $y$ might want to take joy in $x$'s happiness.

This demonstrates that empathy plays a positive role in the moral life. Yet a purely sentimentalist account focuses on how one enters the empathetic process from the affective/intuitive stage. Similarly, the cognitivist emphasizes how one enters the empathetic process from the perspective-taking stage. Therefore, we still need an explanation of how one enters the circle of empathy from the action-oriented disposition stage. I propose an approach from Indian philosophy that offers a more detailed account of empathy's role in forming the motivation to help others in the moral life. While the sentimentalist perspective provides an affective account of human action and the cognitivist perspective provides an affective account of human action and the cognitivist perspective offers reasons for action, these accounts do not start from empathetic action. I contend that Indian philosophy helps complete our account of the circle of

---

[4.] It is important to note that there is no priority or hierarchy between stages. All three stages are necessary and sufficient for empathy to occur.

empathy. Indian philosophy is not focused on metaethical debates, but on improving oneself, finding equanimity and serenity, purifying your mind, and becoming a better person focused on what really matters in life. This approach to philosophy as a way of life will be useful for considering the third aspect of the circle of empathy.

It is important to note that, according to my definition of empathy, all three stages are needed to complete the circle of empathy. Without all three, our understanding of empathy is incomplete. There is no proper order within these stages; it does not matter which one comes first, as long as all three are present. One can be empathic by reasoning first or by feeling first. I will demonstrate that empathy can also begin with action and may be followed by sentiments and reasons for acting. For example, someone might spontaneously act and then later rationalize their action or experience an emotional response to having acted. Empathy can also begin with action, such as engaging in collaborative action or joint activity. For example, two musicians playing the guitar together might start to take the other's perspective by participating in a joint activity, illustrating how the empathetic process can begin with action. Therefore, it does not necessarily begin with intuitive fellow-feeling, or rationalizing a course of action, but with being together in a specific way, such as being involved in a situation which forces one to consider the views of the other.

Consider the following scenario: Imagine someone walking through a public park and noticing a child drowning. Various actions are possible: acting immediately to save the child, calling for help, continuing to walk, or hoping someone else will act. The question is, why does one choose to act immediately? I argue that it is because of empathy. The person who quickly saved the child will reflect on what happened and likely feel compassion or empathy but intended only to save the child's life. Yet empathy was present throughout this process, as long as all three stages were present. This demonstrates that empathy involves much more than just feelings.

This chapter shows how Indian philosophy, through the four yogas, uses the circle of empathy. Firstly, I provide a general background on Indian philosophy and the history of the four yogas. Secondly, I explain the role of the four yogas in Indian philosophy. Finally, I discuss how the yogas, and stages of the circle of empathy, work together, developing scenarios that illustrate how one can enter the circle of empathy at the action-oriented disposition stage. We will see how *karma-yoga* and *bhakti-yoga* are able to complement the Western view of empathy, offering a more complete conception of empathy's place in the moral life.

## Background

In this section, I will introduce some key ideas from Indian philosophy before diving into how the four yogas are relevant to the discourse on empathy. While Indian philosophy has a substantive metaphysical tradition, I will only briefly mention it, as it will not be the focus of our study. A rich metaphysical tradition deserves a study in its own right.

To explore this vibrant intellectual tradition, we will begin with a key text: the *Mahābhārata*. According to Ram Murty, the *Mahābhārata* is concerned with good and evil and issues of social justice.[5] Furthermore, the *Mahābhārata* uses these contexts to discuss deeper philosophical thoughts and yoga systems. The text is written in Sanskrit following the last phase of the *Upanishadic* era (1000 and 600 BCE). It consists of more than 100,000 verses and was composed by the Indian sage-poet Vyasa. This rendition was followed by several versions and translations in all major regional languages of the Indian subcontinent.

After the *Upanishadic* age, some Indian philosophers sought to understand how *Upanishadic* teachings might play a practical role in human existence.[6] These thinkers concerned themselves with issues of ethics and the importance of ethical conduct for humanity. They also focused on a section of the *Mahābhārata* that has since come to occupy an independent status in the Hindu canon known as the *Bhagavad-Gita*. The text speaks of a rivalry between two sides of a family competing for the rulership of a state. It sets out the mental and physical struggles that occur when opposing forces attempt to interpret *dharma* (the moral law) in their own ways.[7] The rivalry commenced between two branches of a family competing for the rulership of a state after the King Dhritarāshtra abdicates in favor of someone other than his son. One side of the struggle is led by the large clan of the Kurus composed of 101 brothers, and the opposing side was represented by the Pandavas, who were five illustrious brothers. On his abdication Dhritarāshtra made Dharmarāja Yudhistra (Arjuna's brother), a member of the Pandavas, the new king, rather than his biological son Duryodhana. Dharmarāja was known to be a virtuous person, one who was interested in a form of *dharma*

---

[5.] Maruti Ram Murty, *Indian Philosophy: An Introduction* (Peterborough, ON: Broadview Press, 2013).

[6.] It is worth noting that central to the Upanishadic thought was the concept of an all-encompassing universal Being (*Brahman*), but this will not be dealt with in this discussion.

[7.] Murty, *Indian Philosophy*, pp. 77–78.

(moral law) founded by wisdom.[8] A power struggle ensued between the new king, Dharmarāja, and Duryodhana, the disfavored son. This led to the great *Mahābhārata* war.

The Pandavas befriended Krishna, the king of a neighboring state. They came to learn that Krishna embodied the teachings of the *Upanishads,* both intellectually, and in the character of his phenomenological experience and intersubjective relations.[9] Krishna became a counselor for the Pandavas, and provided an army assist them in the struggle against the Kurus. Krishna was also Arjuna's charioteer,[10] providing him with timely advice.

The first chapter of the *Bhagavad-Gita* describes Arjuna as a key military commander. As a warrior, he moves through the world with his *Sva-dharma* (self-vocation).[11] When marching with his troops, he does not simply travel with them; he surveys the landscape for potential ambush sites. He does not merely ride in his chariot; his body is prepared for action. He might have to fight at any moment and his body is braced for this eventuality. He always maintains a firm stance to avoid being knocked over; and his memory is attuned to ensure his weapons are within easy reach. Arjuna is not idle; he is already experiencing the battle ahead, including who he might have to kill. Arjuna's lived experience as a warrior—his body, perception, thoughts, and being—is attuned to his *Sva-dharma.* He holds a disposition of military readiness; not always fighting, but always ready to fight. This readiness constitutes Arjuna's action-oriented disposition and establishes his entrance to the circle of empathy.

Arjuna moves through the world enacting his *Sva-dharma* and experiencing this committed disposition of military readiness. Yet he begins to experience an existential crisis on the battlefield. Arjuna feels distraught at the thought of fighting his, and possibly killing, people he grew up with, who were now in the army opposing him. He knows them well, understands their perspectives, and feels their anger, their fear, and their confusion. This weighs heavily on Arjuna. He does not want to confront them. He turns to Krishna, his mentor, in disbelief asking, "How can I slay these people? These people are my teachers, friends,

---

[8.] Ibid., pp. 77–79.

[9.] Ibid.

[10.] It is important to note that that Krishna, a king who is offering his army, takes on the role of the charioteer—which is both menial and extremely dangerous.

[11.] S. Radhakrishnan and Charles A. Moore, *A Source Book in Indian Philosophy* (Princeton: Princeton University Press, 1989), 160.

and loved ones."[12] At this point, Arjuna wants to withdraw from the battle and ascend to a life of solitude in the mountains rather than to "slay [his] honoured teachers."[13] Arjuna struggles with *moha* (attachment) to his loved ones[14] moving through the affective/intuitive stage of the circle of empathy. One could argue that this stems from his conscience because he imagines the people he intends to kill. However, Arjuna's conscience does not usually inhibit him from fighting his enemies. If his conscience is at play here, it is activated by empathy, engaged by the imagination. Empathy is not just a matter of responding to what someone present is feeling in the moment. An empathetic person can respond to imaginary cases.

As a warrior, Arjuna has accumulated vast knowledge about war and warriors. He understands the different perspectives involved in this war: his loved ones committed to fight on the opposing side; his troops' commitment to follow his lead, the strategic and logistical planning for the battle, the consequences of victory and defeat, and the political significance of the war's outcome. Through empathy, Arjuna reaches a richer understanding of what his enemies expect of him, despite their earlier attachment. He appreciates that his family and friends expect him to behave as a soldier ought to behave. In considering all these perspectives, Arjuna understands that he must fight, following his *Sva-dharma* and living as a warrior. By doing so, Arjuna completes the circle of empathy, moving from perspective-taking stage to recognizing his loved ones' are committing to fight, thus deciding to fight rather than retreat.

In the *Bhagavad-Gita*, those who see God in all beings consider the joys and sorrows of others as their own. Empathy is a feature of the perfect yogi, of the one who reaches enlightenment. The clearest example of empathy is found in 6.32: "I regard them to be perfect yogis who see the true equality of all living beings and respond to the joys and sorrows of others as if they were their own."[15] This passage highlights not only the ability to empathize with others but also the element of action that calls for a response to others' joys and sorrows. Empathy, understood as compassion, is even a mark of true devotion in 12.13.

---

[12] Murty, *Indian Philosophy*, pp. 79–81.

[13] Ibid.

[14] Some may argue that Arjuna's decision to continue to carry out his *Sva-dharma* by slaying opposing forces is not in keeping with empathy. Such an objection is taking a literal reading as opposed to a deeper, symbolic understanding and significance of what is transpiring. Also, the narrow familial notion of empathy has to be discarded in favor of a larger global empathy without personal bias.

[15] Swami Mukundananda, "The Bhagavad Gita: The Song of the Lord," Chapter 6: Verse 32. www.holy-bhagavad-gita.org.

One could object that Arjuna simply overcomes the pull of empathy through a reasoning process. One could argue, in keeping with Bloom, that Arjuna's inner struggle is merely a matter of pre-rationally resonating with others' feelings. He is first moved by empathy but overcomes those feelings when considering his duty, his warrior virtues, the needs of his people, and so forth. I argue that Arjuna continues to be empathetic throughout. The story notes how Arjuna does not lose sight of the perspective of his family members fighting against him. Empathy remains in play even when he is motivated by higher concerns than familiar bonds. He is empathetic toward his family, but empathy also informs his decision to fight. Empathy reveals that his family and friends expect nothing less of him. It is not just a purely rational consideration.

The *Bhagavad-Gita* demonstrates a philosophical understanding of empathy through Arjuna's life. Through this case, we see that one can enter the circle of empathy through an action-oriented disposition. Arjuna then moves to the affective/intuitive stage and completes the circle of empathy via perspective-taking.

To explore the significance of this case more fully, it is necessary to understand the co-constitutive stages of the circle of empathy in terms of the four yogas.

## The Four Yogas Within Indian Philosophy

As mentioned in the introduction, the term "empathy" is not explicitly used in the Indian *yogic* tradition; however, we can ground our discussion in an alternative understanding found in the four yogas: *bhakti* (love/devotion), *karma* (action), *jnāna* (knowledge), and *rāja* (psychic control). The Sanskrit word *bhakti* is derived from the root word *bhaj*.[16] Its central tenet is to selflessly share one's love and devotion with fellow humans, as demonstrated in the *Bhagavad-Gita*.[17] *Bhakti-yoga* is concerned with the emotions and innovations of love and devotion, which are aimed at caring for and concerning others.

Similarly, the Sanskrit word *karma* stems from *kri*, which means "to do,"[18] pointing to the fact that our actions define who we are. The intensity of love and devotion is to be combined with *karma,* and in this sense, *karma* cannot be

---

[16.] R. Raj Singh, *Bhakti and Philosophy* (Lanham: Lexington Books, 2006).

[17.] Ibid., p. 8.

[18.] Ibid., pp. 8–10.

separated from *bhakti*.[19] *Bhakti* and *karma-yoga* are interdependent and require *jnāna-yoga* to function successfully.

*Jnāna-yoga* may be equated with inner knowledge, which includes the idea of knowing oneself. We attain wisdom by drawing on what we have experienced, and in this sense, *jnāna* or inner knowledge is best captured by the concept of "introspection." It mainly refers to knowledge of oneself through life experience.

*Rāja-yoga*, finally, emphasizes the importance of concentration.[20] One can view this yoga as a form of empathy with oneself. Through reflection, we not only understand others, but also ourselves. It stresses the need to turn inward and attend to our inner working.[21] *Rāja-yoga* illustrates how we come to know ourselves and thus how we can practice *bhakti, karma,* and *jnāna-yoga*. However, for the purposes of this chapter, I will emphasize *bhakti, karma,* and *jnāna-yoga* as they offer particular insights into practicing empathy.

In the next section, I describe how my circle of empathy, consisting of affective/intuitive, perspective-taking, and action-oriented disposition, aligns with the four yogas by (re)imagining the concept of empathy through the insights of

---

[19.] Ibid., pp. 12.

[20.] Murty, *Indian Philosophy*, p. 83.

[21.] According to Murty, *rāja-yoga* is the kingly path of psychic control. *Rāja-yoga* is also elucidated in the *Gita*, the Gita being the succinct summary of all the major philosophical strands preceding itself. *Rāja-yoga* has an emphasis specifically on meditation and psychic control of the mind and knowledge through concentration. This *rāja-yoga* is present in Krishna's discourse to Arjuna. How is this knowledge acquired? Vivekananda argues that the term "raja-yoga" means concentration of mental activity. We know that human beings are easily distracted, and their minds are constantly bombarded with numerous thoughts. By silencing the mind and calming one's thoughts one can first understand the mind and then gain control over one's mind. Furthermore, *rāja-yoga* when performed properly can enable one to control one's thoughts, emotions, and feelings. For one to attain higher knowledge of reality, one must be inquisitive. Through proper and deeper inquiry, the mind is fully concentrated. *Rāja-yoga* is the path to mind control through understanding. Krishna inspires Arjuna to aim for the steadiness of the mind (*stitaprajna*) and describes the person who has this steadiness of resolve, a perfect sage, in his answer to Arjuna's inquiry concerning how such a man speaks, walks, and sleeps. According to Vivekananda, every science has to have a method based on experiment, observation, and critical analysis. Since *rāja-yoga* is called the science of religion, it too has a method. Thus, he describes the essence of Hinduism simply and practically in his popular writings. Vivekananda describes the study of one's own mind through the process of reflection which is the essence of *raja-yoga*; and this form of understanding is in essence empathy with oneself, based on seeking to understand one's own reality, reflection, and mind control facilitated by *raja-yoga*. Thus, we see an underlying unity in both *rāja-yoga* and *jnāna-yoga* in that they are both based on reflection. This idea is to show how Arjuna still overcomes the reluctance to fight inspired in a kind of empathy with himself. As mentioned above, it would seem that Arjuna overcomes the struggle by considering his duty and other rational arguments. Yet I should stress that it is *rāja-yoga* or empathy with himself that motivates Arjuna to fight. An example of this type of empathy might be found during a flight emergency. Flight attendants advise passengers to put their own oxygen masks on before assisting others. The video usually shows a mother concerned with her child. Empathy would lead her to assist the child in the first place. Yet the flight attendant gently reminds her that in order to succeed in such an emergency, it is necessary to take care of oneself first, before assisting others. This attitude is certainly not motivated by selfishness, but by a type of empathy toward oneself, as illustrated in *rāja-yoga*. Thus, I would like to point out again that while Arjuna struggles with his decision to kill his loved ones because of empathy toward others, it is also empathy toward himself and who he should be, that is present in his decision to go to battle.

Indian thought. My goal is to demonstrate how the co-constitutive elements of the yogas function and how they directly relate to the interconnected components of the process of empathy. To elaborate briefly, *bhakti-yoga* touches on the affective aspect of empathy, while *jñāna-yoga* ties into the idea that empathy involves reflection. *Karma-yoga* points to the importance of action for empathy to be meaningful. Like the yogas, the main aspects of the process of empathy that I identify are inseparable and need to be thought of as constituting a single process rather than being disentangled. In other words, the process of empathy parallels how the four yogas function as a unit, with their features inseparable from one another and considered holistically.[22]

To summarize, there are two levels at which the incorporation of the yogas is helpful for (re)-thinking empathy. First, much like the process of empathy, the yogas must be considered as a whole and not divided into individual parts. They lose their significance when considered in isolation and do not require hierarchical ordering. The term *yoga* in Indian philosophy implies a union, so all the four yogas work in conjunction to create that union. Second, as I have stated above, the content of the yogas directly speaks to the elements of empathy I wish to address. Finally, the four yogas have a central ethical component, consisting of techniques or spiritual/bodily practices designed to purify the mind. The Indian tradition focuses on improving the person, with an openness to others as a way to acquire perfection, making it possible to speak about empathy within Indian philosophy. Perfect yogis, as mentioned above, are those who not only empathize with others, but also act in response to others' joy and sorrows.

## The Yogas and the Circle of Empathy

In this section, I provide an analysis of *bhakti, jñāna and karma-yoga* and how they play a role within the circle of empathy through case study scenarios.

## Gita on Bhakti-Yoga

In the Western philosophical tradition, empathy has been conventionally understood to contain an affective/intuitive state. For this reason, I start with

---

[22] Singh, *Bhakti and Philosophy*, p. 12.

an account of *bhakti-yoga*, as it reflects the affective stage of empathy in the Western philosophical tradition.

The notion of *bhakti* (or devotion) is emphasized in the *Gita*. Its central meaning is to selflessly share one's love and devotion, as demonstrated in the *Bhagavad-Gita*.[23] Here I focus on the relational aspect toward other human beings. As noted above, Arjuna moves through the world as a warrior but also feels the pain of killing his teachers and relatives. Arjuna learns from his *guru* Krishna that his feelings for others is his practice of *bhakti-yoga*.[24] Krishna teaches Arjuna that *bhakti* enables us to live a fulfilled life, one devoted not only to the self but also to others. This devotion requires that we rid ourselves of the "unripe ego," the part of ourselves that is concerned with material goods and worldly possessions. The "ripe ego," is the mark of the mature individual, where we are not devoted to worldly/material attachments but feel that the other—even the stranger—is a deserving of our love and consideration.[25] This attitude of feeling for the other is what the emotivist tradition refer to as "sympathy," and what I argue is the affective/intuitive stage of the circle of empathy. For Hume, sympathy can be extended beyond our family and immediate friends, allowing us to sympathize even with strangers and those we have never met.[26] Here, we find a coincidence from two very different traditions, helping us understand the richness of the notion of empathy.

## Scenario # 1

Betty and Mary met at university twenty years ago and quickly became fast friends. They shared the same academic and nonacademic interests and did everything together. During a trip to Italy, they met their partners Tim and John. Betty and Mary got married around the same time, each serving as the other's maid of honor. Unfortunately, Mary's marriage to John did not work out, primarily due to financial issues. Mary blamed John for what she considered poor job choices, leading to many arguments and tensions. After seeking marriage counseling, Mary

---

[23] It is important to note that in this tradition love and devotion are to be shared with God and fellow human beings. However, an in-depth account of the specifics of metaphysics with regards to the *Gita* is beyond the scope of this chapter.

[24] Murty, *Indian Philosophy*, 94.

[25] Swami Nikhilananda, *The Gospel of Sri Ramakrishna* (New York: Vedanta Society of New York, 1992), 121.

[26] David Hume, *A Treatise of Human Nature*, ed. David Fate Norton and Mary J. Norton (Oxford: Clarendon Press, 2011), 313.

and John decided to get divorced. Mary confided in Betty about her marriage breakup and the reasons behind it.

During the divorce proceedings, Mary and Betty met at their favorite restaurant. While quietly chatting, Lionel Richie and Diana Ross's "Endless Love" began to play over the restaurant's sound system. Suddenly, Mary's mood changed, and she broke into tears. Betty, sensing Mary's sadness, felt flushed, and teary-eyed, experiencing a sinking feeling in her gut. Betty's emotional response exemplified the first stage of the circle of empathy: affective/intuitive, by mirroring Mary's emotions. Betty automatically placed her hand on Mary's shoulder, handed her tissue, and tried to comfort her saying, "Everything will be okay." Betty moved from the first stage to the third stage of action-oriented disposition without pausing to make inferences; she responded spontaneously.

During the comforting process, Betty pondered the specific cause of Mary's breaking down. She considered all of her surroundings: it could not have been the restaurant, as Mary had agreed to come out for dinner. Nor could it have been the food, as they ordered their old favorites, or the other patrons who were quiet and respectful. Betty realized that Mary began to cry as soon as the song "Endless Love" started to play. She recalled that "Endless Love" was the song that Mary and John danced to at their wedding. Betty imagined that the song brought Mary back to her wedding day, now a painful memory. By examining the context and trying to understand Mary's thought process, Betty was attempting to take her perspective. As Betty continued to ponder the situation, Mary, still weeping, said, "I miss John." Hearing this, Betty rose from her chair, walked over to Mary, and gave her a comforting hug saying "I understand what you are feeling. Is there anything that I can do to help you overcome your sadness?" Feeling Betty's closeness, and hearing her comforting words, Mary's mood began to change.

Mary's sadness was triggered by the song, yet the presence of an empathetic friend who understood what was happening and "shared her pain," made the situation more bearable. It was Betty's empathy that prompted her to comfort Mary and assure that everything would be okay. This is a classic example of empathy: when feelings of distress, sadness, or helplessness are shared by someone else, the effective-emotional dimension of empathy prompts the empathizer to think their way into the other's perspective.

Elements of *bhakti-yoga* can be seen in the scenario of Mary and Betty. When Mary began to cry in the restaurant, Betty felt for her friend. This feeling awakened in Betty the urge to respond to Mary with love and consideration. Betty empathized by observing Mary's crying, which awakened the realization that she must respond sympathetically. In this moment, empathy was part of appreciating what Mary was feeling. In the case of Arjuna, however, he responded not to the distress of those he must kill, but to his imagination of what they felt or would feel when confronting them.

Although the context of Arjuna feeling the pain of killing his loved ones is different from Betty feeling the pain of Mary's divorce and sadness, both cases illustrate an entry point into the circle of empathy. Both enter from the affective/intuitive stage and demonstrate that we feel for the other and, in pursuing the circle of empathy, show our love and devotion to the other.

## Gita on the *Jnāna-Yoga*

The perspective-taking aspect of the circle of empathy mirrors *jnāna-yoga*. This form of *yoga* encompasses not only our inner knowledge, which includes self-awareness, but also the reflection that allows us to understand others. It is this second aspect that I would like to highlight in relation to the circle of empathy.

In Indian philosophy, there is a practical element where wisdom draws on our experiences and reflects on them.[27] In this way, *jnāna* or knowledge is not merely about engaging in abstract reasoning or creating philosophical constructs. Individuals with a "ripe ego" need to draw on their extensive reflections and actual experience, applying them to real-world situations, events, and people. This practice of reflection with regard to others is emphasized in the cognitivist tradition and represents the perspective-taking stage of the circle of empathy.

## Scenario # 2

Jenny is a university student living on her own for the first time. She and her friends, Claire, Sam, and Amber are discussing the newfound freedom that living on their own provides compared to the rules their parents enforced at home. They all agreed on what they disliked about living with their parents: (1) curfews (2) doing homework before playing video games, and (3) seeing friends only under certain circumstances. Despite these rules, Jenny's friends' parents were supportive and always there for them. For example, Claire's parents would

---

[27.] Murty, *Indian Philosophy*, p. 92.

drive her to her friends' house, even though she had to be back home at a certain time. Sam's parents would buy him video games, and his father, a fellow gamer, enjoyed playing with him. After visiting with her friends, Amber's parents would ask about the visit, showing interest in her social life without being intrusive.

During the conversation, Jenny reflects on her home life. She recalls that her father was very strict, imposing many rules that were never properly enforced. Her father struggled with alcoholism and was not there for her when she needed him most. "Drunk dad" was different from "sober dad." When sober, her father harshly insisted on rules but did not enforce them. Due to his intoxication, he could not drive her to her friends' house, did not ask about her day, and could not afford to buy video games or other fun things for her. Jenny realized how different her childhood was compared to that of her friends'.

Jenny asks herself, "Why was it so different for me?" She observes that her friends' parents were supportive and involved in their lives, while her father was not. The difference lies in her father's alcoholism and their financial situation. She wonders, "Why was my dad always coming home drunk?" By asking these "why" questions, Jenny begins to enter the perspective-taking stage of the circle of empathy, even though this is not prompted by any prior affective-emotional empathetic identification with her father. She begins to work her way into her father's perspective by questioning his decisions and their impact.

Jenny does not find answers right away, but the question has now been posed. She decides to set it aside, enjoy time with her friends, and revisit later. When she revisits the question, Jenny realizes there must be reasons for her dad's behavior. Although she does not yet understand why her dad is an alcoholic, she knows that there must be some reason. Consequently, Jenny decides to call her paternal grandmother, who invites her for a visit. By doing this, Jenny enters the third stage of the circle of empathy which is action-oriented disposition.

While visiting her grandma's house, Jenny asks about her father's childhood. Her grandmother explains that her late husband was very strict, and favoured Jenny's father's younger brother, who excelled in sports, whereas Jenny's father preferred books. Her grandfather did not relate to her father, and spent little time with him, leading to poor self-esteem and resentment, which fueled her father's struggles. Hearing about her father's upbringing, Jenny starts to make connections. She understands what "strict" and "taught him discipline" mean experiencing involuntary emotional reactions to her father's situation as she now perceives it. When she hears those words, she gets a pang of fear in her gut. It is important to note that with this Jenny starts to enter the first stage—the affective component of the circle of empathy—where she begins to experience involuntary emotional reactions to her father's situation as she now perceives it to have been.

Jenny empathizes with her father's fear and emotional responses. She reflects on her dad coming home drunk and realizes that, while he could have been more supportive and engaged, his behavior had underlying reasons. Understanding her father's upbringing, Jenny's attitude shifts from anger and disappointment to compassion. She decides to reach out to her father with a kinder disposition.

Jenny's father lacked empathy toward her, leading to her original disappointment. His lack of empathy caused him to fail to see the normative significance of a certain feature of a situation. He failed to see that his daughter needed him and that she was hurting as a result of his inattention. This led Jenny to perceive her dad as someone who had failed her. Learning about her father's past, Jenny becomes more empathetic toward him, aiding her healing process.

Aspects of *jñāna-yoga* are evident in the Jenny case. While with her friends, Jenny reflects on her home life, considering her friends' and father's childhood experiences. She considers wider implications and concrete examples. While Arjuna's context of considering different perspectives in war is very different from Jenny's reflection of her friends' and her father's experiences, both cases demonstrate entering the circle of empathy from the perspective-taking stage. They reveal that considering the lived experience of others and pursuing the circle of empathy, involves practicing the tenets of *jñāna-yoga*.

## Gita on Karma-Yoga

The last co-constitutive stage of the circle of empathy involves a call to action. My account of empathy holds that fellow-feeling and perspective-taking are not sufficient; an action-oriented disposition is necessary for the process of empathy to be complete. From the perspective of Indian philosophy, one may argue that this action-oriented disposition is found in *karma-yoga*.

As mentioned above, the Sanskrit word *karma* is derived from *kri*, which means "to do."[28] According to *karma-yoga*, our actions define our moral character. Whom we love or are devoted to are expressions of our *karma*, and it is in this sense, *karma* cannot be separated from *bhakti-yoga*. The *Gita* describes the

---

[28] Ibid., p. 87.

philosophy of *karma-yoga* as "right action," exemplified by Arjuna's situation on the battlefield. Here, we see a clear reference to an action-oriented disposition.

In the *Gita,* Krishna tells Arjuna that despite his misgivings Arjuna must acknowledge and take on his warrior disposition. Krishna says that one must not allow "the fruits of action to be [one's]...motive."[29] It is the fulfillment of *dharma* (moral law) that should be the motivating factor, not considerations of *moha* (attachment). Success may be beyond his control; a sudden gust of wind may well blow the arrow off its intended course.[30] The lesson is that being attuned and enacting one's stance in the world is what counts, not the outcome.

It is important to acknowledge the limitations of my account. It is not my intention to invoke elements of the Indian philosophical tradition to definitively justify my view on empathy and its three co-constitutive stages. Rather, I seek to articulate an opportunity to find ways in which the Western and Indian philosophies can provide mutual support and illumination as similar themes emerge in these philosophical traditions and idioms.[31]

## Action-Oriented Disposition (Scenario #3)

While the case of Arjuna can show how one can live in the world as a warrior, following his *Sva-dharma,* this "living in the world" occurs in many familiar ways. Real-life scenarios can illustrate how an action-oriented disposition can be our entrance to the circle of empathy.

Consider the following case. George is a commercial realtor, and is picking up a client, Kevin, from the airport to show him a property for sale. Kevin sits in the passenger seat so that he can discuss the property details while en route. Despite the important conversation, George keeps his attention and thoughts focused on the road, knowing his responsibilities as a driver are heightened with a passenger in the car. George, a lifelong resident of the city and avid driver, knows all the ins-and-outs of traveling through the city. He is not an idle driver;

---

[29] Radhakrishnan and Moore, *A Source Book in Indian Philosophy,* 110.

[30] Ibid.

[31] Zubin R. Mulla and Venkat R. Krishnan, "Karma-Yoga, the Indian Work Ideal, and Its Relationship with Empathy," *Psychology & Developing Societies* 20:27–49 make a connection between *karma-yoga* (action) and the dimensions of empathy. Both conducted a study using 108 participants. Several of their findings resulted in a correlation between empathetic concern for the other and *karma-yoga.* Zubin and Krishnan argue that persons who scaled high on empathetic concern and low on person distress were more inclined to perform actions for the good of others rather than for their own benefit.

rather he is already anticipating traffic conditions ahead, including potential risks and impediments to a safe and efficient drive.

As they move toward the downtown core, the traffic becomes denser, and they become stuck at a red light in a busy intersection. Even while stopped, George maintains a steady posture and a firm grip of the steering wheel. His foot is poised to move from the brake to the gas pedal whenever needed. George scans the roadway for potential risks: he notices cyclists weaving between the car, a pedestrian engrossed in a phone call crossing the street, and a frustrated diver in the next car. Once the light changes, the traffic flows, and George and Kevin move steadily through the intersection. George's experience as a vigilant driver, like Arjuna's warrior disposition, shows his body, perception and thoughts attuned. George is always ready to take the requisite actions for a safe and efficient journey. It is this readiness that constitutes George's action-oriented disposition, and this establishes his entrance to the circle of empathy. In other words, empathy cannot be viewed through a narrow lens but rather through a wider lens of other factors and influences.

George's disposition, in this case, results in action. He catches sight of a car ahead speeding through the intersection, despite a red light governing that car's lane of traffic. Because of George's vigilant disposition, his foot was already poised for an emergency stop, allowing him to slam on the brakes and avoid the collision. George's readiness to ensure the safety of himself and his passenger permits him to throw his arm across Kevin's chest, protecting his passenger from harm. This physical motion of his arm is what I am describing as illustrative of the action-oriented disposition to empathy.

George's vigilance and readiness made him calm and collected in the moment. His disposition allowed him to anticipate the danger and therefore he was not surprised by it. However, George felt Kevin's shock of the near accident, including his heart thudding in his chest; a clench in his stomach coupled with a flush of heat throughout his body. George is moving to the next stage of the circle of empathy, affective-intuitive, by mirroring Kevin's feelings.

George recalls that Kevin was lost in conversation while they were moving through the intersection. He was discussing his plans for the new property and how much he should initially offer. George understands that Kevin was clearly excited to tour the property, share his plans for the future, and make a good impression on George. In other words, Kevin was not paying attention to the road. By examining the context and trying to understand what Kevin's experience in the car might have been, George is attempting to take his perspective. In other words, he is moving to the perspective-taking stage of the circle of empathy.

This case shows how one can enter the circle of empathy from the action-oriented disposition stage. George is a safe and conscientious driver, but the focus is not on his reaction to protect his client in a potentially dangerous situation. This perspective helps us understand a new approach. While cognitivist theory emphasizes entering the circle of empathy from the perspective-taking stage, stressing the importance of reasons in understanding morality. Emotivist theory focuses on entering the circle of empathy from the affective-intuitive stage stressing the importance of fellow-feeling and desire in guiding our conduct. Indian philosophy, in particular the four yogas, can help us to understand how to enter the circle of empathy from the action-oriented disposition stage, as evidenced by this case. Furthermore, Indian philosophy brings out the importance of the attunement of one's whole being in one's relation to the world and others. Hence the serenity and equanimity that comes from practicing the yogas enables one to have the right orientation to acting in the world, and hence an enduring readiness to act appropriately. This attunement (which one could think of as a kind of empathy (or oneness) with Being) enables spontaneous action, which the agent then seeks to rationalize or come to terms with emotionally after the fact (bringing into play the other two stages of the circle).

Through the *Gita,* we can understand Arjuna's warrior disposition, demonstrating military readiness. Arjuna's *Sva-dharma* is to be a warrior, the four yogas can help us understand this disposition and how one can practice it. To say that Arjuna could not help but follow his *Sva-dharma* does not sufficiently explain what it is like to embody that position. Similarly, in saying that it is Arjuna's duty to fight, we fail to capture the nuances of how one's body, thoughts, and perception are attuned to the disposition. To say that Arjuna is distant or separate from the reality of having to fight his loved ones, we ignore how it is Arjuna's *Sva-dharma.* We overlook how it is Arjuna who has habituated himself to be a warrior and how *he* is the one who must do the fighting. In this way, the *Gita* shows how Arjuna moves through the world as a warrior. By Arjuna's practicing of the yogas, we see how he enters the circle of empathy through the action-oriented disposition stage.

Similarly, George has a disposition of vigilance in his driving. George is not destined to be a safe driver; he has habituated his driving practice toward safety out of empathy for his passengers. George does not simply follow the rules of the road; he is attuned and always ready to take action to ensure safety. George may act selflessly in ensuring his passenger's safety, but he is not distant from the situation. *He* is the driver and *his* vigilance that ensures safety for himself and his passenger. George, then, embodies an action-oriented disposition that leads him into the circle of empathy.

# Conclusion

Empathy as related to Indian philosophy, involves awareness of the mutual coexistence of all life. We must view empathy more broadly, rather than through a limited definition. For example, Paul Bloom's or Jesse Prinz's understanding of empathy provide a one-dimensional view. Bloom and Prinz assert that empathy is not necessary for the making of moral judgments and can be dangerous due to potential bias. Accepting their position limits our understanding of empathy. Indian philosophy brings a nuanced approach, showing that empathy is experience involving emotions, imagination, observation/understanding, and action. The empathetic process moves us to see things and ourselves in a larger context without adapting the other's exact emotional responses. It enables us to see the other's lived experience and reasonably assist them without demanding conformity to our perspective.

Empathy involves three co-constitutive cycles, making it a complex process. It is possible to do the right thing without feeling these responses or taking these perspectives, but empathy is a precondition for living a recognizable moral life. Indian philosophy sheds light on the metaethical debate, showing that empathy is not solely a sentiment, nor should it be avoided altogether. While not necessary for moral judgment, empathy often takes place in human interactions. By bringing in Indian philosophy, we see that empathy is not exclusive to Western moral theory and can enhance our understanding of moral psychology.

Empathy is both a human reality and a complex process. It involves a "circle of empathy" made up of three co-constitutive stages, though not always present. Empathy is complete when the full circle is present, bringing in different philosophical traditions into the conversation with each other.

CHAPTER 7

# Sri Aurobindo on Integral Yoga and Technology

*Jacqueline Kumar*

Sri Aurobindo (1872–1950) developed a form of metaphysical and mystical philosophy in his "Integral Yoga." He is part of the Indian philosophical tradition, which had the express goal of "interpreting and reinterpreting the ancient philosophies of India in the modern context."[1] Aurobindo was not raised in the Indian tradition; for his father, who seemed to be opposed to Indian culture, sent him to England by the age of seven with the intention that he may become part of the Indian Civil Service. After successfully completing his education and graduating from Cambridge University, he returned to India, having purposefully avoided the examination for the position. The reason might have been that, while in England, Aurobindo had taken part of a secret society which aimed at obtaining Indian independence from Great Britain. Upon his return to his homeland, Aurobindo experienced a profound mystical spiritual awakening. He subsequently took a job as a lecturer at Baroda College. Upon his return from England, he applied himself to the study of *Sanskrit* and yoga, which he will later deepen through his mystical philosophy. During a revolutionary period in his life, Aurobindo also spent some time in prison. Once he regained freedom, he gave up those revolutionary ideas of independence, and turned to the study of yoga. He intensely studied the Upanishads and the Ramayana, significant texts derived from the Vedas, thus learning about the silence of the mind which is essential for higher levels of yoga.

In this chapter, I will briefly outline Aurobindo's worldview. Secondly, I will describe Aurobindo's concept of "Integral Yoga." And thirdly, given his intent to revitalize ancient Indian philosophy within a modern context, I will examine the issue of technology in the context of Aurobindo's thought and consider how it may prevent us from attaining what he calls the spiritual transformation of consciousness.

---

[1] M. Ram Murty, *Indian Philosophy: An Introduction* (Toronto, Canada: Broadview Publishing, 2013), 151.

## A Brief Outline of Sri Aurobindo's Worldview

Aurobindo's Integral Yoga includes not only the four yogas of Vivekananda but also a theory of higher levels of consciousness. According to him, we lead a life of reaction and not reflection. Yet, if we can practice reflection, we will have made the first ascent into the higher mind. Beyond the higher mind, Aurobindo states that there are even higher levels: illumined mind, intuitive mind, overmind, and finally supramental consciousness.[2]

Aurobindo's interest in Yoga and meditation started in 1908, when he met with Vishnu Bhaskar Lele (a Maharashtrian yogi). Lele educated Aurobindo on how to meditate, which for Aurobindo was a turning point in his life. Aurobindo testifies to this, when he states that, "It was my great debt to Lele that he showed me this. 'Sit in meditation,' he said, 'but do not think, look only at your mind; you will see thoughts coming into it; before they can enter throw these away from your mind till your mind is capable of entire silence."[3] This experience marked the beginning of yoga for Aurobindo, what he would later call the initial levels of the supramental consciousness. Once one achieves this state, one will have a higher vantage point, as the thoughts and feelings will not affect the mind.

For Aurobindo, "Man is a transitional being; he is not final,"[4] as he is in a process of constant evolution. This process of constant change and perfection is a very important element of Aurobindo's worldview. His doctrine is based on the idea that the *Absolute* expresses itself in the universe through a series of degrees of realities that go all the way from material reality to the *Absolute* spirit. That means, according to Aurobindo, that the *Absolute* also descends into the finite, as it is an inevitable expression of the essential power of *Brahman*.[5] Because of the nature of the *Absolute*, this process is never-ending, leading man to a never final, only transitional being.

Everything in reality, for Aurobindo, is infused by the *Absolute* spirit. This is the reason why he states that "man is a transitional being; he is not final," for the evolution of lower forms into higher forms is inevitable. This however, will

---

[2] Cf. Ibid., Chapter 4, p. 159.

[3] Sri Aurobindo, *The Collected Works of Sri Aurobindo*, Vols. 26, 84 (Pondicherry, India: Aurobindo Ashram, 1972).

[4] Ibid., Sri Aurobindo, *The Essential Aurobindo*, ed. by Robert A. McDermott (Great Barrington, MA: Lindisfarne Books, 2001), 64.

[5] Cf. Sarvepalli Radhakrishnan and Charles A. Moore, *Indian Philosophy* (Princeton, NJ: Princeton University Press, 1967), 575.

require great effort on the part of man, for there is like a veil that separates man, who is finite, from the infinity of the *Absolute*. This is when Aurobindo brings in his notion of "Integral Yoga." The goal of man in this life is to identify himself to the *Absolute*, which he will achieve by rising from the physical world, crossing through the mental world and beyond, in order to effect a supramental change. This process of liberation and union requires a very elaborate technique or discipline of yoga, which he calls "Integral Yoga." This type of yoga is called "Integral," for it is comprehensive in its transformative process, not leaving aside any aspect of the state of mind and the life of the individual. Additionally, it is integral because it combines the four yogas of Vivekananda into a synthesis of yoga.

Aurobindo states: "This illumination and change must take up and re-create the whole being, mind, life and body; it must be not only an inner experience of the Divinity, but a remolding of both the inner and outer existence by its power."[6] Integral Yoga will be the discipline that will enable man to prepare himself for this ascent, yet, it will only be through the assistance of the *Absolute* that man will be enabled to achieve his ultimate destiny.

Thus, Aurobindo's Integral Yoga is considered to be one of the most comprehensive approaches to the transformation of consciousness.[7] It is thus that matter, spirit, man, and the *Absolute*, the finite and the infinite reality, the one and the many, will be reconciled. Through the practice of Integral Yoga, man will achieve progress, that is, will rise from the state of mind to that of the supermind. Aurobindo states: "For in man and high beyond him ascend the radiant degrees that climb to a divine supermanhood."[8]

## Aurobindo's Integral Yoga

According to Aurobindo, the *Absolute* manifests itself, in its creative energy, as the supramental consciousness. We can say that this supramental consciousness is an intermediary between the world and the *Absolute*. In this way, human beings attain progress by reaching this stage of divine life through the practice

---

Sri Aurobindo, *The Life Divine* (Twin Lakes, WI: Lotus Press, 1920), Book 2, Part 2, Chapter 28, 1019.

Cf. Masayuki Kobayashi, *On the Triple Transformation in the Integral Yoga of Sri Aurobindo* (San Francisco: California Institute of Integral Studies, 2005), 3.

Ibid., Sri Aurobindo, *The Collected Works of Sri Aurobindo*, Vols. 26, 84.

of "Integral Yoga."[9] Through Integral Yoga, the individual will seek an integral and total change of consciousness and nature not just for the individual himself, but for humankind as a whole and the entire cosmos. This is one of the main differences with some prior forms of yoga. Aurobindo does not present Integral Yoga as pursuing a release from the cycle of birth and death. What Integral Yoga pursues is a kind of transformation of life and existence as a whole by the *Absolute,* through it, and for it. The ascent of man to the supermind, however, is only the first step. The final goal will be the descent of a new consciousness, once it has been attained in the process of ascent of the mind. Thus, we can say that the Integral Yoga is the discipline and practice by which man consents to cooperate with the *Absolute* that manifests itself in nature and seek the process of ascension and descent.

Now, this process of ascent has five levels, and in each one of them the human mind is still undergoing a process of evolution. Aurobindo envisioned the evolutionary process through a series of gradations of the mind achieved through the practice of Integral Yoga: the mind first ascends to the higher mind, then to the illumined mind, then the intuitive mind, followed by the overmind, and finally, the mind reaches the state of the supermind. The tool to enhance this evolutionary process is through Aurobindo's Integral Yoga.[10]

The first step in this process of evolution is that of the higher mind. Here, the mind is still dependent on the instrumentality of ideas, yet these ideas take a more vast, universal and comprehensive character.[11] According to Aurobindo, man can use "his thinking mind and will to restrain and correct his life impulses." Thus, the result will be to "bring in the action of a still higher luminous mentality aided by the deeper soul in him, the psychic being" in order to bring about the regulation of desire.[12]

The second step is that of the Intuitive Mind. At this point, according to Aurobindo, the Intuitive Mind is "fully formed in the mental being and is strong enough to dominate if not yet wholly to occupy the various mental activities."

[9] Cf. Sanjyot D. Pai Vernekar, "Aurobindonian Ontology: Salient Peculiarities," Twentieth World Congress of Philosophy, Boston, August 10–15, 1998, last accessed on October 5, 2018, https://www.bu.edu/wcp/Papers /Onto/OntoVern.htm.

[10] Ibid., Radhakrishnan and Moore, *Indian Philosophy*, p. 578.

[11] Indra Sen has argued that examples of the content of the higher mind are the ideas of "practical or pure reason," the idea of "God," the "soul," "nature" as a totality, etc. Cf. Indra Sen, *Sri Aurobindo's Theory of the Mind* (Honolulu: University of Hawaii Press, 1952), 49.

[12] Sri Aurobindo, *The Synthesis of Yoga*, Part 1: "The Yoga of Divine Works," Chapter 2, "Self-Consecration" (Madras, India: Sri Aurobindo Library, 1948) 73.

Thus, it is possible for the mind to lift "the centre and level of action above the mind and the predominance of the supramental action."[13]

Aurobindo then presents the third step in the rise of the mind, that of the "illuminated mind." In its rise, the mind, which is a mixed power, has to be purified of all "mental dependence and mental forms" in order to convert all willing and thinking into thought-sight and truth-seeing will by an illumined discrimination, intuition, inspiration, revelation.[14] According to Aurobindo, this is the final purification of the intelligence. This mid-stage, according to Sen, shows transcendence of ideas, but not yet the mastery of intuition. Thus, "it is characterized by a general illumination, clarity, and certitude, which readily take form in ideas."[15]

At his point, a series of steps or gradations, the ascent of consciousness beyond the mind takes us through the Higher Mind, to the Illumined Mind, and from there to the Intuition and to the Overmind.[16] Once the mind reaches the Overmind, it breaks out of the consciousness from the individual to the cosmic level and thus overpasses the instrumentalization of the ego.[17] Thus, knowledge is not "produced" by the mind, but originates in the *Absolute*. Aurobindo states:

> Thought, for the most part, no longer seems to originate individually in the body or the person but manifests from above or comes in upon the cosmic mind-waves: all inner individual sight or intelligence of things is now a revelation or illumination of what is not in one's separate self but in the universal knowledge; the feelings, emotions, sensations are similarly felt as waves from the same cosmic immensity breaking upon the subtle and the gross body and responded to in kind by the individual centre of the universality; for the body is only a small support or even less, a point of relation, for the action of a vast cosmic instrumentation.[18]

The mind, then, experiments a transition to the "supermind." Aurobindo explains this as a shift of standpoint, to that of the divine awareness. From looking at reality from one's artificial perspective, the divine takes over the individual, who now

---

[13] Ibid., p. 789.

[14] Sri Aurobindo, *The Synthesis of Yoga*, Part 4: "The Yoga of Self-Perfection," Chapter 7, "Purification–Intelligence and Will" (Madras, India: Sri Aurobindo Library, 1948) 645–646.

[15] Ibid., Sen, *Sri Aurobindo's Theory of the Mind*, p. 49.

[16] Ibid., Sri Aurobindo, *The Life Divine*, Book 2, Part 2, Chapter 26, "The Ascent Towards Supermind."

[17] Ibid.

[18] Ibid.

sees things in a new light. Aurobindo explains: "The limitations of our individual life being break down and we live no longer with a personal life force, or not with that ordinarily, but in and by the universal life energy."[19]

Thus, when the mind has reached this final stage, and is not only united with the *Absolute* but also takes this new standpoint, man will be able to see the universe from a different perspective, one in which there are no contradictions, there is harmony, and everything is revealed "in its truth and totality of power and delight." Thus, man becomes a channel "of the reactions of the active life force through us working as an instrument of self-manifestation."[20]

## Technology and Its Impact on Man's Transformative Process

In this section, I will ask the question on how Integral Yoga may help us avoid the problems that seem inherent with the use of technology. Aurobindo believed that we can train the mind the way we train our creative faculty, such as writing.[21] In order to achieve this level of discipline, a high level of concentration is required, which in the case of Aurobindo, it was provided by the practice of Integral Yoga.

One of the problems of the modern world, is that technological devices and the internet have become too disruptive for even our basic daily routines and activities. People are seen on their cellphones while dining with someone else, while working at the library, or even in classes. Here we are dealing not even with an obstacle to raise the level of mind, but even an obstacle to fulfill basic obligations. The distractions caused by constant messaging, Facebook notifications, Instagram pictures, tweets, or Snapchat streaks, don't allow the student to even complete his or her homework. What is left for the life of the mind? Aurobindo would be dismayed by the actual state of affairs. What would he say or recommend to today's human beings? He would probably answer: "We need to be constantly aware of our primary goals. We need to remind ourselves that goalless life is a meaningless life. Sri Aurobindo says: For the spiritual seeker this change of consciousness is the one thing he seeks and nothing else matters in life."[22]

---

[19.] Sri Aurobindo, *The Synthesis of Yoga*, Part 4, Chapter 24, "The Supramental Sense", p. 841.

[20.] Ibid., p. 842.

[21.] Testimonies attest to the amount of writing he did every night: "From six in the evening till six in the morning." See Satprem, *Biography of Sri Aurobindo*, Vol. 26 (Pondicherry, India: Sri Aurobindo Ashram, 1964), 95.

[22.] Sanjeev Patra, *Technologies- Boon or Bane for the Sadhaks of Integral Yoga (Pondicherry, India: Sri Aurobindo Ashram, 2018)*, Ref. 1. Savitri, Kireet Joshi Books, 3.

Are we hypnotized by technology? Of all the realities of the modern world, this seems to be an impediment for progress, an element hard to integrate within the cosmic evolutionary process presented by Aurobindo. In order for one to reach beyond the ordinary mind, we need to remove obstructions from our minds. For example, there seems to be an overuse of technological advancements. Unless we are not careful about it, it could lead to a halt in the progress of man toward the *Absolute*.

The internet age has brought with itself the largest amount of information in the history of humanity. Man, curious by nature, tends to get distracted too many times in his desire to satisfy his thirst for knowledge. Yet, as Aurobindo would certainly agree with, we should say that:

> What is important is not so much information, but the power of concentration which can command information at will. Unfailing concentration and irresistible will. This twin power has to be the basis of our life and has to be applied to the various functioning of the mind, life-force and body. Apart from these powers and functioning, there are the domains of the inner and higher personality. Will this device help me in finding my true being, can I come into direct and living contact and then into a union with the Divine?[23]

Aurobindo has offered a worldview that presents man in constant progress toward the supramental consciousness through the practice of Integral yoga. Perhaps it is time to integrate this practice in programs of education in order to help students achieve both immediate and long-term goals. If Integral Yoga can help us to transcend to the ultimate state of consciousness, as Aurobindo believe it does, then it certainly will be a great tool to deal with the obstacles that technology causes in our modern day. Even at an individual level Aurobindo's ideas can be embraced by thoughtful readers.

## Conclusion

This chapter provides a comprehensive account of Aurobindo's Integral Yoga within the context of his ontological framework. It elucidates his vision of the mind's ascent through successive levels of consciousness, ultimately culminating in the supermind. Aurobindo's Integral Yoga emerges as a holistic and transformative practice aimed at achieving the spiritual transformation of consciousness.

---

[23] Ibid., p. 3.

In considering the contemporary relevance of Aurobindo's philosophy, particularly in the context of technological advancements, Integral Yoga offers a pathway to address modern challenges. Technology, with its pervasive distractions, poses significant obstacles to mental discipline and spiritual growth. Aurobindo's emphasis on concentration and willpower over mere information accumulation underscores the importance of maintaining focus amidst technological noise.

Aurobindo's vision of continuous human evolution toward supramental consciousness invites a revaluation of our relationship with technology. By integrating Integral Yoga into educational programs, we can foster a balanced approach that combines technological proficiency with spiritual growth. This integration can help students and individuals achieve both immediate academic and long-term spiritual goals, thereby harmonizing technological use with the quest for higher consciousness.

Moreover, Aurobindo's philosophy offers a profound critique of modern life's fragmented nature. His call for a comprehensive transformation of consciousness challenges us to look beyond superficial advancements and seek deeper, more meaningful progress. The practice of Integral Yoga, with its emphasis on unity and holistic development, serves as a counterbalance to the divisive and distracting tendencies of contemporary technology.

Aurobindo's insights into the nature of consciousness and the evolutionary potential of humanity provide a framework for understanding and overcoming the limitations imposed by technological dependence. By cultivating the discipline of Integral Yoga, individuals can aspire to transcend the ordinary mind, achieving a state of harmony and higher awareness that integrates both the material and spiritual dimensions of existence.

Ultimately, Aurobindo's Integral Yoga represents a synthesis of ancient wisdom and modern aspirations. It offers a path to reconcile the finite with the infinite, the individual with the universal, and technology with spirituality. As we navigate the complexities of the modern world, Aurobindo's vision of a transformative consciousness remains a beacon of hope, guiding us toward a future where technology serves as a tool for spiritual evolution rather than an impediment.

In conclusion, Aurobindo's Integral Yoga is not only a philosophical doctrine but a practical guide to living in harmony with the universe. It provides a robust framework for addressing the challenges of technological distractions, emphasizing the need for inner discipline and spiritual focus. By embracing Aurobindo's teachings, we can aspire to a higher state of consciousness that transcends the limitations of our current technological age, paving the way for a more integrated and enlightened existence.

# PART II

## Studies in Comparative Philosophy

# CHAPTER 8

# Schopenhauer and Indian Thought

*R. Raj Singh*

Schopenhauer's philosophy shows a remarkable connection with Hindu and Buddhist thought systems. Through his rigorous studies of Eastern philosophy and religious texts available in his times, he became more and more appreciative of the relevance of Indian thought for philosophy in general. Indeed, he was one of the first European philosophers to show a consistent appreciation of the role of Indian thought and endeavored to incorporate many of its concepts into his own system. However, a reassessment of Schopenhauer's connection with Indian thought is necessary in view of the neglect of this topic in the secondary literature on Schopenhauer.

Despite the indisputable evidence of the influence of Hindu and Buddhist thought on Schopenhauer's philosophy and his creative amalgamation of Western and Eastern concepts within his own metaphysical system, the study of these influences has received only a scanty and casual attention from the various Schopenhauer scholars of our times. This neglect of the Eastern dimension of this thinker's work has also resulted in several misunderstandings of his basic standpoints and has greatly contributed to some extreme assessments of his obviously pessimistic outlook. A lack of study of his Eastern sources makes Schopenhauer more pessimistic and outlandish than any other philosopher of his day and age.

This essay will begin with a brief account of Schopenhauer's connections with Eastern thought in his early and later writings. He will also take stock of the remarkably different approach that Schopenhauer had toward the role of Indian thought in European philosophy that distinguishes him from many of his predecessors and contemporary thinkers who also had an abiding interest in Indian thought and some of whom became full-fledged German ideologists. Beginning with the Romantic thinkers like J. G. Herder 1803), Friedrich Schlegel (1772–1829) and his brother August Wilhelm Schlegel (1767–1845), G. W. F. Hegel (1770–1831) and F. W. J. Schelling (1775–1854) were the leading figures in German philosophy who wrote about Indian thought approvingly or critically in their own original manners.

Secondly, after a brief history of Schopenhauer's engagement with Indian thought and a brief inquiry regarding his destructive approach toward it which was unlike that of any other Indologists of his times, we will focus on the content of his actual treatment of Hindu and Buddhist thought within his works. Without going into the futile controversies on whether he preferred Buddhism over Hinduism and how he might have modified his standpoints in the light of more and more studies of Eastern sources in his later works, we will concentrate on the issue of how his philosophical work reflects and treats some of the critical concepts and outlooks of various Hindu thought systems. This is not to deny or minimize the deep impact of Buddhism on his thought. A study of Schopenhauer's connections with Buddhist thought is equally valuable for a fuller understanding of his philosophical standpoint.

Thirdly, some issues will be raised and pursued concerning Schopenhauer's interpretations of Indian thought as well as the role played by the Eastern ways of thinking in his own thoughts system. Some of the major problems to be discussed are as follows: (a) Did Schopenhauer know the fundamentals of Vedanta and Buddhism deeply and comprehensively enough prior to the publication of the first edition of *The World as Will and Representation* (*WWR*) in order for us to conclude that these Eastern philosophies influence the first enunciation of his metaphysical system? (b) If Schopenhauer's study of the Eastern texts available in Europe grew gradually through his career, what impact this renewed scholarship had on his later works? (c) Was Schopenhauer's exposition of Vedantic and Buddhist thought comprehensive enough or reasonable enough for his day and age, given that the translated texts were still far fewer and limited? (d) Did Schopenhauer misuse Eastern concepts to sub-serve his own standpoints in philosophy particularly to revalidate his pessimistic worldview? (e) Since the relation between Schopenhauer's philosophy and Indian thought is still an uncharted territory in the current secondary literature, what kinds of misinterpretations of this thinker's concepts and standpoints have taken place typically among the Western scholars of his work?

## Schopenhauer and German Indology

In order to understand Schopenhauer's connection with Indian thought it is important to examine the growing interest in Indian and German thinkers of the late

18th and early 19th centuries. This spadework in the field of Indology must have provided a fertile ground for the growth of Schopenhauer's own passion for Indian thought. As early as in 1813, he attended the lectures of F. Mager (1771–1818) and responded to them in his intellectual diary (Handliche Nachlass). Mager was himself influenced by Herder who had overseen some German translations of Indian texts appearing in English, French, and Latin. As Wilhelm Halbfass informs us in his excellent work *India and Europe*.[1] The motivation regarding self-criticism or criticisms of Christianity along with the issues of common origins of mankind, characterize the romantic awareness of India and the Orient. Herder was both a pioneer of the Romantic Movement in general but was particularly responsible for the polarizing awareness of India within the Romantic Movement. Herder was impressed with the idea that the Oriental thought had its autonomous structures in the Orient represented Europe's childhood. He described the core of Hindu thought as followers; "the idea of one Being in and behind all that there is, the idea of the unity of all things in the absolute, in God."[2] Herder was, however, critical of the impact of the caste system on the free evolution of the arts in the myth of metempsychosis, which promoted compassion for all living things but lessens sympathy with the sufferings of fellow human beings. Thus, he recognizes the preeminence of Christianity over India and the Orient, since only Christianity was "the religion of purest humanity." Nevertheless,

> India became the focal point of an enthusiastic interest, occasionally bordering on fanaticism, within the German Romantic movement developed detail opinions about Indian thought more or less independently of one another, including Schelling, Novalis, Görres, Cruzer, Goethe, Claudius, and, more than any of the others, the Schlegel Brothers. Mager served as a catalyst through the translations he made, and…also helped in shaping Schopenhauer's interest in India.[3]

G. W. F. Hegel (1770–1831) and F. W. J. Schelling (1775–1854) were other significant figures among Schopenhauer's contemporaries, who made their original philosophical analysis of Indian thought. Hegel and Schelling were fellow students and roommates at the University of Tübingen and her close friends, until about

---

[1] Wilhelm Halbfass, *India and Europe: An Essay in Understanding* (Albany, NY: State University of New York Press, 1988), 69.

[2] Ibid., p. 70.

[3] Ibid., p. 73.

the time of the publication of Hegel's masterpiece *The Phenomenology of Spirit* (1806) when doctrinal split happened between them.[4]

Hegel's focus into Indian thought did not evolve any interest or approval from ideological scholars. In the words of the author of *Indrenbild,* H. Von Glasenapp, "Hegel was a bookman, living in a world of abstractions speculations…He was the prototype of a Westerner, who saw Western thought as the measure of all things…Therefore, whatever he knew to say about the Indian world, turned out to be very insufficient, and the result was a caricature."[5] Hegel, being a critic of the Romantic Movement, was committed to an irreversible direction of history, necessarily judging the past from the standpoint of the present matured state of the spirit of world history that has accomplished greater richness and complexity. Unlike the Romantics he did not engage in the glorifications of origins and early stages. The orient might be the Morgan land (land of surprises) of early origins and childhood but the West cannot and need not return to it says Hegel in his *Lectures on the Philosophy of World History*[6] as well as in his Lectures on the History of Philosophy.[7] Hegel was not an Indologist like the Schlegel Brothers had no knowledge of Sanskrit but relied on translations of the Indian texts. Although he read some of the latest secondary literature on Indian thought, by the likes of H. Th. Colebrooke and P. Buchanan, he did not gain detailed knowledge of the six classical systems of Hindu thought such as Samkhya and Nayaya-Vaisesika of Buddhism. Hegel's basis for the study of Indian thought was Vedanta in general, that is, selections from the Vedas and Upanishads and through study of the *Bhagavad-Gita.* He wrote an almost 100-page-long review of W. Von Humboldt's essay on the *Bhagavad-Gita.*[8] Hegel maintains that the "Orient is the beginning…The way of the 'Weltgeist' (world spirit) leads from East to the West. The Occident supersedes the Orient."[9]

Hinduism is the prototype of the "religion of substance" lacking in transcendence according to Hegel. In his view Indian philosophy is inseparable from religion. Substantiality applies to philosophy as well as religion. Pure substance means indeterminate

---

[4] Ibid., p. 100.

[5] Ibid., p. 84.

[6] Georg Wilhelm Friedrich Hegel, *Lectures on the Philosophy of World History* (Cambridge: Cambridge University Press), 158.

[7] Ibid., p. 263.

[8] Halbfass, India and Europe, p. 86.

[9] Ibid., p. 88.

being-in-itself. This is exactly what Hegel finds in the Indian conception of *Brahman*. It is formless, indeterminate, unspeakable and unsinkable. An attempt to describe or think it will lead away from it…The Indian mind has thus found its way to the one and the universal, which Hegel too seems as the true ground of religion and philosophy. But it has not found its way back to the concrete particularity of the world.[10]

Schopenhauer's contemptuous remarks on Hegel and Hegel's philosophy are well known and his unfair and imbalanced invectives against Hegel constitute a low. He described Hegel as a crude charlatan and his philosophy as a "confused empty verbiage" point in Schopenhauer's personality.[11] Such harsh words were certainly spoken out of personal contemptuousness as well as due to clear-cut doctrinal differences. Schopenhauer's philosophy is remarkably free of any acknowledgment of history and his metaphysical system is supposedly equally applicable to all periods of history. Historical and cultural differences do not affect the validity of the connection between the human entity and the will-to-live. In Hegel, however, the historical evolution of the world-spirit (Weltgeist) is an important factor and modern Western philosophy is a matured version of all ancient philosophies including ancient Indian philosophy which has failed in producing its matured stage as it continues to function as a bunch of eternal verifies. Thus, he calls Indian thought as constituting the childhood of the world-spirit whereas the Modern Western philosophy represents its full maturity. Oriental thought remains at a static and petrified state whereas modern Western thought supersedes the Orient through a useful, new, more developed and comprehensive stage. There is no such idea in Schopenhauer's view of Indian thought. He does not regard it as an infantile version of modernity but approaches it as a full comparable storehouse of ancient wisdom, whose ideas are still applicable and valuable in discovering the true nature of the will-to-live. It may also be noted that Hegel primarily relied on Indian sources pertaining to Vedanta that are the insights of Vedas and Upanishads. He does not comment on the six philosophical systems of Hinduism, regarding which he learned only at the end of his career. He has had hardly any familiarity with or commentary on Buddhism. In this respect, Schopenhauer, being eighteen years younger than Hagel, has more access to the sources on the six systems and especially on Buddhism which exercise a major influence on his thought.

---

[10.] Ibid., p. 89.

[11.] Ibid., p. 106.

F. W. J. Schelling (1775–1854), who was initially a good friend of Hegel and later a vehement critic of Hegelianism, offered an analysis of Indian thought in his *Philosophy of Mythology*. In this book, Schelling has extensive sections on India and other Eastern traditions, although his analyses are done from a critical standpoint. He, however, shows a clear-cut commitment to the Christian revelation.12 Schelling developed the idea of the world as a falling off (Abfall) from the absolute, and calls the absolute is the only reality and finite things as lacking in reality, somewhat like the Vedantic notion of the world as *maya*. He refers to the etymological connection between *maya* and *magia* or magic as well as with *Macht* (power and Moglichkeit or potentiality). He also calls Vedanta as "nothing but the most exalted Idealism or spiritualism."[13] However, he finds in the Upanishads "a very unsatisfactory reading" because in them "a positive explanation of the supreme unity is not found anywhere."[14] Halbfass remarks that Schelling's response to Indian thought is not that of a neutral scholar but, just like Hegel's, "a philosophically and theoretically committed response."[15] (WH, 102). Schelling is clearly fascinated with *Advaita Vedanta* which he calls the Indian system of absolute identity, "the highest point to idealism could rise without proper revelation." Thus, we may notice that Schopenhauer was a more neutral scholar without theological commitments to Christian revelation or monotheism, and was unlike Schelling. The Upanishads to him were the most elevating reading than these can be for him, and not unsatisfactory due to their lack of monotheism as they were for Schelling.[16]

## Schopenhauer and Indian Thought

Schopenhauer's numerous references and elucidations in the three editions of *WWR* and in his later works shows a unique harmony between a system of Western philosophy and ancient Eastern thought systems. Indeed the way some Indian philosophical concepts are incorporated in Schopenhauer's own work shows a deep-seated conviction that various philosophies of the world, both ancient and

---

[12.] Ibid., p. 100.

[13.] Arthur Schopenhauer. *Samtliche Werke* (Leipzig, Germany: 7 Banden, 1988), II/2, 482.

[14.] Ibid., p. 480.

[15.] Halbfass, *India and Europe*, p. 102.

[16.] Arthur Hubscher, ed. *Samtliche Werke* (Leipzig, Germany: F.A. Brockhaus, 1988).

modern, are outcomes of the same human quest to fathom the perennial issues of Being, existence, worlds, real and unreal. It also shows that the thinker himself was over searching for Eastern terms comparable to his own basic concepts such as the will-to-live, the denial of the will, *principium individuationis*, etc. perhaps without success of finding exact equivalents. However, the process of such comparisons seems to have delivered its own rewards and contribute to the originality of his own system.

Whether Schopenhauer freely adopted the Indian concepts in his writings or use them to re-authenticate his already developed concepts of the will-to-live and its denial, one thing is certain no other Western philosopher has studied, elucidated and incorporated his own system, the Indian philosophies as vigorously as he did. He did not subscribe to the usual notion that Indian philosophy is inseparable from religion, the kind of view held by Hegel but seems to regard the philosophies of the world as one body of knowledge in which the systems of Hindu thought and Buddhism hold a distinctive place. It was a remarkable step by a Western philosopher in his day and age when Eastern philosophies were still barely known and their texts were inadequately translated. Although Schopenhauer recognize the loftiness of the New Testament Christianity in providing a thought for worldview, he never regarded Vedanta and Buddhism being inferior or less-developed in contrast to a supposed superior and fully matured status of the Christian worldview such as a tendency is clearly visible in the writings of several Indologists and Indian philosophy scholars of his times, including Schlegel, Schelling, and Hegel with respect to the connection of Schopenhauer's philosophy with Eastern thought, a question is bound to arise. Do Vedanta and Buddhism really contain the elements of pessimism and extreme asceticism that Schopenhauer's philosophy seems to uphold at first sight? How exactly did he match his own concepts with the classical notions of Indian thought such as *brahman, atman, samsara, maya, trsna* (craving), *upadana*, etc. was Schopenhauer's interpretations of India good enough even for his age? Did he twist, turn and simplify perennial Indian concepts to match his own terms and preoccupations? Some of these and similar questions are posed and analyzed by Wilhelm Halbfass in his scholarly work *India and Europe*.

Halbfass points out that responding to these questions is not an easy matter in Schopenhauer's own ongoing quest to match his own concepts with Indian ideas and the search for exact equivalents is recorded in his handwritten intellectual diaries (Handliche Nachkass) as well as his remarks within his writings, make it a complex issue. It will be neither fair nor justified to equate the all-important notion of will-to-live to one of the seemingly similar Indian concepts such as *brahman*, *maya*, *trsna*, and *upadana*. "How his knowledge of the Indian material was related to the genesis of Schopenhauer's own system is a question which cannot be answered with complete clarity and certainty; his own explicit remarks, in any case, do not provide a sufficient basis for answering it."[17] Halbfass is referring to Schopenhauer's own frustration in discovering an equivalent Indian concept for the will-to-live, and his many declarations concerning the issue. Some such statements of Schopenhauer in his writings, letters, and diaries are quoted by Halbfass as follows.

Halbfass also points out that Schopenhauer considered the concept of *maya* is comparable to his notion of *principium individuationis*.[18] Schopenhauer also believes that basically "the sages of all times have always said the same"[19] "Buddha, Eckhardt and I all teach essentially the same."[20] Schopenhauer found the Buddhist concept of *upadana (*attachment) comparable to the will-to-live.[21] Turning, now, from Schopenhauer's own search for Indian concepts parallel to the will-to-live, to the speculations of his interpreters, simplistically equated to *brahman*, *atman*, *maya*, *trsna*, *upadana*, etc. make the issue, even more unresolved. However, we must take into account that Schopenhauer's concept of the will-to-live was not produced merely in response to Indian philosophy but primarily to counter certain tendencies that had emerged in Western philosophy of his times. Halbfass maintains that:

> Schopenhauer's doctrine of the will implies a critique of the European tradi-
> tion of representational and rational thinking, of calculation and planning…he
> continued a critique of some of the most fundamental pre-suppositions of the
> Judeo-Christian tradition such as the notion of a personal God, the uniqueness
> of the human individual, and the meaning of history.[22]

This clearly implies that while Indian concepts did influence Schopenhauer's thinking, they were not used to build his own system. Reactions to various devel-opments in the European philosophy of his times including to the historicism

---

[17.] Halbfass, *India and Europe*, p. 107.

[18.] Arthur Schopenhauer. *The World as Will and Representation*, Vols. I and II, trans. E. F. J. Payne (New York: Dover Publications, 1969), vol. II, 378; vol. 2, 160.

[19.] Arthur Schopenhauer. *Parerga and Paralipomena*, ed. Paul Deussen (Cambridge: Cambridge University Press, 1908, 2014), vol. V, 348.

[20.] HN, Deussen, IX, p. 89.

[21.] Deussen, XV, p. 46.

[22.] Halbfass, *India and Europe*, p. 120.

of Hegel, Judeo-Christian dogmas and rationalism, were the main initial
impetus behind the writing of *WWR*. Indian philosophy, especially played a
part offering examples of an alternative way of thinking, which seem to match
Schopenhauer's own approach to reality. The will-to-live seeks to correct the
well-established Western assumptions regarding the idea of personal God, the
supremacy of the rational and the dismissal of the instinct of the virtues of the
heart, a Schopenhauer calls them. Indeed, the Vedantic notions of *maya* and
*mamta* (mineness), *moha* (attachment), and *aham* (ego) all contain the characteristics of the will-to-live, and so do the Buddhist notions of *trsna* (craving)
and *upadana* (attachment). However, it would be wrong to equate the will to
the Vedantic notion of *brahman*. This characterization of the divine Being as
everlasting, pure consciousness and bliss (*sat-chitta-ananda*) is certainly not
comparable to the blind, irrational urge to live and live it up. Also the concept
of the denial of the will-to-live touches upon him metaphysical dualism and
extreme asceticism and a pessimistic rejection of the world, which is contrary
to the spirit of Vedanta and Buddhism. Did Schopenhauer shift his philosophical standpoint in the light of his growing knowledge of Vedanta and Buddhism
after 1818? Moria Nicholls in her article "The Influences of Eastern Thought on
Schopenhauer's Doctrine of the Thing-in-Itself" offers some useful information
about Schopenhauer's citations of Eastern thought, even though her thesis about
the shifts in Schopenhauer's philosophical position after the first publication of
*WWR* (1818) is flawed and unconvincing:

> Volume I of *WWR* (1818) contains about 80 references to Buddhist thought, five
> of which are added in later editions (1844) and (1859) of that volume. By com-
> parison in Volume II, first published in 1844 (when a second edition of Volume
> I was also published), there are at least 30 references to Buddhism. References
> to Hindu thought in Volume I number over fifty, seven of which are added in
> later editions, and in Volume II there are over 55 references to Hinduism. While
> these figures are only approximate, the indicate of marked rise in Schopenhauer's
> knowledge and interest in Buddhist thought from 1818 on, and strong and con-
> sistent in Hindu thought from 1813 until his death in 1860...[This] indicate[s]
> that Schopenhauer had an abiding interest in Eastern philosophy, and that he was
> keen to demonstrate parallels between his own doctrines and these of the east.[23]

---

[23] Moira Nicholls, "The Influences of Eastern Thought on Schopenhauer's Doctrine of the Thing-in-Itself," in *Cambridge Companion to Schopenhauer*, ed. Christopher Janaway (Cambridge: Cambridge University Press, 1999), 176.

So far Nicholls' assertions are factually true. We should keep in mind, however, that a statistical analysis can only reveal a part of the truth and can very easily lead us astray. Nicholls' subsequent conclusions are seriously flawed and pre-sumptuous. They are enough to make Schopenhauer turn in his grave:

> Three identifiable shifts in Schopenhauer's doctrine of the thing-in-itself occur between the publications of the first volume of *WWR* in 1818 in his later works. The first shift concerns the knowability of thing-in-itself, the second...[Its] nature, the third...Is explicit attempt to assimilate his own doctrine...With eastern doctrines. Schopenhauer asserts numerous times throughout his work that the thing-in-itself is will or will-to-live and he claims that we know this through direct intuition in self-consciousness...However...In his later works...He seems to withdraw the claim that in self-consciousness we are aware of the will, suggesting indeed that in self-consciousness we are aware of no more than our phenomenal willings.[24]

> The second shift [occurs when he] introduces the idea that thing-in-itself has multiple aspects, only one of which is will. Other aspects of the objects of aware-ness of such persons as mystics, saying and ascetics, who have denied the will.[25]

> [Regarding the third shift]...I have identified six passages in which Schopenhauer asserts that the thing-in-itself can be described as will, but only in a metaphorical sense...[as] similar views are expressed in eastern thought.[26]

In response to Nicholls' speculation, it may be said emphatically that there are no such ships in Schopenhauer's doctrine of the will which he identifies as the thing-in-itself, for which his enhanced knowledge of eastern thought or anything else is responsible. Nothing is clearer than the fact that Being of all beings is named will-to-live by Schopenhauer. This thing-in-itself (a Kantian term) was never claimed by him to be entirely unknown or entirely and precisely known in human consciousness. If further attempts are made by the thinker to compare the will with *brahman, nirvana,* or more specifically to *maya* or *trsna,* this by no means indicates a shift in Schopenhauer's basic doctrine of the will. It is well known that despite dismal sales, Schopenhauer rewarded *WWR* as the ultimate and complete metaphysical system, from which all his later works originate, requiring

---

[24.] Ibid., pp. 171–176

[25.] Ibid.

[26.] Ibid., 176.

no emendations or changes. He calls the contents of Volume II (in 1844) merely "supplements in concordance with the already existing for books of the original, to which only further explications and examples can be added but no changes to it are ever necessary." His later works, other than *WWR* are also from his point of view, further elaborations of his original metaphysical masterpiece. Nicholls' assertion that in later works Schopenhauer "seems to withdraw the claim that in self-consciousness we are aware of the will" has no credibility. Not only is such a withdrawal uncharacteristic of Schopenhauer's consistent pride in his fundamental work, but such a claim shows a misunderstanding of his basic definition of the will. The Being of beings is named after its most excellent species, namely, human will. However, one is not clearly aware of the will being the source of one's needs, wants, and urges but knows his existence vaguely or fuzzily. However, human beings have the possibility of knowing the will's operations and machinations when knowledge, which usually plays second fiddle to the will, surmounts the will and inspires the subject to deny the will. The ascetics and mystics from Western as well as Eastern traditions seem to be practitioners of the denial of the will, if we ignore their various dogmatic beliefs and religious commitments. Thus, the will is never missing from self-consciousness but is seldom known with all its implications. Schopenhauer never shifted or changed this account of the will. As far as Nicholls' reference to another shift of will being known "only in a metaphysical sense" supposedly due to the thinker's advanced readings of Eastern thought, we may again assert that no such shift ever happened in the later works.

Although Schopenhauer made use of the biographical or the hagiographical materials concerning the saints and the ascetics theistic (Christian, Hindu) as well as aesthetic (Buddhist, Jain) religious traditions, he did so without losing sight of his own secular metaphysical system. That is why he wants the reader in the Book IV of *WWR* that religious dogmas and superstitions of these saints must be disregarded. A denier of the will-to-live knows the will and it demands full well and not just "metaphysically," although anyone will find it difficult to find the thing-in-itself precisely or completely, according to Schopenhauer's early as well as later works.

Another extensive study of Schopenhauer's Eastern sources was done by Bikkhu Nanajivako, who is a practicing Buddhist monk, in his book *Studies in Comparative Philosophy.*[27] This book provides some useful data and insights on Schopenhauer's connection with Indian philosophy in general and Buddhism in particular. Nanajivako begins with a critique of the Euro-centric interpretations

---

[27] Bikkhu Nanajivako, *Studies in Comparative Philosophy* (Columbo: Lakehouse Publishers, 1983).

of Schopenhauer's thoughts and demonstrates through numerous citations, the central role of Indian thought in it. The bulk of the book is devoted exclusively to Schopenhauer's references to Buddhism, and the author clearly deemphasizes the roots of Vedanta in his highly favored treatment of Buddhism and puts forward the thesis that although "fragmentary" Upanishads were initially a significant influence on Schopenhauer, he grew out of "mutually discordant." Hindu systems and his more mature years opted for the more methodical and cohesive Buddhist philosophy. Thus, Nanajivako focuses on Schopenhauer's comments on Buddhism sprinkled throughout his early and later works. In fact, all the statements of Schopenhauer on Buddhism are reproduced, making those approximately 100 pages a useful research tool.

However, an open-minded reader will not find any credibility for Nanajivako's thesis. There is no evidence that Schopenhauer even lost his admiration for Vedanta and allied Hindu systems. Nor did he ever show an overall preference for a certain Buddhist notion. For example, in his essay on death in Volume II of *WWR*, he praises the Buddhist notion of rebirth being better than that theories of metempsychosis in ancient Greek and Hindu thought. "We find this doctrine in its subtlest form coming nearest to truth in Buddhism"[28] perhaps Buddhist theory of rebirth comes nearest to Schopenhauer's own theory of "indestructability of the will," which according to him, lives on in the species rather than in the individuals. Sporadic observations of this kind should not lead us to conclude that Schopenhauer preferred Buddhism over Vedanta on the whole in his later phase, for in the same essay on death, he has this to say: "the conviction here described and arising directly out of the apprehension of nature must have been extremely lively in those sublime authors of the Upanishads of the Vedas, who can scarcely be conceived as mere human beings."[29] Schopenhauer admires and cites the *Bhagavad-Gita*[30] as well as the Buddha[31] in the same work, composed in the later years (1844 onward) of his career.

Nanajivako correctly points out that Schopenhauer, like Goethe and Schelling, had attended Friedrich Majer lectures in Oriental thought in 1813. In the same year, he received a copy of the Upanishads from Weimar library. In section 192, there is this: "the wiser Indian started from the subject, from *atman, jivatman*." In

---

[28.] Schopenhauer, *The World as Will and Representation*, vol. II, trans. E. F. J. Payne (New York: Dover Publications, 1969) p. 504.

[29.] Ibid., p. 475.

[30.] Ibid., p. 473.

[31.] Ibid., pp. 504, 508.

the notes made by Schopenhauer in his *MR* in the next two years, there are further reflections on *maya*.[32] These earliest references may suffice to show how deep the first impact of Indian thought was on Schopenhauer at the very time when the idea of his system was beginning to germinate in his mind. However, Nanajivako thesis that Schopenhauer grew out of his initial fascination with Vedanta and Hinduism, and regarding Buddhism as the most worthwhile philosophy is unconvincing and clearly biased. Why would anyone consider Schopenhauer as dismissive of Vedanta, when as late as in 1851 he will pay the following tribute to the Anquetil-Duperron translation of the Upanishads: "[It is] the most edifying reading, with the exception of the original text that could be possible in this world; it has been the solace of my life and will be the solace of my death."[33]

More unconvincing and misleading conclusions such as the following are drawn by Nanajivako: at later stages it can be seen how *this expansion of the Vedic* idea of *maya* subsided and "was taken over by more explicitly Buddhist connotation of *samsara*." Nanajivako's attempts to claim *samsara* is exclusively a Buddhist notion is quite strange. *Samsara* is a perennial concept of the Indian tradition, which is a colloquial form for the "world." This term is connected with the mess of reincarnation and is older than the Buddhist faith itself. Thus, in Schopenhauer's thought, there is no such thing as a break with Vedanta and full endorsement of Buddhism. There was no abatement of his admiration of Eastern concepts from either Vedanta or Buddhism.

However, Schopenhauer's own interpretation was somewhat slanted toward pessimism and he does not show adequate attention to detail in his reading of the four noble truths. He focuses on the mention of the term (*dukkha*), the literal meaning of which is suffering or pain. The more philosophical meaning, namely, existential un-satisfactoriness is not fully present in Schopenhauer's interpretation. In the ancient Buddha *sutras* (discourses) the standard statement of the first noble (Aryan) truth is as follows: "now this o monks, is a noble truths of *dukkha* ; birth is *dukkha*, old age is *dukkha*, sickness is *dukkha*, sorrow, lamentation dejection and despair are *dukkha*. Contact with unpleasant things is *dukkha*, not getting what one wants is *dukkha*. In short, five skandhas of grasping are *dukkha*."[34] The repeated use of the term *dukkha*, if taken in its literal meaning, may create the impression

---

[32] Ibid., Nanajivako, *Studies in Comparative Philosophy*, p. 22.

[33] *Parerga and Paralipomena*, II, Section 184.

[34] "Samyutta-nikaya," in *A Sourcebook of Indian Philosophy*, ed. S. Radhakrishnan and C. A. Moore (Princeton, NJ: Princeton University Press, 1973), 274.

that the Buddha took a gloomy view of human existence and said that "all life is suffering." This would also create the impression that Buddhism is a pessimistic philosophy that turns a blind eye toward possible happiness and glorious potentials of human existence.

But when we recognize that Buddha took pains to specify some specific occasions of inevitable suffering, the accusation of pessimism is no longer credible. We should add to the fact that three noble truths affected diagnosis, as well as a remedy out of *dukkha*; it is not fair to call it pessimistic on the whole.

Nevertheless, suppose pessimism and asceticism combined with seeming reflection of *samsara* (worldliness) may be the main attractions that draw Schopenhauer to Buddhism. He seems to oversimplify the four noble truths in Volume II of *WWR*:

> In (Buddhism) all improvements, conversion and salvation to be hoped from this world, from this *samsara* proceed from knowledge of the four fundamental truths: (1) *dolor* (suffering), (2) *doloris ortus* (origin of suffering), (3) *dolris inferitus* (cessation of suffering), (4) *Octoparite via ad doloris sedation* (eightfold path to the calling of suffering)...

> Christianity belongs to the ancient true and sublime face of mankind. The state stands in contrast to the falls, shallow and pernicious optimism that manifests itself in Greek paganism, Judaism and Islam.[35]

Schopenhauer admires Buddhism, Hinduism, and Christianity for their supposed rejection of pernicious optimism that prevails in the Old Testament and Islam. At the same time, he clearly oversimplifies the noble truths, especially the first one. He describes the essence of the first noble truths in one world, namely, suffering. The question arises, if the Buddha wanted to say all human existence is nothing but suffering, why did not he say so? It was easy to say "life is suffering," skip the remaining descriptions of the specific locations of suffering. Buddhists believe that their account was realistic rather than pessimistic. For the noble truths identify a cause of *dukkha*, namely, *trsna* (craving), assert that this cause can be "removed without a remainder." They also prescribed an eightfold path that will remove suffering. Thus, Schopenhauer chooses to overlook the hopeful spirit of the second, third, and fourth noble truths. The sermon of the Buddha, which contains a statement of four truths, begins with an admonition of the Buddha the five former disciples:

---

[35]. Schopenhauer, *The World as Will and Representation*, vol. II, p. 623.

> These two extremes, O monks, are not to be practiced by one who has gone
> forth from *samsara*...That conjoined with passions...and that conjoined with
> self-torture...Avoiding these extremes, the *Tathagata* (Buddha) has gained the
> knowledge of the middle way, which gives site and knowledge and tends to
> claim, to insight enlightenment, Nirvana.

Thus, neither the thoughtless and pursuit of passions, nor other extreme of
asceticism and mounting self-torture, can deliver a higher thoughtful life and/
or the glimpses of truth. Thus, Buddhism does not advocate other pessimism or
asceticism or the denials of the will in its extreme form.

## Some Hasty Critiques of Schopenhauer

Schopenhauer is not exactly an admired figure in the history of modern philosophy. The tag of being a rapid pessimist too readily applied to him. However,
the reasons for his pessimism are often oversimplified and the extent of his
pessimism is unduly exaggerated, as many of his concepts and standpoints are
misunderstood. Many such misunderstandings are rooted in a lack of appreciation
of his connections with Eastern thought. A lack of even a basic familiarity with
Vedanta and Buddhism on the part of many of his modern critics, has driven
them to draw some hasty conclusions not only about Schopenhauer's thought but
also about his personality. The fundamental positions of this thinker regarding
the sufferings and the undesirable status in this world, the concepts of eternal
justice, death and salvation are grossly misunderstood in the secondary literature.
This is so because an assessment of the same or similar concepts in Vedanta and
Buddhism is seldom carried out, and the roots of the seemingly discordant notions
of Schopenhauer's system are seldom traced in Eastern thought. This is not to say
that Schopenhauer simply borrowed these concepts from Eastern thought, nor is
it an attempt to exaggerate the role of Eastern influences on Schopenhauer. But
an assessment of similar notions in Eastern thought helps us to understand the
original way of thinking that Schopenhauer had. Many of Schopenhauer's modern
interpreters have misunderstood and oversimplified this thinker's fundamental
positions on the status of this world, human existence and suffering, or account
of remaining silent on the Eastern dimension of his thought.

One of the most bewildering aspects of Schopenhauer's thought for many of
his interpreters has been his apparent disdain of the world, human existence, and

human nature. His condemnation of individualism, on all important Western values, as well as his focus on suffering and overlooking the possibilities of happiness are viewed as quite anomalous. Thus, the labels of extreme pessimism, absurdity, perversity, and hypocrisy are applied to Schopenhauer by some well-established scholars. Schopenhauer is widely known as a pessimistic thinker and he himself is never shy of calling optimism a pernicious philosophy and of rejecting the notion that ours is the best of all possible worlds. Nevertheless the current secondary literature often judges him as more pessimistic than he is and caricatures both his life and work as odd, eccentric, and puzzling. The statements such as these have raised many eyebrows: "To desire immortality for the individual is to perpetuate an error forever, for at bottom every individuality is really only a special error, a false step, something that it would be better should not be, in fact, something from which it is the real purpose of life to bring us back."[36] This kind of assertion is so difficult for many Schopenhauer scholars to accept at face value. They usually attribute such conviction of the thinker to his pessimism or begin to see contradictions in his standpoints. For example, Michael Fox in his article "Schopenhauer on Death, Suicide and Self-Renunciation" frustratingly remarks:

> The doctrine of palingenesis as promulgated by Schopenhauer is indeed difficult to comprehend and there is more than one lacuna in his account...After all Schopenhauer makes perverse claim that for mankind it would have been better not to have come into being and to exist; life is just a disturbing interruption of the blissful non-existence. Schopenhauer's doctrine of self-renunciation must be examined independently of his entirely perverse and absurd position...That man is guilty and inexpugnably sinful, not because of his deeds but merely because he exists.[37]

In a similarly unsympathetic and literal reading of Schopenhauer's statement "we are at bottom something that ought not to be,"[38] David Cartwright writes, "We suffer and die because we deserve it. The world is perfectly retributive. We deserve what we receive because we are guilty. We are guilty because we exist. Schopenhauer's logic is now as clear as it is unconvincing."[39]

---

[36.] Ibid., vol. 2, p. 432.

[37.] Ibid., pp. 504, 508.

[38.] Ibid., vol. 2, p. 507.

[39.] Ibid.

A misunderstanding of Schopenhauer's analysis of *samsara*, consistent with his reading of Vedanta and Buddhism, a failure to distinguish between "excessive worldliness" and the "world as such," a refusal to take seriously the wisdom behind the myth of reincarnation, a living belief of the two thirds of humanity, has driven many interpreters of Schopenhauer to extreme judgment of not only this man's philosophy but of the man himself. For example, Bryan Magee in his *Philosophy of* Schopenhauer,[40] writes:

> In the light of the present day knowledge there can be little doubt that Schopen-
> hauer's despairing view of the world, above all, his conviction of terribleness
> of existence as such, were in some degree neurotic manifestations which had
> roots in his relationship with his mother...If actions speak louder than words,
> his life as he in fact lives it...tells us of a man in whom protean pleasures are
> being experienced side by side with mountainous frustration, misanthropy and
> desolate miseries of neurosis.

> Although John Atwell does not offer an adequate analysis of Schopenhauer's
> connections with Eastern thought in his book *Schopenhauer: The Human Charac-
> ter*,[41] he offers an important rejoinder to scholars who advocate selective reading
> of Schopenhauer, and wishes to rub out the sections, usually those aligning with
> Eastern worldviews, from Schopenhauer's writings. Atwell cautions that passages
> deemed as "absurd," "perverse," and "unconvincing" from Western perspectives
> cannot simply be disregarded.

> Now if the doctrine of eternal justice is "absurd" or "perverse," then it is not so
> in itself, but only because Schopenhauer's entire metaphysical thesis—the world
> as will—is absurd or perverse; for the doctrine of eternal justice follows with
> strict necessity from the metaphysical thesis...Consequently one cannot logically
> accept the metaphysical thesis or even regarded as plausible or worthwhile or
> insightful (as critics often suggest) and then reject the doctrine of eternal justice
> or regarded as nonsense (as the very same critics often do).

Atwell correctly identifies the tendency to show irritation with some parts of Schopenhauer's writing by his modern critics. It is to be noticed that the passages in the concepts taken to task are frequently those that emanate from Schopenhauer's

---

[40] Ibid.

[41] Ibid.

affinities with Indian thought, which is an area of knowledge that these critics have not adequately taken into account. Thus, often some fundamental rationales, presuppositions, and concepts of Schopenhauer are cast aside due to a critic's unfamiliarity with Eastern thought.

In response to these hasty and severe critiques, we must assert that there is nothing absurd or perverse about Schopenhauer's appreciation of the Vedantic and Buddhist standpoint that continued life of *samsara* (attachment to the world-liness) is not something to be celebrated otherwise higher life of detachment and seeking of salvation will be rendered meaningless. The bliss of *moksha* (salvation, freedom) must be contrasted with the vulgarity of *samsaric* existence or what Schopenhauer calls life of a philistine. This is necessary to inspire oneself toward a higher life of detachment, that is, life of denial of the will. The portrayal of *nirvana* as a release from the cycle of rebirth is a mythological exposition of the philosophical standpoint that *samsara* or worldliness ought not to be valued in a philosophical lifestyle. To desire perpetuation of one's individuality is to give in to mineness (*mamta*) and *moha* (attachment). It is tantamount to saying yes to *samsara*, which is neither philosophically desirable nor praiseworthy. Schopenhauer's statement that "at bottom every individuality is a special error, a false step, something that it would be better not to be"[42] is consistent with the Vedanta message that to take the ego (*aham*) as real is to dismiss one's larger self (*atman*). All individualities and diversity are superficial and in contrast to oneness of *brahman*. Agreeing with Vedanta, Schopenhauer maintains that the real purpose of human life is to bring ourselves back from the individuality-based, vulgar living which continues to affirm that the seemingly rational pursuits of the irrational urges of the will-to-live, which produce *samsara* for us. In essence, Schopenhauer is revalidating what Socrates said, "it is not just living that counts but living well."

## Schopenhauer and Vedanta

It may be noted that any thesis regarding his alleged preference of Buddhism over Hinduism, or any alleged revision of his positions in the light of his new knowledge of Buddhism, will be nothing but scholarly quibbling. Furthermore, it is hard to write two separate essays on "Schopenhauer and Hinduism" and

---

[42.] Ibid., vol. 2, p. 492.

"Schopenhauer and Buddhism." It is hardly possible to detach his allusions to Hinduism out of his general comments on Indian thought. Even though Schopenhauer's knowledge of Hindu thought came to him much earlier than that of Buddhism and his respect for it never diminished throughout his life, he developed an equal degree of respect for Buddhism, as well. As quoted by Halbfass[43] the following autobiographical remarks, make it clear that his knowledge of Vedanta came to him before the literature on Buddhism even became available in Europe:

On the whole the harmony (of Buddhism) with my teachings is wonderful, all the more so because I wrote the first volume (of *WWR*) between 1814 and 1818 it did not nor could have known all that[44] "Nor, could have known all that" (about Buddhism) indicates that not much was even available in print about Buddhism between 1814 and 1818. But the following remarks in manuscript remains (1816) show that admission that he was already exposed to Hindu thought, perhaps after attending lectures of F. Mager, during the writing period of the first volume of *WWR*: by the way, I admit that I do not believe that my doctrine could have ever been formulated before the Upanishads, Plato and Kant were able to able to cast their light spontaneously onto a human mind."[45]

However, the fact that Schopenhauer's exposure to Hindu thought was earlier than that of Buddhist thought, should not lead us to the conclusion that he preferred one over the other, or that he revised doctrinal positions in any way due to his subsequent studies of Buddhism. It is evident to any careful reader of his later editions and later works that quoted from these two Eastern traditions together and in the same breath. Thus, the texts and commentaries of Hindu thought only gradually advanced his knowledge of Buddhism, as more and more translations and studies of Buddhism became available in Europe. However, he was far more advanced than Hegel, whose commentaries on Indian thought were based exclusively on a study of Hindu texts, and who had little or no knowledge of Buddhism. Schopenhauer, however, developed a deep interest in Buddhism and read everything that was being published on the subject in Europe in his lifetime. Regarding the rapid advancement of Indian studies in Europe during his times, one of his footnotes in the later addition of *WWR* quite instructive: "in

---

[43] Halbfass, *India and Europe*, p. 107.

[44] Briefe, Deussen XV, p. 470; Schopenhauer, *The World as Will and Representation*, p. 388; Halbfass, *India and Europe*, p. 107.

[45] HN, Deussen, XI, p. 459.

the last forty years Indian literature has grown so much in Europe, that if I now wished to complete this note to the first edition, it would fill several pages."[46]

Schopenhauer, like other Indologists, studied first and foremost, the philosophy that he maintained a life-long admiration and deep interest in Vedanta. This is evident in his numerous references to the Vedic concepts and doctrines throughout his early and later works. This does not mean that his perceptive and creative accounts of Vedic thought were always comprehensive as well as indisputable in their interpretations. Schopenhauer's validation of atheism, asceticism and above all, pessimism are obviously in discord with the spirit of Vedanta. That is why it will be most objectionable to compare his concept of the will-to-live with either *brahman* or *atman*. It may be more comparable to *maya*. Although *brahman* is described as beyond everything while being within everything, neutral and indifferent, it is also called *sat-chitta-ananda* (everlasting, pure consciousness, blissful). Thus, atheism and pessimism are ruled out by Vedanta. According to popular views, Hinduism became explicitly theistic and devotional in the post-Upanishadic period in which the epics and *Bhagavad-Gita* were written. *Bhagavad-Gita*, a favorite text of Schopenhauer, was frequently quoted in his writings. Although Schopenhauer correctly celebrates the contributions of Hindu and Buddhist ascetics such as *sadhus*, *samanas*, *munis*, and *rishis* for their remarkably other-worldly lifestyles of the denial of the will-to-live, it is still hard to say whether Hinduism recommends the extreme asceticism of the kind described as prototype of the denial of the will. For the pursuit of *dharma* is not a simple matter of affirmation and denial in various shades and schools of Hinduism. It is not merely a decision to deny stifle worldliness or *maya*. The Vedanta tradition includes in itself the practice of *bhakti* (devotion, love) which is to be combined with (*yoga*) action (*karma*) and knowledge of the divine (*jnana*). In other words the way of *bhakti* is not exactly the path of asceticism but perhaps an alternative to asceticism, a spontaneous embracing of the other-worldly in this world, an invitation to higher love in this life. The work of the bhakti-saints that appeared in India as part of the southern (6th century onward) and northern (13th century onward) *bhakti*-movements of Hindu revivalism, show a personal and passionate longing to identify with the object of devotion (*Ish*). The role as well as the superiority of the way of *bhakti* is very succinctly outlined in the following words of the 16th-century *bhakti*-saint Eknath (1548–1608):

---

[46.] Schopenhauer, *The World as Will and Representation*, vol. I, p. 388.

Though one restrains, the senses, yet they are not restrained. Though one re-
nounces sensual desires, yet they are not renounced. Again and again he return
to torment one. For that reason "the flame of *hari-bhakti* was lit by Veda." There
is no need to suppress the senses, desire of sensual pleasure ceases of itself. So
mighty is the power that lies in *hari-bhakti*.

The senses that *yogis* suppresses *bhaktias* devote to the worship of *bhagvat*
(Blessed-One, Lord), offer to *bhagvat. Yogis* suffer in the flesh…the followers of
*bhakti* become forever emancipated. Though he has no knowledge of the Vedas,
still buy one so ignorant may the real *atman* be apprehended. The condition of
*brahman* may easily be attained and realized.

Women, *sudras* (lower castes) and all the others…can be borne by the power of
*sraddha* (faith) and *bhakti* to the other shore (of the ocean of *samsara*).[47]

It is obvious that Schopenhauer paid hardly any attention to *bhakti* as an important
aspect of Hinduism. However, he does mention that *Kural* is an important text of the
Southern *Bhakti* movement in Tamil language. "The passion of the mind directed
onwards and that of the I directed inwards should cease," he quotes to compare
it with a saying of Madame de Guyon in *German theology*: "In true love, there
remains neither I nor me, mine…and the like".[48] In the next line, Schopenhauer
quotes the Buddha, "My disciples reject the idea that I am this or this is mine." For
the lack of analysis of *bhakti*, neither Schopenhauer nor other early 19th-century
Indologists can hardly be blamed. Hinduism of the intellectual variety alone or
various treatments of *jnana* (knowledge) alone were offered in Europe of those
times. By and large, *bhakti*, which is what makes Indian philosophies "living
philosophies" or guidelines to higher living is given hardly any importance even
today. Most Western and Eastern scholars continue to offer intellectualized systems
of Hindu thought in Western terminology, although some translations of the work
of *bhakti* masters have appeared in recent times. Obviously, such accounts of the
practice of *bhakti* were not available to Schopenhauer although he was able to
capture the essence of Hinduism in his own original fashion.

In the fourth book of the *WWR*, Schopenhauer while discussing the denial of
the will-to-live, finds much to admire about Christian mystics and ascetics as
well as about the saints, ascetics and monks of Hinduism and Buddhism:

---

[47] Ibid.

[48] Ibid., vol. 2, p. 613.

> We cannot sufficiently wonder at the harmony we find…[between] a Christian pertinent or saint and that of an Indian. In spite of such fundamentally different dogmas, customs and circumstances, the endeavor and the inner life of both are absolutely the same…The Christian mystics and the teachers of the Vedanta philosophy agree in regarding all outward works and religious practices as superfluous for the man who has attained perfection.[49]

Schopenhauer's remarks indicate that the field of religion can also offer much by way of philosophical insight and guidelines for philosophical life, provided the different religious dogmas, rituals, and customs are set aside and what is common to practitioners of the denial of the will-to-live from Western and Eastern religions is studied carefully. Being a secular minded and atheistic philosopher, unlike Hegel and Schelling, what he admired in Hindu thought was the notion of *brahman*, which cannot simply be equated with that of God, and also the fact that Buddhism remains free of the obsession with God. Thus, he was not merely admiring the Indian systems of thought that was also trying to free the philosophical investigations of modern Europe from its hidden agendas based on monotheistic Christian ideology and the concept of God. Thus, his opposition to Hegel and Hegelianism was not merely a personal dislike but rooted in doctrinal differences. He was also trying to correct the assumptions of Indologists like Schlegel brothers and Schelling:

> It was necessary to find out whether the ancient and non-European notions especially Hindustan, and many of the oldest Greek philosophers, actually arrived at those concepts, or whether only we, by translating *Brahma* (*brahman*) of the Hindus and the *Tien* (*Tao)* of the Chinese quite falsely as "God" charitably describe such concepts to them,…whether it is not the case that theism proper is to be found only in the Jewish religion and the religions that have sprung from it.[50]

Schopenhauer was sharp enough to foresee that the work of the Indologists gratifying complementary as it was to the Indian scholars, also did a great harm to the study of Indian philosophies and religions by providing some foundational interpretations which were based on Christian and theistic presuppositions. An example of this is some classical interpretations of the *Bhagavad-Gita* which

---

[49] Ibid., vol. I, p. 389.

[50] Ibid., vol. I, p. 486.

was hailed as the first theistic work of Hindu thought, as its connections with Vedic and Upanishadic thought was dismissed in view of its supposedly theistic message. Due to the same line of thinking, the concept of *bhakti* (the soul of love, religious or secular) was simplistically understood as "worship of God," and its origins were traced in the *Bhagavad-Gita* rather than the Vedas, where it actually began. It is amazing to see that in the early 19th-century, Schopenhauer was free from such theistic dogmas and largely recognized Hindu thought in independence from Western presuppositions.

With respect to the relative existence governed by of sufficient reason, Schopen-hauer offers one of the most lucid definition of *maya* reminds us the way *maya* was defined by Sankara, 13th-century Hindu philosopher:

> It is *maya* the veil of deception, which covers the eye of the mortals and causes them to see a world of which one cannot say either it is or that it is not, for it is like a dream, like the sunshine on the sand...or like the piece of rope on the ground which [one] regards as the snake" (These similes are repeatedly found in innumerable passages of the *Vedas* and *Puranas*). But what all this meant... is nothing else but...the world as representation subordinated to the principle of sufficient reason.[51]

This is an example of how Schopenhauer often found parallels for his own concepts in the doctrines of Vedanta. In the fourth book of *WWR,* Schopenhauer devotes almost two pages comparing his concept of eternal justice and "vivid knowledge (which) will always remain inaccessible to the majority of men," comparing it with Vedanta and allied myths of reincarnation.[52] He explains the great truth *tat tvam asi* (that art thou) "was translated into the way of knowledge following the principle of sufficient reason...This way of knowledge is indeed quite incapable of assimilating that truth...yet in the form of a myth, it received a substitute."[53] Schopenhauer highlights the importance of the myth of rebirth in Hinduism. This myth serve as a guide to conduct by making clear the ethical significance of human conduct through a figurative description, according to the "principle of sufficient reason which is eternally foreign to this significance":

---

[51] Ibid., vol. I, p. 8.

[52] Ibid., vol. I, pp. 355–356.

[53] Ibid., vol. I, p. 355.

Never has a myth been, and never will be, more closely associated a philosophical truth accessible to so few, than this very ancient teaching of the noblest and oldest of peoples...We, on the contrary, now send to the *Brahmans* English clergymen and evangelical linen-weavers...But this is just the same as if we fired a bullet at a cliff...The ancient wisdom of the human race will not be supplanted by the events in Galilee. On the contrary, Indian wisdom flows back to Europe, and will produce a fundamental change in our knowledge and thought.[54]

Schopenhauer repeatedly wonders why Hindus were so resistant to the attempts made by the foreign missionaries to convert them continues to show his regard for Vedanta philosophy in Hinduism in general in *Parerga and* Paralipomena,[55] his major work, which finally made him famous throughout Europe. This book is a collection of essays and random thoughts on a variety of subjects written in a popular format. Schopenhauer shows grasp of the world of Hinduism by interpreting its philosophies, religious texts, and mythologies. He does not miss the role of Hinduism as a unique worldview and a way of life. He looks at Hindu mythology as a mirror of Hindu thought, as his studies of the primary and secondary texts gave him a unique expertise. He found its concepts of Vedanta, along with those of six classical systems and of Buddhism, as valuable ways of thinking about the grounds of reality. His own slant to reality is often unhittable, as in the following analysis of Hindu trinity (*Trimurti*):

Vedas also teach no God creator but a world-soul called *brahma* (*brahman*) in the center. *Brahman*, sprung from the navel of Vishnu with the four faces and as part of the Trimurti, is only a popular personification of *Brahma* (*Brahman*) in the extremely transparent Indian mythology. He obviously represents the generation...just as Vishnu does their acme, and Shiva their destruction and extinction. Moreover, his production of the world is a sinful act, just as is the world incarnation of *Brahma* (*Brahman*).[56]

The last sentence shows Schopenhauer's pessimistic bias. The production of the world by *Brahman* is not described as a sinful act, nor is the world on the whole, a sinful reincarnation of *Brahman* according to Hindu scriptures. As explained by *Sankara,* the

[54] Ibid., vol. 2, p. 357.

[55] PP II, pp. 223, 225, 328.

[56] PP, I, p. 127.

world was created as a sport (*leela*), as a playful act of *Brahman* the Being of beings that is not lacking in anything before and after the supposed creation of all things.

There are numerous quotes in the two volumes of *PP* regarding the philosophical issues related to the meaning of death. He brings home the idea that birth, life and death have to be considered as inter-connected. The following remarks regarding life and death and growing old are indicative of the thinker's ability to express profound thought in a simple metaphor:

> Human life cannot really be called either long or short as it is at bottom standard whereby we measure all other length of time. In the Upanishad…the normal duration of human life is stated to be a hundred years. I think this is correct because I have noticed that only those who have passed their nineteenth year… die without any illness. The older we grow, the smaller human affairs seem to be, one and all…The vanity and emptiness of the whole stands out.

The remark that life is the standard measure of all other durations shows an understanding of Time as existential reality, similarly to Heidegger's existential theory of time, which is opposed to Aristotle's notion of Time as a series of nows. It is so difficult for the human entity to view life as either too short or too long. We assume these general characterizations alternatively depending on our own judgment of the way life strikes us.

The Vedantic insights from the Upanishads play a central role in the culmination of Schopenhauer's system. The identification of one's individuality with all and all the others is an insight of the Upanishads that quotes numerous times in his later works:

> The readers of my Ethics know that with me the foundation of morality rests ultimately on the truth which has its expression in the Veda and Vedanta in the established mystical formula *tat tvam asi* (that thou art) which is stated with reference to every living thing, whether man or animal, is then called the *Mahavakya* or Great Word.[57]

Thus, Hindu thought remained an enduring influence on Schopenhauer since his first introduction to it in the time period of the composition of his chief work. Even

---

[57] Arthur Schopenhauer. *Parerga and Paralipomena*, ed. Paul Deussen (Cambridge: Cambridge University Press, 1908, 2014), vol. II, 219.

though he learned about Buddhism and about various systems of Hindu thought in later years, his respect for the Upanishadic Hindu thought stayed with him to the end of his time. He had great regard for the philosophy for the philosophical schools of Hindu thought. But he had equal interest in the mythologies and broad outlooks of the Hindu people as well as in the art, music, and literary works of that tradition. No wonder that Hindu thought lies underneath the foundations of the system in a special and creative way.

# CHAPTER 9

# Schopenhauer on Suffering and Nirvana

*R. Raj Singh*

Transcultural philosophy is a variant of the so-called comparative philosophy. The value of comparative philosophy is increasingly being recognized, and its methods reflected upon in philosophical circles today. The dialogue among the various philosophical traditions, labeled on the basis of their origins in distinctive civilizations and/or geographical regions of the world, is deemed extremely valuable at present. For the most part, individual philosophers have philosophized in response to the history of ideas and concepts of their own respective traditions and have enriched their own traditions as well as contributed to the body of human knowledge. However, there have been from time to time in all traditions, certain thinkers who did not confine themselves strictly to their own heritages in the name of some assumed and self-glorified standards of purity and rigor. The ability to borrow from and contribute to the so-called foreign traditions was not only exemplified by some great classical thinkers and literary masters such as Plato and Shakespeare but also by many creative minds in the 19th and 20th centuries, when more and more translations of foreign texts were becoming available. The intellectual lives of this class of modern thinkers was not confined within cultural boundaries as they identified themselves and their work beyond the limits of their own traditions. A transcultural thinker is one who not only compares and contrasts the ideas and concepts of different traditions but treats a chosen foreign tradition as his own, makes it his own by employing its concepts within his own philosophical projects and problematics. Such a thinker shows the ability to transplant philosophical concepts of two or more traditions in a creative and thoughtful manner and somehow treats world philosophy as one body of knowledge.

Schopenhauer (1788–1860) was a pioneer in transcultural thinking. Philosophies of India particularly Vedanta and Buddhism were his favorite sources for composing and revalidating the universality of his own system. He admired philosophies and religions of India and cited extensively from their texts, which were beginning to be known in Europe in his times. His chief work *The World as Will and Representation* (*WWR*) was published in 1819 and two subsequent enlarged editions appeared in 1844 and 1859. The second edition contained fifty supplementary chapters on the themes discussed in the first edition. The later editions of this chief work and Schopenhauer's other later works contain numerous citations, illustrations, and comparative analyses of Indian concepts.

In this chapter, we will trace the connection between Schopenhauer's thought and the systems of Vedanta and Buddhism with special reference to the problems of suffering and its final remedy proposed by Schopenhauer. This exposition will illustrate the transcultural nature of Schopenhauer's method for philosophizing. At the same time, this exercise in comparative philosophy will hopefully overcome some problems and misunderstandings of Schopenhauer's thought that abound in contemporary Schopenhauer scholarship largely due to the inability of his several interpreters to fully acknowledge his Eastern way of thinking.

## Suffering or "Dukkha"

Schopenhauer is widely recognized as a pessimistic thinker and he himself is never shy of rejecting optimistic notions such as this being the best of all possible worlds, as well as optimistic systems and optimistic thinkers of all hues. Nevertheless, for the most part, the secondary literature on Schopenhauer makes him even more pessimistic than he is and caricatures both his life and work as odd, eccentric, and puzzling. This has happened largely due to a lack of appreciation of Schopenhauer's sources, especially his Eastern sources.

What is suffering according to Schopenhauer. How and to what extent it is part and parcel of human existence? Schopenhauer gives us both theoretical and descriptive answers to these questions. Before beginning his discussion of the denial of the will-to-live in the fourth book of the *WWR*, he defines suffering in terms of his central concept of the will-to-live:

> We have long since recognized this striving that constitutes the kernel and in-itself of everything, as the same thing that in us, where it manifests itself most distinctly in the light of the fullest consciousness, is called "will." We call its hinderance through an obstacle placed between it and its temporary

goal, "suffering"; its attainment of the goal, on the other hand, "satisfaction," well-being, happiness.[1]

According to Schopenhauer, striving penetrates everything that is, including ourselves. Every entity, every organism is on its way, evolving, striving toward its own telos and its own goals. These goals are repeatedly thwarted and goal-lessness remains an elusive state.

> All striving springs from want or deficiency, from dissatisfaction with one's own state or condition, and is therefore suffering so long as it is not satisfied. No satisfaction is, however, lasting; on the contrary, it is always merely the starting point of a fresh striving. We see striving everywhere impeded in many ways, everywhere struggling and fighting, and hence always as suffering. Thus, that there is no ultimate aim of striving means that there is no measure or end of suffering.[2]

It may seem like life contains possibilities of accomplishments and happiness, just as it has pitfalls of suffering. But, in fact, suffering is the rule and happiness is exceptional, elusive, and short-lived. The existence both human and nonhuman is imbued with striving. This striving in itself is endless and meaningless, for one is born incomplete and one dies incomplete. The ground of existence is therefore appropriately called the will, for existence is never bereft of willing this or that. Besides this theoretical account of suffering, Schopenhauer refers to various kinds of sufferings that this so-called best of all possible worlds is replete with. In Volume II of the second edition of *WWR*, he reflects on the sufferings of human life:

> We feel pain but not painlessness; we feel care but not the absence of care; fear, but not security…We do not become conscious of the three greatest blessings of life, health, youth and freedom so long as we possess them, but only after we have lost them.[3]

Human life is beset by poverty and/or boredom. Poverty is the bane of the poor man, whereas boredom, customary pleasure being no pleasure, assails the rich

---

[1] Arthur Schopenhauer, *The World as Will and Representation*, Vols. I and II, trans. E. F. J. Payne (New York: Dover Publications, 1969), Vol. I, 309.

[2] Ibid., Vol. I, p. 309.

[3] Ibid., Vol. II, p. 575.

man. "Nine-tenths of mankind live in constant conflict with want, always bal-
ancing themselves with difficulty."[4]

> The truth is that we ought to be wretched and are so. The chief source of the
> most serious evils affecting man is man himself. Man is a wolf for man…The
> archfiend is fitted more than the rest, and appears in the form of a conqueror, he
> sets several hundred thousand men facing one another and exclaims to them: "To
> suffer and die is your destiny, now shoot each other with musket and cannon."[5]

Schopenhauer cites human beings' injustice toward each other and their boundless
egoism that necessitates state and legislation. He also refers to slavery and child
labor as instances of man's cruelty toward man.

> At bottom optimism is the unwarranted self-praise of the real author of this
> world, namely of the will-to-live which complacently mirrors itself in its work.
> Accordingly optimism is not only a false but also a pernicious doctrine, for it
> presents life as a desirable state and man's happiness as its aim and object…It
> is far more correct to regard work, privation, misery and suffering, crowned by
> death as the aim and object of our life (as is done by Brahmanism and Buddhism,
> and also by genuine Christianity) since it is these that lead to the denial of the
> will-to-live. (W II, 584)[6]

Schopenhauer's descriptions of the suffering and undesirability of this world
are graphic, creative and comprehensive, spanning through his chief work, its
supplements and in his later works. A few pages of exposition cannot summarize them all. It is obvious that he makes frequent references to Vedanta and
Buddhism and invokes their doctrines to seek support for his clearly pessimistic
conclusions concerning the nature of the human world as well as the destiny of
human existence.

Schopenhauer's use and misuse of Indian systems gives rise to some troubling
issues (a) Since according to Schopenhauer, the wisdom of the sages of India
is in accord with the basic underpinnings of his own philosophy, are Indian
thought-systems also as pessimistic as Schopenhauer. (b) Is Schopenhauer's

---

[4.] Ibid., p. 584.

[5.] Ibid., p. 578.

[6.] Ibid., p. 584.

understanding of Vedanta and Buddhism fair, acceptable, and rigorous even for his times? (c) What is Schopenhauer's contribution to the introduction of Indian philosophy in the West? Keeping in mind these issues, let us continue to focus on the problem of suffering and examine how it is presented in Vedanta and Buddhism.

The problem of *dukkha*, generally translated as pain or suffering, is a central problem in Buddhism. The Buddha mentions it in his very first sermon as part of the four noble truths. What the Buddha says as a prelude to the enunciation of the four fundamental truths is also relevant to the Schopenhauerian reading of Buddhism:

> These two extremes, O monks, are not to be practiced by those who have gone forth from *samsara*. What are these two? That conjoined with passions…and that conjoined with self-torture. Avoiding these extremes, the *tathagata* has gained the knowledge of the middle way.[7]

The Buddha recommends the path of moderation and the middle way both in thought and in living. In the realm of thought, it means no philosophies rooted in either Being or in Nothingness, that is, no metaphysics, no nihilism. In living it means neither extreme indulgence nor extreme asceticism. In advocating denial of the will-to-live Schopenhauer extols the path of asceticism clearly not recommended by the Buddha. However, Schopenhauer is right in picking up the rejection of *samsara* and the necessity of overcoming it very much recommended by both Buddhism and Vedanta. Regarding suffering or dukkha, the Buddha is reported to have said the following in the script of the four noble truths:

> Now this O monks is the noble truth of dukkha. Birth is dukkha, old age is dukkha, sickness is dukkha, death is dukkha, sorrow, lamentation, dejection and despair are dukkha. Contact with unpleasant things in dukkha, not getting what one wishes is dukkha. In short, the five *skandhas* are dukkha.
>
> Now, this O monks, is the noble truth of the cause of *dukkha*: that craving (*trishna*) that leads to rebirth, combined with pleasure and lust, finding pleasure here and there, namely craving for passion, craving for existence, craving for non-existence.[8]

---

[7.] S. Radhakrishnan and C. A. Moore, ed., *A Sourcebook in Indian Philosophy* (Princeton, NJ: Princeton University Press, 1973), 276.

[8.] Ibid., p. 274.

The Buddha gives a list of inevitable events of *dukkha* in life, thereby implying that, of course, there are pleasant moments in life too. If he wished to say all of human life is *dukkha*, he could have easily said so (monks, life is *dukkha*). He said birth is *dukkha* because *nirvana* means release from *samsara* not coming back into it and staying in it. What is at stake is overcoming of *samsara* vs. clinging to it, both as possibilities of this very life, life of *dharma* vs. vulgar worldly life. Of course, Schopenhauer takes condemnation of *samsara* and condemnation of *dukkha* as one and the same thing, and pays scant attention to the Buddha's emphasis on moderation, middle path and his optimistic and firm belief in *nirvana*. Not only the notion of *dukkha*, a philosophical translation of which is "unsatisfactoriness" rather than pain, but also the term for the identified cause of *dukkha*, that is, *tanha* or *trishna* can be misunderstood by extreme interpretations. *Trishna* (that causes *dukkha*) is immoderate desire or craving rather than desire as such. Thus, a literal and extreme understanding of these two central concepts of early Buddhism can lead one to the wrong conclusion that Buddhism is pessimistic and the Buddha paints a black picture of life.

In the same way the undesirability of *samsaric* existence as emphasized in Vedanta as well as in the Hindu myth of reincarnation does not mean a pessimistic outlook. The presence of *brahman* (Being) and its everlasting replica (*atman*) in human existence makes it an optimistic doctrine. The yoga or path of *bhakti* or loving devotion to the deity is not exactly asceticism but a joyful contemplation of God in the Hindu systems.

## Will-to-Live or "Trishna"

Whether Schopenhauer freely adopted the Eastern concepts in his later supplementary writings or he simply found in Vedanta and Buddhism, a reauthentication of his already developed notions of the will-to-live and its denial, one thing is certain. No other Western philosopher has studied, elucidated and adopted Eastern, especially Indian philosophies as rigorously as he did. To be so appreciative of a foreign tradition, to treat philosophies of the world as one, was a remarkably bold step, especially in his day and age, when Eastern philosophies were still barely known and inadequately and scantily translated.

> As Wilhelm Halbfass in his recent scholarly work *India and Europe* points out, it will not be proper to simply equate Schopenhauer's concept of will-to-live

to one of several Indian concepts such as *maya*, *atman*, *trishna*, or *upadana*. Halbfass also refers to Schopenhauer's own frustration in finding an equivalent Indian concept to his all-important notion of the will.[9] Some of Schopenhauer's own statements quoted by Halbfass on this matter are as follows:

On the whole, the harmony [of Buddhism] with my teachings is wonderful, all the more so because I wrote the first volume [of *WWR*] between 1814 and 1818 and did not and could not have known all that.[10]

By the way, I admit that I do not believe that my doctrine could ever have been formulated before the Upanishads, Plato and Kant were able to cast their light simultaneously on to a human mind.[11]

The Sages of all times have always said the same.[12]

Buddha, Eckhard and I teach essentially the same.[13]

Thus, Schopenhauer himself was far from being decisive about the exact Indian philosophical equivalent of will-to-live, but nevertheless found several Indian concepts valuable in exposing the inner workings of the will and the ultimate human potential of will's denial.

If we take into account the simplistic equivalence of the will to Indian concepts such as *atman*, *maya*, *trishna*, or *upadana* by Schopenhauer's interpreters, the matter becomes even more complex. However, it should not be overlooked that will-to-live was not propounded primarily for the purpose of comparative philosophy. Halbfass seems to have hit the nail on the head:

Schopenhauer's doctrine of the will [primarily] implies a critique of the European tradition of representational and rational thinking of calculation and planning... which foreshadows more recent developments...He continued a radical critique of some of the most fundamental pre-suppositions of the Judeo-Christian tradition

[9] Wilhelm Halbfass, *India and Europe: An Essay in Understanding* (Albany, NY: State University of New York Press, 1988), 107.

[10] Ibid.

[11] Ibid.

[12] Ibid.

[13] Ibid. Also Schopenhauer, *The World as Will and Representation*, Vol. II, Chapter 48.

such as the notion of personal God, the uniqueness of the human individual and the meaning of history.[14]

This means that while Indian concepts did cast a spell on Schopenhauer's thinking, he did not simply borrow them to build his own system. He used them primarily to reauthenticate his worldview and enrich its exposition. The concept of the will-to-live was enunciated to critique and correct the Judeo-Christian and Western metaphysical assumptions, which had taken both Christian religion and Western philosophy in its grip, Hegel's system being one example of a full adoption of these assumptions.

Indeed, the Vedic notions of *maya*, *moha* (passionate love), *aham* (ego) all illustrate the nature of the will-to-live and so do the Buddhist notions of *trishna* (craving) and *upadana* (attachment). However, it will be most objectionable to equate the will-to-live with the Vedic notion of *brahman* (Being). The ever enduring (*sat*), pure consciousness (*chitta*), and blissful (*ananda*) reality as defined by Sankara, has hardly anything in common with the blind, irrational urge to live as conceived by Schopenhauer.

Furthermore, the concept of the denial of the will-to-live touches a degree of metaphysical dualism and advocates extreme asceticism combined with a pessimistic dismissal of the world. This is not exactly the true message of Vedanta and Buddhism. To wean the human entirely away from excessive worldliness (*samsara*), the Vedic tradition proposes a fusion (*yoga*) of *karma* (action), *bhakti* (devotion, love), and *Jnana* (knowledge) as enunciated by the *Bhagavad-Gita*. The method of *bhakti* (love) is not merely a denial of the world (*samsara*) but a spontaneous reorientation of the mind toward the loved and loving deity, a drive that leaves *samsara* behind. Schopenhauer's reading of Vedanta is almost silent on the method of *bhakti*.

Similarly, as mentioned earlier, idea of moderation, middle path and non-metaphysical thinking, so central to the Buddhist worldview, and emphasized by the Buddha in his first sermon, seems to be absent in Schopenhauer's concept of the denial of the will-to-live and in his project to construct an all-encompassing metaphysical system as well as in his dualistic account of the will and its denial.

Thus, the traditions of Vedanta and Buddhism clearly transcend metaphysics, pessimism, and extreme asceticism of the kind that Schopenhauer seems to uphold in his system. Nevertheless, Indian philosophy is but richer with the contribution

---

[14.] Halbfass, *India and Europe*, p. 120.

made by Schopenhauer. He transmitted its insights in the Western metaphor in a manner that is unmatched by any other Western thinker. The bridge that he built between the Western and Eastern shores is still standing. At the same time perhaps, no other modern philosopher can combine more skillfully the serious-ness of a philosophical insight with the simplicity and beauty of expression. See, for example, how he sums up the problem and lessons of death through his East–West thinking: "you are ceasing to be something which you would have done better never to become."[15]

## Denial or Nirvana

Will-to-live that appears in the human entity has a unique possibility which is unavailable to animals, plants, and inanimate things. It is the possibility of will's knowledge of itself. In man, the will has the potential of not only knowing itself but denying itself or rendering itself quiet.

> Knowledge of the whole, of the inner nature of the thing-in-itself…becomes the quieter of all and every willing. The will now turns away from life; it shudders at the pleasures in which it recognizes the affirmation of life. Man attains to the state of voluntary renunciation, resignation, true composure and complete will less ness.[16]

This voluntary denial of the will involves indifference to all worldly goals and projects, one "gives lie to one's phenomena" that is, refuses to be act in subservience to the world, and "gives lie to the body," that is, seeks no sexual satisfaction and/or comforts for the body. Schopenhauer says that such asceticism also necessitates voluntary and intentional poverty. "He therefore endures such ignominy and suffering with inexhaustible patience and gentleness, returns good for all evil without ostentation, and allows the fire or anger arise within him as little as the fire of desires."[17]

Schopenhauer not only seeks the support for such a denial by citing the lives of Christian saints and mystics but also refers to practices and lifestyles of Hindu

---

[15] Schopenhauer, *The World as Will and Representation*, Vol. II, p. 500.

[16] Ibid., Vol. I, p. 379.

[17] Ibid., p. 382.

and Buddhist saints, sadhus, samanas, bhikkus, and holy men. What he wants us to appreciate is not just the religious zeal of these holy lives, but their decision to give up the matter of course human subservience to the urges and commands of the will-to-live.

> And what I have described here with feeble tongue, and only in general terms is not some philosophical fable, invented by myself and only of today. No, it was the enviable life of so many saints and great souls among the Christians, and even more among the Hindus and Buddhists, and also among believers of other religions.

> Thus it may be that the inner nature of holiness of self-renunciation, of mortification of one's own will, of asceticism, is here for the first time expressed in abstract terms and free from everything mythical, as denial of the will-to-live.[18]

Schopenhauer responds in advance to the possible criticism that knowing so much about the evils and decadence of the will-to-live why his own life was not that of perfect denial.

> It is just as little necessary for the saint to be a philosopher as for the philosopher to be a saint; just as it is not necessary for a perfectly beautiful person to be a great sculptor, or for the great sculptor to be himself a beautiful person. It is a strange demand on a moralist that he should commend no other virtue than that he himself possesses.[19]

Schopenhauer's fundamental assumptions concerning the sufferings and undesirable status of the world are rooted in his thoughtful and rigorous reading of the Vedantic and Buddhist texts in the available translations. Schopenhauer's Western interpreters, for the most part, being innocent of even the basics of Indian philosophies, have grossly misunderstood this thinker's fundamental positions on the status of this world, existence, death, and suffering. Although these same interpreters have done a good job in tracing Schopenhauer's connections with the Platonic and Kantian systems, they are either silent or too brief on Schopenhauer's Eastern studies, and transcultural experiments. One of the most bewildering aspects of Schopenhauer's thought for his Western readers is

---

[18.] Ibid., p. 383.

[19.] Ibid.

his apparent disdain of the world and existence as such. His condemnation of individualism, an all-important Western value, and his emphasis on suffering and overlooking of happiness are viewed as equally puzzling. Thus, labels of extreme pessimism, absurdity, perversity, and hypocrisy are applied to Schopenhauer's thought by some of the well-established scholars.

Schopenhauer's thought concerning individual existence and the human potential for salvation is largely misunderstood in the secondary literature. The statements such as the following have caused much confusion:

> To desire immortality for the individual is to perpetuate an error forever, for at bottom every individuality is really only a special error, a false step, something that it would be better should not be, in fact something from which it is the real purpose of life to bring us back.[20]

This is a kind of statement that is so hard for many Schopenhauer scholars to accept at its face value. They often attribute such convictions of the thinker to his pessimism or begin to see superficial contradictions in his standpoints. For example, Michael Fox in his article "Schopenhauer on Death, Suicide and Self-Renunciation" frustratingly remarks:

> The doctrine of palingenesis as promulgated by Schopenhauer is indeed diffi-cult to comprehend, and there is more than one lacuna in his account...After all Schopenhauer makes the perverse claim that for mankind it would have been better not to have come into being than to exist; life is merely a disturbing interruption of the blissful non-existence. Schopenhauer's doctrine of self-re-nunciation must be examined independently of his entirely perverse and absurd position...that man is guilty and inexpungeably sinful, not because of his deeds but merely because he exists.[21]

In a similar unsympathetic reading of Schopenhauer's statement "we are at bottom something that ought not to be"[22] David Cartwright in his article "Schopenhauer on Suffering, Death, Guilt and Consolation of Metaphysics" remarks:

---

[20] Ibid., Vol. II, p. 492.

[21] Michael Fox, ed., "Schopenhauer on Death, Suicide and Self-Renunciation," in *Schopenhauer: His Philosophical Achievement* (New Jersey, NY: Barnes & Noble Books, 1980), 161.

[22] Schopenhauer, *The World as Will and Representation*, Vol. II, p. 507.

> We suffer and die because we deserve it. The world is perfectly retributive. We
> deserve what we receive because we are guilty. We are guilty because we exist.
> Schopenhauer's logic is now as clear as it is unconvincing...If we explore these
> claims they seem highly implausible.[23]

A misunderstanding of Schopenhauer's attitude toward *samsara* consistent with
his reading of Vedanta and Buddhism, a failure to distinguish between "excessive
worldliness" and "the world," a refusal to take seriously the wisdom behind the
myth of reincarnation, a belief of the two-thirds of humanity including that of
ancient Greeks, has driven many contemporary interpreters of Schopenhauer to
extreme judgments of not only this man's philosophy but of the man himself. For
instance, Bryan Magee in his recent book *The Philosophy of Schopenhauer* says:

> In the light of the present day knowledge there can be little doubt that Schopen-
> hauer's despairing view of the world above all his conviction of the terribleness
> of existence as such were in some degree neurotic manifestations which had
> roots in his relationship with his mother...If actions speak louder than words,
> his life as he in fact lives it...tells us of a man in whom protean pleasures are
> being experienced side by side with mountainous frustration, misanthropy and
> desolate miseries of neurosis.[24]

In response to these half-baked critiques, I must say that there is nothing absurd
or perverse about Schopenhauer's deep appreciation of the Vedantic and Buddhist standpoint that having to be reborn in *samsara* is no event for celebration.
The bliss of *nirvana* has to be contrasted with the unsatisfactoriness and vulgarity of *samsaric* existence. The need for salvation must be understood as an
unsatisfactory status of thoughtless worldliness. The portrayal of *nirvana* as a
releasement from the cycle of rebirth is a mythological exposition of the philosophical standpoint that *samsara* or downright worldliness ought not be valued.
Thought and thoughtful life must overcome immoderate worldliness. To desire
perpetuation of individuality, to give in to self-love (*mamta*), ego (*aham*), and
*moha* (attachment) is the same thing as saying yes to *samsara*, and hence neither

---

[23] David E. Cartwright, "Schopenhauer on Suffering, Death, Guilt and the Consolation of Metaphysics," in
*Schopenhauer: New Essays in Honour of His 200th Birthday*, ed. Eric von der Luft (Lewiston, NY: Edwin Mellen
Press, 1988), 54.

[24] Bryan Magee, *The Philosophy of Schopenhauer*. Revised Edition (Oxford: Clarendon Press, 1977), 260.

desirable nor praiseworthy. Schopenhauer's statement that "at bottom every individuality is a special error, false step, something that it would be better not to be" is a reiteration of the Vedantic message that taking ego (*aham*) as real is to dismiss one's larger and real self (*atman*). All individualities and diversities are superficial in contrast to the oneness of *atman* says Vedanta. To remain caught up in individuality is to overlook the oneness of subjects and objects or the truth of "that thou art" (*tat twam asi*). Agreeing with Vedanta, Schopenhauer maintains that the real purpose of human life is to bring ourselves back from the individuality based, narrow-minded living that affirms and remains involved in the rational pursuits of the irrational and blind urges of the will-to-live that produce *samsara* for us from moment to moment.

# CHAPTER 10

# Schopenhauer and Tagore: On Universal Aesthetics

*R. Raj Singh*

The prospects of all philosophical traditions include their dialogue with each other, so that questions are asked, and answers are found from the widest and deepest possible perspectives. Philosophers no longer have to confine their thinking to strictly their own traditions in the name of some self-assumed and traditional standards of consistency or rigor. The ability to freely borrow from and contribute to so-called foreign traditions was not only exemplified by great classical thinkers and literary masters such as Plato and Shakespeare but also exhibited by many creative minds of the 19th and 20th centuries. Their love of knowledge was not confined within their cultural boundaries, as they identified their concepts both within and beyond the places of their origins.

This chapter will outline the profiles of two such transcultural thinkers: Schopenhauer and Tagore, who modernized and globalized the insights of the Indian philosophical heritage, and freely deployed both Eastern and Western sources in their contributions toward the foundation of a universal aesthetics. At the same time, we will assess the actual and potential role of perennial Indian philosophical concepts in the development of a universal aesthetics. The term "universal aesthetics" is used in the sense of being applicable to all branches of fine arts as well as to all kinds of art traditions, namely, European, Indian, Chinese, Japanese, etc. The work of Schopenhauer and Tagore illustrate the potentials of transcultural thinking as well as the capacity of Indian philosophy to have a universal appeal. Universal aesthetics is not only vital for the aesthetic understanding and delight of a closely knit world community but also offers a remarkable theoretical rigor to the discipline.

Arthur Schopenhauer (1788–1860) was a pioneer in transcultural thinking. The philosophes of India, particularly Vedanta and Buddhism, were his favorite sources for composing and revalidating the universality of his own system. He admired the philosophies and religions of India and cited extensively from their texts, which were beginning to be known in Europe in his time. His chief work, *The World as Will and Representation* Was published in 1819 and two subsequent editions were published in 1844 and 1859. Volume 2 of the second edition contained 50 supplementary chapters on the themes discussed in the first edition, republished as Volume 1. Thus, the later editions of *The World as Will and Representation* and Schopenhauer's other leader works contain numerous citations, illustrations and comparisons from Indian philosophies.

Aesthetic considerations occupy more than one quarter of Schopenhauer's chief work. It is because aesthetic contemplation accompanied by knowledge of the Platonic Ideas Seems to him a uniquely human capacity. It is a moment in which knowledge escapes its usual service of the will-to-live. The will-to-live is the central reality of Schopenhauer's worldview. It is the inner being of all that exists. Here is a definition of the will in his own words:

> All representation, be it of whatever kind it may, all object is phenomenon. But only will is thing-in-itself...It is that of which all representation, Object, is the phenomenon...It is the innermost essence, The kernel of every particular thing and also of the whole. It appears in every blindly acting force of nature, and also in the deliberate conduct of man.[1]

According to Schopenhauer, art experiences a momentary withdrawal of the will, which enables human knowledge to contemplate Ideas in their purity. The notion of the will-to-live and its manifold implications, including the unique possibilities of its withdrawal and its denial, has an intimate connection with the creation and experience of art.

Schopenhauer claims that the first edition of his *magnum opus* Was composed while he was completely innocent of Indian philosophy. It was only later that he found a remarkable similarity between his ideas and the ancient systems of Vedanta and Buddhism. Nevertheless, the entire corpus of Schopenhauer's works contains so many references to Indian philosophy that it can be regarded as one great influence on his thought as a whole. Before we examine Schopenhauer's remarkable achievement as a transcultural Western thinker, let us consider the chief features of his aesthetics, which of course revolve around the central notion of the will its denial, for the fuller expositions of which Schopenhauer draws

---

[1] Arthur Schopenhauer, *The World as Will and Representation*, trans. E. F. J. Payne (New York: Dover Publications, 1969), Vol. I, 110.

upon numerous sources of Indian thought. Schopenhauer discusses at length, the essence of art, the creation of artworks and the art experience in *The World as Will and Representation*, as well as in some of his later essays. He links art activity and art experience to the intuition of (Platonic) ideas. Great art, which is often the work of a genius, plays the role of communicating or "repeating" the external Ideas better apprehended through pure contemplation by the artist:

> But what kind of knowledge is it that considers what continues to exist outside and independently of all relations, but which alone is really essential to the world, the true content of its phenomena, that which is subject to no change, and is therefore known with equal truth for all time, in a word, the Ideas that are the immediate and adequate objectivity of the thing-in-itself, of the will? It is art, the work of genius. It repeats the eternal Ideas apprehended through pure contemplation, the essential and abiding element in all the phenomena of the world. According to the material in which it repeats, it is sculpture, painting, poetry, or music. Its only source is knowledge of the ideas; its sole aim is communication of this knowledge.[2]

Regarding the pure knowledge of the Ideas and its reproduction in the works of art by a genius, Schopenhauer presents his own version of Idealism. The artist's genius lies in his ability to contemplatively apprehend the Ideas beyond the orbit of mundane thinking, that is, beyond the pale of the principle of sufficient reason. Artists of genius are also able to communicate these ideas of entities through their artworks to ordinary observers of art. But the ordinary and innocent observers are spectators of artworks and do not possess genius equal in measure to that of the artist. How can the observers even begin to enjoy, comprehend, and share the artist's vision?

> Genius consists in the ability to know independently of the principles of sufficient reason, not individual things…but the Ideas of such things, and in the ability to be, in the face of these, the corrective of the Idea, And hence no longer individual but pure subject of knowing. Yet this ability must be inherent in all men in a lesser and different degree, as otherwise they will be just as incapable of enjoying works of art as of producing them…We must therefore assume as existing in all men that power of recognizing in things their Ideas, of divesting themselves for a moment of their personality.[3]

---

[2] Ibid., p. 184.

[3] Ibid., p. 194.

However, human knowledge for the most part remains subservient to the will-to-live and given up to the throng of desires and constant hopes and cravings produced by the will. The tyranny of the will is not without respite. There are moments when

> an external causer inward disposition suddenly raises us out of the endless stream of willing, and snatches knowledge from the thralldom of will, the attention is now no longer directed to the motives of willing, but comprehends things free from their relation to the will. Thus, it considers things without interest, without subjectivity, purely objectivity.[4]

A deep devotion to philosophical contemplation as well as a higher life of the denial of the will-to-live succeed in overcoming the oppression of matter and, of course, willing. But art experiences another occasion of the will's momentary retirement. The moments in which one enjoys the being or performance of a work of art, the deliverance of knowledge from an oppressive and demanding will, produces such a joy that one has a magical feeling, as if one has stepped into another world. Great objects of nature are also works of art, and produce a feeling of the sublime in us. When we experience being external subjects of pure knowing, or intimacy with all that it reveals itself. Schopenhauer compares this with the experience of *brahman*.

> Many objects of our perception excite the impression of the sublime; by virtue both of their spatial magnitude and of their great antiquity...we feel ourselves reduced to nought in their presence, and yet reveal in the pleasures of beholding them. One of this kind are very high mountains, the Egyptian pyramids, and colossal ruins of great antiquity...Against Such a ghost of our own nothingness... there arises the immediate consciousness that all these worlds exist...as modifications of the external subject of pure knowing...It is...what the Upanishads the Veda express repeatedly: "I am all this creation collectively, and besides me there exists no other being."[5]

Schopenhauer's central concept of the will-to-live and the human possibility of its denial, spontaneously in art experience and deliberately in asceticism, seem

---

[4] Ibid, p. 196.

[5] Ibid., p. 206.

to be heavily influenced by the Vedanta and Buddhist worldviews that he intimately studied and consciously adopted in the formulation of his own system of
philosophy. Whether Schopenhauer freely adopted the Indian concepts in his later
supplementary writings or he simply found in them a revalidation of his already
developed notions of the will-to-live and its denial, one thing is certain—no other
Western philosopher had studied, elucidated, and adopted Eastern, especially
Indian philosophies, as rigorously as he did. To be so appreciative of a foreign
tradition, and to treat philosophers of the world as one, was a remarkably bold
step, especially in his day and age, when Eastern philosophies were still barely
known and inadequately and scantily translated.

A question is bound to arise in our minds. Was Schopenhauer's comprehension
and use of Eastern concepts fair, rigorous, and valid, or were they merely an
exotic ornamentation of his own system, for the elaboration of which the Eastern
concepts were simply pressed into service? The nagging question of pessimism
will also arise. Do Vedanta and Buddhism really support the tendencies of pessimism and extreme asceticism that Schopenhauer's philosophy seems to promote?
Was Schopenhauer's knowledge of Eastern philosophy good enough even for
his age? Some of these and similar questions are posed by Wilhelm Halbfass in
his recent scholarly work, *India and Europe*.

Halbfass' assessment of Schopenhauer's connections with Indian thought
points out that this matter cannot be dealt with simplistically. It will not be fair to
simply equate the will-to-live to one of the several Indian concepts such as *maya*,
*brahman*, *trisna*, or *upadana*. "How his knowledge of the Indian material was
related to the genius of Schopenhauer's own system is a question which cannot
be answered with complete clarity and certainty; His own explicit remarks, in
any case, do not provide a sufficient basis for answering it."[6] What Halbfass is
referring to, is Schopenhauer's own frustration in finding an equivalent Indian
concept to his all-important will-to-live and his many declarations concerning
the originality of his own system vis-à-vis Vedanta in Buddhism.

Halbfass also points out that Schopenhauer alternatively consider the concept
of *maya* equivalent to his notion of *principium individuationis and* express the
belief that the Vedantic notion of *brahman* corresponded with his own theory of
cosmic will, for it meant "force, will, wish and propulsive power of creation."
Schopenhauer's basic position was, in general, that the sages of all times have

---

[6] Wilhelm Halbfass, *India and Europe: An Essay in Understanding* (Albany, NY: State University of New York Press, 1988), 107.

always said the same: "Buddha, Eckhardt, and I all teach essentially the same." Speaking of the results of his own thought, he explained that they corresponded with the most ancient of all worldviews, namely, the Vedas. Halbfass it points out that Schopenhauer saw the Buddhist concept of *upadana* (attachment to the world and worldly objects) possibly as an equivalent of his will-to-live.[7]

If we take into account the simplistic equivalence of will-to-live to concepts such as *brahman*, *atman*, *maya*, *trisna*, and *upadana* by Schopenhauer's interpreters, the matter becomes even more complex. However, we cannot ignore the fact that the will-to-live was not propounded primarily for the purposes of comparative philosophy. This means that while Indian concepts did cast a spell on Schopenhauer's thinking, he did not simply borrow them to build his own system. The concept of the will-to-live was primarily enunciated to critique and correct the fundamental Judeo-Christian and Western metaphysical assumptions that had taken both the Christian religion in Western philosophy in their grip. The will-to-live indeed corrects all entrenched Western assumptions concerning the idea of a personal God, the supremacy of the rational, and the dismissal of instinct. The Indian concepts are alluded to by Schopenhauer to elucidate not only the inner nature of the will-to-live but also to exemplify how an authentic denial and overcoming of it is possible and was deemed desirable by the saintly thinkers of all world traditions, of noble religions and philosophies.

Indeed, the Vedic notions of *maya*, *mamta* (mineness), *moha* (passionate love), and *aham* (ego), all illustrate the nature of the will-to-live with the Vedantic notion of *brahman*, which seems to have hardly anything in common with the blind, irrational urge to live, as conceived by Schopenhauer. It is hard for us to elaborate here, but the concept of denial of the will-to-live touches the degree of metaphysical dualism and extreme asceticism combined with the pessimistic dismissal of *samsara*, that Vedanta and Buddhism do not advocate. The *bhakti* method of loving involvement with the deity as an authentic way to salvation (*moksha*), the yoga *bhakti*, which is so extensively exposed in the *Bhagavad-Gita* and in the Vedas, is almost absent in Schopenhauer's reading of Vedanta. Similarly, the idea of moderation, the middle path, and nonmetaphysical thinking, so important to Buddhism and stressed by the Buddha in his first sermon, seems to be absent in Schopenhauer's emphasis on "denial" and in his metaphysical and dualistic account of the strife between the will and its denial.

---

[7] Ibid., pp. 111–112, 119.

Nevertheless, Indian philosophy is but richer for the contribution made by Schopenhauer. He transmitted its insights in the Western metaphor as no one else did. The bridge that he built between Western and Eastern shores is still standing. At the same time, perhaps no other philosopher can combine more skillfully the seriousness of a philosophical problem with simplicity and beauty of expression.

Rabindranath Tagore (1869–1941) was not only an outstanding representative of the heritage of India but also served as a bridge between East and West. Although he shied away from the title "philosopher" and called himself primarily a poet, his writings do contain treatments of various philosophical issues carried out in a unique and poetic style of his own. Being an artist of the first rank and a man of letters, he was quite interested in aesthetics. Some scholars believe that modern Indian aesthetics begins with Tagore.[8] Not only do ancient Indian conceptions of art and aesthetics peep through Tagore's essays on aesthetics, but he was also especially adept in showing the rooted Ness of ideas of aesthetics in the perennial philosophical concepts of the Indian tradition, particularly Vedantic and Upani-shadic concepts, such as *atman*, *Brahman*, *ananda*, *maya*, *leela*, and *bhakti*. This Tagore did, not by mimicking the classical Vedanta systems or classical Indian aesthetic theories, but by presenting his original aesthetic interpretations of the Upanishadic worldview from a contemporary cosmopolitan standpoint. Thus, his aesthetic and general philosophical analysis are remarkable not only for their simplicity and contemporary relevance but also for their jargon-free, poetic prose. Besides his deep contact with the Upanishads, Tagore was also influenced by the mediaeval *Vaishnava* poetry, as well as Baul and Sufi saints. He had a full realization of the fact that in Indian tradition, *bhakti* is as important as *jnana* to realize the full potential of thought. He was especially drawn toward the *bhakti* poets Kabir and Tukaram, and translated some of Kabir's couplets in English.

Tagore not only makes ancient Indian thought come alive in his work for a world audience but also prepares Indian aesthetics to offer its concrete contribution to the body of a universal aesthetics. He was especially well equipped for this task due to his well-balanced self-education and literature and philosophes of the West. Tagore was also aware of the popular aesthetic theories and issues in contemporary Western aesthetics. All aspects of European culture—poetry, philosophy, art—were known to Tagore. His sensibility became broader through his studies of European authors. Being a popular figure in the world of literature, Tagore had the privilege of having personal conversations concerning the problems

---

[8.] S. K. Nandi, *Studies in Modern Indian Aesthetics* (Simla, India: Indian Institute of Advanced Study, 1975), ix.

of philosophy with some of the important thinkers of his age, including Croce, Bergson, Einstein, Rolland, Russell, Schweitzer, Dewey, Keyserling, and others.[9]

It is difficult to do justice to Tagore's ideas on art and art experience in one section of a short essay. But the following account aims at showing Tagore's substantive contribution to aesthetics based on his remarkable ability to reinterpret some fundamental concepts of Indian philosophy and to make his aesthetic theories and concepts ready to take their place in a universal aesthetics.

In his essay "What Is Art?" Tagore remarks on the futility of seeking a definition of art. "Definition Of a thing which has a life growth is really limiting one's vision to be able to see clearly. And clearness is not necessarily the only or the most important aspect of truth."[10] "Therefore I shall not define art," says Tagore, "but question myself about the reason of its existence, and try to find out whether it owes its origin to some social purpose, or to the need of catering tour aesthetic enjoyment, or whether it has come out of some impulsive expression, which is an impulse of our being itself."[11] in this passage, Tagore forecasts his intention to contemplate the reason of the being of are in terms of delight, expression, and personality, some of the chief concepts of his aesthetics. He would trace the relationship of art to Being as such an the Being of the human being rather than defining art as one of the many activities of the human entity.

Tagore traces the origin of art through a reference to the genesis of creation as posited by the classical Vedanta systems of Indian philosophy in his essay "Religion of an Artist":

> Brahman is boundless and is superfluity which inevitably finds its expression in the external world process. Here we have the doctrine of the genesis of creation, and therefore the origin of art. Of all living creatures in the world, men has his vital and mental energy vastly in excess of his need which urges him to work in various lines of creation for its own sake; like Brahman himself, he takes joy in productions that are unnecessary to him...Art reveals man's wealth of life, which seeks its freedom and forms of perfection which are ends in themselves.[12]

---

[9] V. S. Narvane, *Modern Indian Thought: A Philosophical Survey* (Bombay, India: Asia Publishing House, 1964), 120.

[10] Rabindranath Tagore, *Angel of Surplus* (Calcutta, India: Visva-Bharti, 1978), 29.

[11] Ibid., p. 30.

[12] Ibid., p. 8.

The idea of *leela* or divine-play, illustrative of the truth that *brahman* created this world not due to a lack but as a sport, is clearly behind Tagore's notion that "the living atmosphere of superfluity in man" is the one upon which art thrives. Is an aspect of the soul within men that he has an impulse to participate in art:

> This living atmosphere of superfluity in man is dominated by his imagination, as the earth's atmosphere by the light. It helps us to integrate desultory facts in a vision of harmony and then to translate it into our activities for the very joy of its perfection; It invokes in us the universal man who is the seer and doer of all times and all countries. The immediate consciousness of reality in its purest form, unobscured by the shadow of self-interest, irrespective of moral or utilitarian recommendation, gives us joy as does the self-revealing personality of our own.[13]

It may be noticed that Tagore is as fascinated with the word *leela* as he is with the word *maya*. The word *maya* appears in his poems carrying different shades of meaning. The word *leela* and *kreeda* (playfulness) are also frequently used in his poems.

The Vedanta worldview with its rich conceptions of *brahman, atman, leela,* and *ananda* are all present in Tagore's contemporary exposition of the reason of being of art. His reference to the invocation by art of the universal man is particularly interesting period in pressing into service the age-old concepts of the tradition, Tagore does not, however, mimic any of the classical Vedanta Schools, which, as Hiriyanna points out, had "applied their own fundamental principles to interpretations (of *rasa*) so that in the course of time, there came to be more than one theory of *rasa*."[14] Obviously, instead of using the ready-made classical Indian theories of aesthetics, Tagore offers his own contemporary aesthetic interpretations of the Upanishadic Concepts, an interpretation which is meant for a world audience and partly written in English and translated into several European languages. He uses the simple term "personality" rather than the more religious and scholastic term *atman* in order to enunciate the truth opened up by art and the delight that it generates by intensifying a sense of unity indicative of the truth that the difference between "I am" and "Thou art" is superficial.

Tagore seems to be impressed with the fact that the ancient Vedic name of the highest God was *purusha*, which literally means "the person." The ancient name came to be a synonym for *brahman*, and, within the later theistic and *bhakti*

---

[13] Ibid.

[14] M. Hiriyanna, *Art Experience* (Mysore, India: Kavyalaya Publishers, 1954), 7.

traditions such as Sikhism, *akal purusha* (deathless person) is the name of God. Tagore can be viewed as subscribing to the personal God (*ishvara*) rather than *nirguna brahman*, without ceasing to have a high regard for Sankara's thought. The idea of "personality" and "expression," which are the cornerstones of Tagore's aesthetics, seem to be modern and simplified versions of the classical Vedic notions.

> Limitation of the unlimited is personality: God is personal where he creates. He accepts the limits of his own law and the play goes on, which is this world whose reality is in its relation to the Person. Things are distinct not in their essence but in their appearance; in other words, in their relation to one to whom they appear. This is art, the truth of which is not in substance or logic, but in expression.[15]

The concept of "personality" is fully elucidated by Tagore in its relation to art activity, in which the world's human or personal significance is fully realized. The stamp of personality is fixed on an abstract world, as he remarks in his essay, "The Artist":

> In the dim twilight of our insensitiveness a large part of our world remains to us like a procession of nomadic shadows. According to the stages of our consciousness we have more or less been able to identify ourselves with this world...In art we express the delight of this unity by which the world is realized as humanly significant to us.[16]

The expression of personality is the true impetus behind art activity, according to Tagore. Man never receives passively in his mind the appearance of things around him, but rather adopts, transforms, and makes his own the facts of the physical environment "through constant touches of his sentiments and imagination." Thus, man by nature is an artist. But art happens when the human being intentionally expresses its personal reality. Tagore seems to say that art is an attempt to put on record or make permanent the artist's version of what is real to him or her. It is a record of one's personality over the world. Tagore illustrates this by referring to the homage that a throng of Eastern artists paid to the Buddha:

> There come in history occasions when the consciousness of a large multitude becomes suddenly illumined with the recognition of a reality which rises far above the dull obviousness of daily happenings. Such an occasion there was

---

[15.] Tagore, *Angel of Surplus*, p. 10.

[16.] Ibid., p. 22.

when the voice of Buddha reached distinct shores across physical impediments. Men, in order to make this great human experience memorable, determined to do the impossible: they made rocks to speak, stones to sing, caves to remember; their cry of joy and hope took immortal forms along the hills and deserts, across barren solitudes and populous cities. Such heroic activity over the greater part of the eastern continents clearly answers the question: what is art? It is the response of man's creative soul to the call of the Real.[17]

The above accounts of the transcultural nature of the aesthetic theories of two celebrated thinkers show abundantly groundbreaking contributions toward universal aesthetics. They show that aesthetics theories rooted in combinations of different philosophical traditions can be creatively or original and theoretically sound. They also show that established philosophical issues in one tradition can be analyzed through the concepts of another tradition.

In inaugurating the modern phase of Indian aesthetics, Tagore seems to have taken stock of the typical problems of contemporary Western aesthetics and responded to them using the perennial concepts of the Indian heritage. He has done so by answering in a creative, original, simple, and poetic way to the age-old basic enigmas aesthetics: what artist, the reason of being of art, the relation between human nature and art activity, etc. At the same time, Tagore seems to have made a concrete contribution to universal aesthetics by adopting a truly cosmopolitan style, consistent with his role as a transmitter of Eastern ideas to the West, and by using a terminology with which the Western reader is quite conversant.

Schopenhauer, who came before Tagore, was a pioneer in transcultural thinking. Although the Indian sources available to him were scanty, he shows us how philosophy can work as a universal body of knowledge. He sought authentication of his own system and his chief concepts by comparing them to those of Indian thought, and hoped that the truth of his metaphysics would be revalidated by the scriptures of the Indian sages of antiquity. We have alluded to various problems of interpretation and the comparison of Eastern and Western concepts and Schopenhauer's thought to illustrate how, these problems notwithstanding, he is one of the founding fathers of transcultural philosophizing.

The contribution of Indian thought to a universal aesthetics does not come merely in the shape of classical theories of art and art forms such as the *rasa* theory of Bharta, the various other *rasa* theories, or theories of poetry, music,

---

[17.] Ibid., p. 25.

dance, etc. In fact, it is the unique concepts of Indian philosophies themselves, particularly Vedanta, Buddhism, Jainism, and other allied systems, that have served as reservoirs of aesthetic insight and provided material for the formulation of modern and contemporary theories of art, both within and outside the purview of Indian thought. The theoretical frameworks of the systems themselves, their inner messages, and most notably, their fundamental concepts, provide endless resources for modern universal aesthetics. As we have shown above, modern Indian thinkers with a cosmopolitan outlook, such as Tagore and Sir Aurobindo, have shown us how the inner depths of Indian thought can rise to the challenge of resolving the enigmas of contemporary aesthetic inquiries. These thinkers freely use perennial concepts such as *bhakti, leela, ananda,* or *moksha,* thematically as well as literally. However, it is noteworthy that they refrain from attempting to formulate newer *rasa* theories. In his exposition of "art experience" in the pioneering book of the same title, Hiriyanna reflects as follows:

> The aesthetic attitude stands higher than that of common everyday life, which is generally characterized by personal interests of one kind of another…It is for this reason that Indian philosophers, especially the Vedantins…compare the experience of our with that of the ideal state…as *moksha.* But the two experiences are only of the same order and not identical…to begin with, art experience is transient… Secondly, art may prove so seductive that [one]…may grow negligent of [one's] obligations to fellow-men…Lastly, the impersonal joy of our experience is induced artificially from outside whereas that of the ideal state springs naturally from within.[18]

We may notice here that the concept of *moksha* (salvation) along with a subsequent reference to *ananda* (delight) have been evoked by Hiriyanna to explain art experience, an explanation that attributes, on the whole, to Vedantin Indian philosophers. What we have studied of Schopenhauer above is quite comparable to Hiriyanna's account, except that the denial of the will-to-live is the ideal state according to Schopenhauer whereas art experience is a transient removal of the will's all-embracing hold over the human entity. The perennial Indian concepts of *maya, moha, trishna, moksha,* and *nirvana* are as embedded in Schopenhauer's thought as they are in Hiriyanna's theoretical attempt to resolve the enigma of art experience.

---

[18.] Hiriyanna, *Art Experience*, p. 27.

As I have shown in my analysis in my essay "Bhakti as the Essence and Measure of Art,"[19] *bhakti* is an outstanding perennial concept of Indian thought that penetrates all systems of philosophies from India. The notion of *bhakti* is all-important in the realm of art and arts. The attempts to infuse *bhakti* as one of the *sthayi-bhavas* (dominant emotions) or as one of the *rasas* appearing frequently in *vaisnava* literature of the Hindu tradition, have been a grave misunderstanding of the role of *bhakti* in art. Hiriyanna correctly reflects that "Indian aesthetics has had its own history and the process of its own evolution…followed closely that of general (Indian) philosophy."[20] If these systems themselves were imbued with *bhakti*, then *bhakti* must have penetrated not only the aesthetic theories but also the aesthetic endeavors as such. That *bhakti* incorporates all aesthetic endeavors in classical Indian art, is a fact. However, the obsessive preoccupation with the notion of *rasa* masks the presence of *bhakti* as a driving force of art. Art is not merely a description of the peculiar manifestations of the human world. In the Eastern tradition, the outlining of the life of higher love has been one of the basic aims of art.

---

[19] R. Raj Singh, "Bhakti as the Essence and Measure of Art," in *Frontiers of Trans-Culturality in Contemporary Aesthetics*, eds. G. Marchiani and R. Milani (Turin, Italy: Trauben, 2001).

[20] Ibid., p. 27.

CHAPTER 11

# Heidegger and Gandhi: Ontology and Technology

*R. Raj Singh*

Some of the most original analyses of the technological times are to be found in the writings of Heidegger and Gandhi, two of the leading thinkers of Western and Eastern streams of thought in the 20th century. Their philosophies concerning the phenomenon of technology are rooted in their respective fundamental onto-logical standpoints reflectively pursued and elucidated in their prolific writings. At the same time, their fundamental ontological insights, and their comparable positions on ontology vis-à-vis ethics offer original theoretical insights on the ground of ethics as such. The work of these thinkers also brings to the fore the weak foundations of the various brands of applied ethics and well meaning by theoretically facile labors of those who aspire to clean up the messy impacts of technology and save the environment. To claim that their analyses of technology as well as their inquiries into the meaning of Being have something in common will immediately raise some eyebrows. How can the work of Eastern mystical political activist be compared with the philosophical achievement of a Western academic philosopher? How can an armchair philosopher and political novice who might have shied away from his political responsibilities be compared to a servant of the people and a philosopher king like Gandhi?

The phenomenon of technology as the spirit of the 20th century was already visible to Gandhi from his South African days. He had already begun to comment on the relation between man and machine and on the problems associated with the impacts of technology. His probes into the spirit of the times in terms of technology as a phenomenon are largely misunderstood and over simplified in the secondary literature. It is true that in his South African days, Gandhi spoke against modern civilization in his deeply original and fundamental commentary on modernity and materialism in his book *Hind Swaraj*. In his analysis of the oncoming technological times Gandhi called the so called material progress both evil and satanic. However consistent with his readiness to revise his own relative

154 New Studies in Indian and Comparative Philosophy

truths while holding on to the absolute truth, he subsequently sought to deal with problems of modernity and the machine age as an insider, fully acknowledging that technology cannot be wished away even though we must accept that there are no technological solutions to the problems of technology. For Gandhi the remedy lies in the moral realm.

Their glaring contrasts notwithstanding, these two representative thinkers of our age openly declare that their chief thought-quest is nothing but the meaning of Being and both strive to outline the subtle but far-reaching impacts of technology based on remarkably similar concerns. Both seemed to longingly envision and outline the features of what could have been and can be a truly nonviolent and poetic human life, without having to wish technology away.

The first prejudice that needs to be overcome is concerning the widespread impression that Gandhi was merely a political leader who advocated and put in practice the methods of nonviolence. While all this is well known and true about Gandhi, what is not well known is that Gandhi was also an original thinker who made an outstanding contribution not only toward a reinterpretation of some important concepts of Eastern philosophy, but also to ontology as such. At the same time, it is also not wise to dismiss Heidegger's thought as entirely academic, to be kept clear of its possible practical relevance. Although Heidegger expresses reservations concerning hasty applications of philosophy under the umbrella of recently mushroomed applied philosophies,[1] His thought goes a long way toward providing the conceptual framework for the self-understanding of the contemporary human entity consumed and overawed by the supremacy of the technical. While Heidegger does not pretend to be a savior and leaves that metaphorically to a god to come, he is open to a possibility of us being saved in our humanity. However, he does not believe that it is up to a philosopher to change the world on a piecemeal basis.

According to Heidegger, a thinker must be preoccupied with a single foundational object of thought. This ground-concept is both an inspiration and the pursuit of one who "thinks." Heidegger says, in a nutshell, "to think is to confine yourself to a single thought,"[2] and "thoughts courage stems from the bidding of

[1] Matthew Heidegger, "Letter on Humanism," trans. Edgar Lohner in *Philosophy in the Twentieth Century*, Vol. 3, ed. William Barret and Henry D. Aikin (New York: Random House, 1962).

[2] Martin Heidegger, "The Thinker as Poet," in *Poetry, Language, Thought*, trans. Albert Hofstadter (New York: Harper & Row, 1975), 4.

Being."[3] This single ground is the innermost energy of the craft of philosophizing, which begins from a wonder about Being and turns into a preoccupation
with an investigation of the meaning of Being. This is why Heidegger is never
tired of saying that philosophy must hold on to and repeatedly raise the question
concerning Being.

Gandhi's original discovery of the meaning of Being as nonviolence or *ahiṃsā*
should be considered as a major contribution to ontology. He clearly confines
himself to a single thought and never ceased to respond to the bidding of Being.
Gandhi's name for Being is especially chosen simple expression *satya* or Truth.
What Heidegger calls Being in the temporal and existential implications of which
he traces in his writings is not essentially different from what Gandhi calls *satya*
and regards it as a coin the other side of which is *ahiṃsā*.

It is well known that Heidegger's original contribution lies in his rekindling
of the issue of Being within Western philosophy. According to him, thinking
about Being must remain part and partial of the philosophical activity or more
appropriately, thinking. Even though Heidegger clearly states his openness to
other possible meanings of Being,[4] he begins his project by focusing on an
exposition of the temporal meaning of Being, in accordance with the traditional
Greek understanding of Being lodged in a temporal span. This is quite evident in
the title of his magnum opus *Being and Time*. Gandhi, however, offers an entirely
new ground for a fundamental understanding of Being not only for the masses
but also for the field of Ontology. this new point of departure for ontological
contemplation is what he calls *ahiṃsā* (nonviolence), the other aspect of *satya*
(truth), Which is a popular version of the philosophical term *sat* (Being). Gandhi's
originality lies in proposing an alternative framework for an understanding of
Being to its age-old temporal meaning followed within Western philosophy. Thus,
he offers a new challenge to "thinking about Being" with its infinite possibilities
in practical prospects for "thought." Furthermore, although Gandhi borrows
the concepts of *satya* and *ahiṃsā* from his own tradition of Indian philosophy,
particularly from the Hindu and Jain traditions acknowledging these as "as old
as the hills,"[5] What remains his original contribution is as follows: (i) he uplifts
*ahiṃsā* in its traditional Hindu and Jain characterization as a paramount ethical
virtue (*ahiṃsā parmo dharma*) to its new level as the ontological ground of

---

[3] Ibid., p. 5.

[4] Martin Heidegger, *What Is Called Thinking*, trans. F. E. Wrick and G. G. Gray (New York: Harper & Row, 1968).

[5] M. K. Gandhi, *All Men Are Brothers*, ed. Krishna Kriplani (New York: Continuum, 1987), 1 (*Harijan*, March 28, 1939).

Being as well as Being human, (ii) He posits *ahiṃsā* as fundamental telos for the practical problems of human existence as well as to the social and political problems of our technological times. Thus, *satya* to Gandhi is what Being is to Heidegger. Gandhi's contribution to human thought lies in his exposition of *ahiṃsā* as an ontological ground in which human being by nature participates in order to be essentially human. In other words, "*ahiṃsā* is the law of our Being." He explains that *ahiṃsā* is not mere ethical value, not a mere policy but a creed, and violence and nonviolence are not two equally open alternatives of conduct. Violence is but of violation for it violates the core of Being. It is inhuman because it is a violation of what is, as a matter of course, our basic Being.

Gandhi uses the term *satya* or truth for the ultimate reality and calls it "his pole star all along during life's journey."[6] *Satya* is "one absolute truth which is total and all embracing…indescribable because it is God."[7] Gandhi's choice of the term *satya* or truth for what essentially is Being of beings is based on several considerations: Firstly, truth is a concept well known to all, even to the most innocent villager, i.e., it is not a term merely for scholars and intellectuals. Secondly, it is not a sectarian or even religious term confined to a particular religious or cultural tradition. It makes sense even to atheists. However, there is no doubt that what Gandhi means by *satya* is *sat* which is the first attribute of what Vedanta calls *Brahman*:

> The word *satya* comes from *sat* which means "to be" "to exist." Only God is ever the same through all time…I have been striving to serve the truth.[8]

> The word *satya* is derived from *sat*, which means that which "is." *Satya* means a state of Being. Nothing is or exist in reality except truth. That is what *sat* or *satya* is the right name for God. In fact, it is more correct to say that truth is God than to say God is truth.[9]

The equation of truth with God is not only indicative of Gandhi's *bhakti*, an affirmation of a devotional pursuit of truth, but also an attempt to desectarianize God. Gandhi's elevation of *given ahiṃsā* to the level of Being makes it much

---

[6] M. K. Gandhi, *The Essential Writings of Mahatma Gandhi*, ed. Raghavan Iyer (Delhi: Harper & Row, 1993), 229 (*Young India*, December 10, 1925).

[7] Ibid., p. 224 (*Navjivan*, November 20, 1921).

[8] Ibid., p. 225.

[9] Ibid., p. 231 (Letter to Narandas Gandhi, July 22, 1932).

more than mere "non-inquiry." It is given a positive meaning which is posed as a challenge to human thought. Thus, it is not easy for everyone to tell *himsā* and *ahimsā* apart:

> Non-violence is not an easy thing to understand, still less to practise, weak as we are.[10]

> I have never claimed to present the complete science of non-violence. it does not lend itself to such treatment.[11]

Violence is not just bloodshed and killing, but also in humanity and slow killing all around. To recognize violence and the causes of violence is the first task of citizens and policy-makers. All cases of injustice inequality are cases of violence. Violence is the result of systemic inequality is prevalent in the world today.

> The first condition of non-violence is just as all round in every department of life. Perhaps it is too much to expect of human nature. I do not, however, think so. No one should dogmatize about the capacity of human nature for degradation or exaltation.[12]

Gandhi recognizes that perfect nonviolence is impossible. Our breathing, eating, moving about necessarily involve some violence. He admits that even taking life sometimes maybe a duty. But to actively seek to reduce the cycle of violence, as far as possible, is part and parcel of the creativity and self-advancement of the human entity.

## Heidegger on Technological Times

Heidegger's Analysis of the phenomenon of technology is explicitly discussed in his famous lecture essay, "The Question Concerning Technology," composed in 1949 and published in 1954. But his insights on the basic features of our technological times appear in several of his later works, most notably in

---

[10] Gandhi, *All Men Are Brothers*, p. 89 (*Young India*, February 7, 1929).

[11] Ibid., p. 79 (*Harijan*, February 22, 1942).

[12] Ibid., p. 77 (*Mahatma*, V, April 1940).

*An Introduction to Metaphysics* (1953), "The Age of the World Picture" (1954), "Building, Dwelling, Thinking" (1956), "Poetically Man Dwells" (1954) etc.

Heidegger confronts the issue of the essence of technology in his celebrated essay, "The Question Concerning Technology," and maintains that "everywhere we remain unfree and chained to technology whether we passionately affirm or deny it. But we are delivered over to it in the worst way when we regard it as something neutral."[13] Technology is not a mere means at the disposal of man nor a merely human activity but "a way of revealing" a particular disclosedness of truth.[14]

> Therefore we must take that challenging that sets up on man to order the real's standing reserve... We now name that challenging claim... *Ge-stell* (En-framing)[15]

> The Revealing concerns nature, above all as the chief storehouse of the standing energy reserve.[16]

> The rule of Enframing threatens man with the possibility that it could be denied to him to enter into a more original revealing.[17]

According to Heidegger, technology is a kind of disclosedness that has enframed our age in an overwhelming way and rendered other ways of knowing as inferior. So that "everything will present itself only in the unconcealment of the standing-reserve." Technology is a dominant way of knowing has the nature of displacing all other ways of knowing and constitutes the destiny of our planet. It is obvious from Heidegger's analysis that alternative worldviews do not stand a chance against the stream ruler of technology which is bound to crush and flatten all rival ways of knowing. And all this is happening while technology is still being taken as a mere means at the disposal of man.

Gandhi's exhortations to his people not to ape the West and to be wary of the blind applications of the machine technology assume a new meaning in the light of Heidegger's analysis. Gandhi warned that "if the village perishes, India will

---

[13] Martin Heidegger, "The Question Concerning Technology," in *The Question Concerning Technology*, trans. William Lovitt (New York: Harper & Row, 1977), 4.

[14] Ibid., p. 12.

[15] Ibid., p. 19.

[16] Ibid., p. 21.

[17] Ibid., p. 28.

perish too. India will be no more India. Her own mission in the world will get lost."[18] This indicates that Gandhi understood and four saw the impending self-sameness of technology and its threat to the Eastern ways of knowing and living.

However, both Heidegger and Gandhi remain optimistic. Heidegger quotes Hölderlin, "But where danger is, grows the saving power also,"[19] and expresses a deep conviction about the basic human being-in-the-world having something poetic about it. Heidegger expands on the Hölderlin's words "poetically dwells man on this earth" in an essay under the same title and profoundly states:

> Dwelling can be unpoetic only because it is in essence poetic. For a man to be blind, he must remain a being by nature endowed with sight...That we dwell unpoetically, and in what way, we can in any case learn only if we know the poetic...How and to what extent our doings can share in this turn, we alone can prove, if we take the poetic seriously.[20]

Thus it is possible to interpret Heidegger's elucidations of a basic human "dwelling" and his deployment of the metaphor of the fourfold (*Geviert*) in his later works as expositions of a fundamental nonviolent and innocent human way of Being.

## Gandhi on Man and Machine

In the case of Gandhi, the phenomenon of technology as the spirit of the 20th century was already visible to him in his South Africa days, as we can see in his earliest writings and journal articles. He had begun to comment on the relation between man and machine and on the problems associated with the impacts of technology in. his probes into the spirit of the times. Gandhi is often dismissed by many as an orthodox thinker who advised India against aping the West and is taken as one whose economic thought is based on a rejection of the modern civilization. Such a view is a gross oversimplification of Gandhi's thought. A relation between Gandhi's thoughts on man and machine and his central concepts of *satya* and *ahiṃsā* is seldom undertaken. It is true that in his South Africa years

---

[18.] Gandhi, *All Men Are Brothers*, p. 116 (*Harijan*, August 29, 1936).

[19.] Heidegger, *The Question Concerning Technology*, p. 34.

[20.] Martin Heidegger, "Poetically Man Dwells," in *Poetry, Language, Thought*, ed. Albert Holfstadter (New York: Harper & Row, 1975), 228.

Gandhi spoke out against modern civilization in rather radical terms. However, consistent with his ongoing experiments with Truth or *satya*, and being always willing to revise his relative truths, he sought throughout his later life to grapple with the problems of modernity as an insider under the glow of his pole-star *satya*.

Gandhi may be one of the first Eastern philosophers who have analyzed the essence of technological times and who have emphasized that since technology is here to stay, we must study its human and societal impacts. The purpose of such a study according to him are as follows. Since the return to a machineless state is neither possible nor desirable, the violence embedded in technology and industrialism can be and should be reduced through a nonviolent restructuring of human society. In the midst of our craze for machines, the basic, innocent, and spiritual aspects of human life, which have nothing to do with technology, ought not be dismissed.

Gandhi understood quite well that the overwhelming advance of technology will not only complete the process of the Europeanization of all standards and standardization of all measures of reality. The world will be a poorer place if the steamroller of Westernization in the form of technology transfers, levels off and crushes the heads of Eastern alternatives to living. Gandhi's concerns about the East–West meltdown and most especially the impending demise of the Indian village republics are captured in his very simple warning: "If the village dies, India will die too." Gandhi's originality as an analyst of our times is acknowledged in the following words of Chester Bowels, the former US ambassador to India:

> It has been said that there is scarcely an individual on this earth whose life has not been affected in some essential way by Gandhi. This is so because no other public figure of our era so clearly understood or so confidently welcomed the implications of the revolutionary age in which we live.[21]

Along with thinkers like Ortega y Gasset, Karl Jaspers, and Heidegger, Gandhi strove to claim the unbridled passion for technology, which was already underway in his lifetime. In his early South African days, Gandhi in his pursuit of the simple life as well as *moksha* (salvation) from materialism or mammon-worship, opposed machine technology's part in what he thought were the ills of modern

---

[21.] Chester Bowles, "Gandhi as I Understood Him," in *Gandhian Thought and Contemporary Society*, ed. J. S. Mathur (Bombay, India: Harper & Row, 1974).

civilization. In an article written in response to a disastrous fire in a Metro train in Paris, Gandhi said:

> Nothing that the modern civilization can offer in the way of stability can ever make any more certain that which is inherently uncertain; that, when we come to think of it, the boast about the wonderful discoveries and the marvelous inventions of science, good as they undoubtedly are in themselves, is, after all, an empty boast. They offer nothing substantial to the struggling humanity.[22]

While retaining his fascination for the splendor of the simple, Gandhi revised his attitude toward machine technology during the course of his life of experiments with truth. He came to realize and accept that machinery is here to stay and technology is bound to penetrate the remotest corners of the earth. His main concern with it was the displacement of human labor. As he wrote in 1924 and 1925:

> Machinery has its place; It has come to stay. But it must not be allowed to displace necessary human labour…what I object to is the craze for machinery, not machinery as such. The craze is for what they call labour-saving machinery… Today machinery merely helps a few to ride on the backs of millions. The impetus behind it all is not the philanthropy to save labour, but greed.[23]

But Gandhi's real concern with technology was twofold: (i) that technology was a threat to East–West diversity. That is, its blind introduction will lead to a supersession of the Eastern way of life as well as the Eastern worldviews. (ii) Too much fascination with technology will result in obstructing from our view the simple graces of human life. The atechnical life will be dismissed as inferior to the technological conveniences and distractions. The second consequence or what he calls "superstition" is explained by Gandhi as follows:

> It has still to be proven that the displacement of the hand by the machine is a blessing in every case. Nor is it true that that which is easy is better than that which is hard. It is still less proved that every change is a blessing or that everything old is fit only to be discarded.[24]

---

[22.] Gandhi, *The Essential Writings of Mahatma Gandhi*, p. 86 (*Indian Opinion*, August 20, 1903).

[23.] Gandhi, *All Men Are Brothers*, pp. 114–115 (*Young India*, November 5 and 13, 1924).

[24.] Gandhi, *The Essential Writings of Mahatma Gandhi*, p. 398 (*Young India*, July 2, 1931).

The first consequences of technology, the selfsameness as well as exploitation and promotion of inequalities, which necessarily lead to violence, is exposed by Gandhi as follows:

> What is the cause of present chaos? It is exploitation, I will not say, of the weaker nations by the stronger, but of sister nations by sister nations. My fundamental objection to machinery rests on the fact that it is machinery that has enabled these nations to exploit others.[25]

Gandhi realized, just as Heidegger did, that technology has the nature of being all encompassing. It trivializes alternative worldviews, centralizes power structures that depend on violence to protect themselves and standardizes all measures of reality. Heidegger defines technology "as a singular way of revealing entities, overwhelming man and entities in all other ways of revealing."[26] this is exactly what Gandhi finds alarming in the advance of technology, "for the other ways up revealing" which includes Eastern worldviews must not be allowed to disappear. Gandhi exhorted India to remain being India and not to lose its soul in aping the West, not because he loved only India as his own but because the world must continue to be diverse and have equally strong alternative worldviews. Otherwise, we will have nowhere to come from and nowhere to go.

Both Heidegger and Gandhi remind us there is more to life than catching the technology express. There is an atechnical life and there are atechnical goals of human society. These must be reckoned with. The notion of Being in its various fundamental interpretations must remain the pole star of those who think and aspire after a poetic dwelling for all, a *sarvodaya*, as Gandhi called it.

---

[25] Gandhi, *All Men Are Brothers*, p. 114 (*Young India*, October 22, 1931).

[26] Heidegger, *The Question Concerning Technology*, pp. 3–35.

CHAPTER 12

# Death and Authentic Life: Socrates and the Katha Upanishad

*R. Raj Singh*

The connection between implications of death and genuine philosophizing remains visible in the legend of Socrates. Among the Eastern philosophical texts, *Katha Upanishad* surpasses others in elucidating the enigmatic role of death contemplation toward a truly contemplative living. Thus, the Platonic report of Socrates and the ancient author of the *Katha Upanishad*, both inform us why death is to be recognized as the inspiration for philosophizing. Many philosophers in the West as well as in the East seemed to have realized the importance of the bond between death contemplation and philosophical enterprise in the ages that follow Socrates and authors of the Upanishads.[1] Not only does the work of this class of philosophers appear to be the outcome of genuine death contemplation, but the phenomenon of death is accorded its due philosophical role in their systems. Along with Schopenhauer, Martin Heidegger is to be regarded as an heir to Socrates as far as death contemplation is concerned.[2] In the Indian tradition,

---

[1] A distinction is to be made between thinkers who treat death as one of the many themes of philosophy and those who realize and show in their work the conviction that genuine philosophical thinking cannot be done without death contemplation.

[2] Schopenhauer traces the deeper connection with death of his central concept "will to live" repeatedly in his works. Heidegger can be named a true heir to Socrates because he realizes, i.e., acknowledges, and practices the bond between death contemplation and thinking in his chief work *Being and Time* as well as in his later works. The consideration of death is not confined to sections 46–53 of Division II, which deals with *Dasein's* Being-toward death explicitly, but is taken up again and again throughout this division. Heidegger considers death contemplation or "anticipation" (*Vorlaufen*) is inseparable from authenticity (*Eigentlichkeiti*) resoluteness (*Entschlossenheit*) and temporality (*Zeitlichkeit*) in general. In his later works, Heidegger drops the term *Dasein* and prefers to call human beings "mortals." Death is called the "shrine of Being" in his essay on "The Thing" and in several of his later essays the "worlding" of the world is explained in terms of the gathering of the fourfold (*Geviert*) of the earth and sky, the divine and the mortals. Morality is given its due fundamental status in the emergence of all worldly reality. James M. Demske is wrong when he attempts to contrast Heidegger's position on death with that of Socrates in his *Being, Man and Death: A Key to Heidegger* (Lexington, Kentucky: University Press of Kentucky, 1970). Heidegger's work calls for a reinterpretation of the *Phaedo*, a matter thoroughly investigated by Henry G. Wolz in his *Plato and Heidegger* (London: Associated University Presses, 1981). For a more detailed treatment of why Heidegger can be viewed as a Socratic practitioner of death contemplation, see my book, R. Raj Singh, *Heidegger, World and Death* (Lanham, MD: Lexington Books, 2013).

the thinker-poets of the Bhakti movement (13th century onward) emphasized in their work the necessity for a thoughtful life to remain consistently aware of its morality. In the writings of Kabir (15th century), the theme of death contemplation is especially pronounced and seems to be an elaboration of the insight of the *Katha Upanishad*.[3]

The aim of this chapter is not, however, to survey the aspects of death contemplation in the works of the abovementioned modern thinkers, for that would require a careful thanatological elucidation of their respective philosophical contributions. Instead, its purpose is to expose and briefly outline Socratic and Upanishadic insights pertaining to the bond between death and philosophy. In the following study of these outstanding Western and Eastern classical reminders concerning the philosophical and existential merit of being thoughtfully cognizant of death, we are seeking first and foremost answers to questions such as: how can philosophy be the practice of death? How can death be a thinker's living concern? What philosophical benefits can death contemplation bring? Thus, the primary aim of this elucidation is not to claim that Socratic and Upanishadic systems are entirely comparable, but merely to show that they both provide valuable and comparative insights on the connection between death contemplation and philosophy.

The bond between the contemplative practice of death and being an authentic philosopher was exposed lucidly by Socrates, rightly called the martyr of philosophy, who made his final statement on the bond by drinking the hemlock poison readily and cheerfully. To learn about Socrates' singular way of living, philosophizing and dying scholars have good reasons to rely upon Plato's testimony.[4] It is in reading Plato's *Phaedo* that one realizes but the answer to the question concerning death contemplation and philosophizing is neither obvious nor simple:

*Simmias:* The many when they hear your words will say…that philosophers are moribund, and that they found them out to be deserving of the death which they deserve.

---

[3] See my paper, R. Raj Singh, "The Pivotal Role of *Bhakti* in Indian World-Views," *Diogenes* 39, no. 156 (Winter 1991): 65–85.

[4] Cf. J. Burnet, *Plato's Phaedo* (Oxford: Oxford University Press, 1972), ix–lvl. Burnet maintains that Plato's "opportunities for learning to know Socrates as he really was were vastly greater than those of Xenophon" (p. xxix).

> *Socrates:* And they are right Simmias in thinking so, with the exception of the words "they have found them out," for they have not found out either in what sense the true philosopher is moribund and deserves death, or what manner of death he deserves.[5]

To learn what Socrates maintained concerning death contemplation, and to reflect upon the motives behind his words, *Phaedo* remains an authentic source. In this work, not only an account of Socrates' views is given, but the goings-on of his death day are presented in a way that sketches his whole personality. Most analytic philosophical interpretations of this dialogue concentrate on the reported statements of Socrates and ignore what the drama suggests. When it comes to outlining Socrates' view of death too much attention is given to the various proofs of the immortality of the soul. In fact, these proofs do not constitute the vital content of Socrates' fundamental attitude toward death. Some statements of Socrates suggest that he was hardly convinced of their credibility himself.[6] The major theme of the work, which also constitutes its lasting value, is Socrates' explanation of why death contemplation must be cultivated by a true philosopher, and this explanation lies not only in his reported words but also in what we know of his exemplary life and death.

In the introductory conversation between Echecrates and Phaedo when the former implores the latter to describe the manner of Socrates' death, the reply includes the remark: "philosophy was the theme of our conversations."[7] The dialogue tells us that Socrates chose to spend his last moments philosophizing with his friends. As death was looming in his as well as in everybody else's mind in this heavy hour, philosophy did not fail to be around. Socrates informed his friends that by being ready to die he was not doing anything strange. "The true votary of philosophy is…of his own accord…always engaged in the pursuit of dying and death."[8] To describe the kind of death the philosopher practices all his life; Socrates speaks about the distinct nature of the body and soul. A true philosopher is said to be concerned about the life of the soul which is obtained at the cost of the death of the body. This death of the body is not achieved either by torturing or annihilating the body but by attaining a freedom from the excessive

---

[5] Plato, *Phaedo*, trans. Benjamin Jowett, in *The Dialogues of Plato* (Chicago: Encyclopaedia Britannica, 1952), 64b.

[6] Ibid., pp. 63c, 70b.

[7] Ibid., pp. 58c, 59a.

[8] Ibid., p. 64a.

concern with the body and matters bodily. It is achieved by freeing one's soul
from bodily involvement and making it ready for "pure thought":

> Thought is best when the mind is gathered into itself…when it takes leave of
> the body and has as little as possible to do with it, when it has no bodily sense
> or desire, but is aspiring after true being.[9]

A superficial reading of the above may lead us to believe that Plato is describing
Socrates as an enemy of the body, and as one who really emphasized the separation
between the body and the soul. However, this simplistic interpretation withers as
we think about Socrates' purpose in positing this distinction. The autobiographical
remarks in the dialogue inform us that after his early disappointment with the teachings of Anaxagoras and with the science "that tries to apprehend things by the help of
particular senses," Socrates decided to "retreat to the domain of reasoning and seek
there the truth of existence."[10] Thus he widened and philosophically defined the Greek
conception of the soul (*psyche*) to teach that one could attain neither true knowledge
nor virtue by relying upon the bodily senses. The true being of things could only be
apprehended by the soul's dwelling in thought, "dwelling in its own place alone, as in
another life, so also in this, as far as it can."[11] The phrase "as in another life, so also in
this" is significant. It indicates that Socrates believes that as the philosopher practices
such as death, the soul sustains itself in a "here" and a "hereafter" in this very life.

The body here should be understood in its broader context, as representing the
worldly involvements of the human being realized through human senses. It is
suggested that for the most part, man's soul is in bondage when it is absorbed
in mundane concerns. The task of philosophy is to obtain the release of the soul
from the concerns of the sense-world, for it is only in this freedom of thought
that a deeper and fundamental (i.e., ontological) knowledge can be gained. It is
this death of the body, i.e., death of one's absorption in worldly concerns, that
he prescribes for the philosopher. In this state the soul dwells "as if in another
life" without relinquishing "this" life and is able to "aspire after the true being
of things" for the philosopher, it is a matter of constant practice to let his soul
dwell "as far it can" from bodily concerns, for it is impossible to dismiss "matters
bodily" altogether. Besides its ontological rewards, this practice also enables the

---

[9] Ibid., p. 65c.

[10] Ibid., pp. 97d, 99c.

[11] Ibid., p. 67c.

philosopher to be ready for death, for he or she has already realized that not-being is not evil. Obviously, Socrates' performance on his death day was well rehearsed.

The simple distinction between the body and the soul was posited by Socrates to impress upon people from all walks of life the ethical and ontological role of philosophy. In Plato's reports, he often seems to choose his words and his analytical methods appropriate to his audience. In the *Phaedo* He is shown as trying to impress upon his friends but the hereafter is in many ways better than this world, and as alluding to the myths of the times. It is not hard to notice that he is doing so primarily for the sake of his audience. He is basically appealing to the credulity of his friends, whereas his own skepticism and indifference is apparent from remarks such as, "I am as certain as I can be of such matters," "Shall I suggest that we speculate a little together about the probabilities of these things?"[12] It is clear that the chief reason for his ready acceptance of death is not that he has found a valid proof of the immortality of the soul. The foremost reason for his cheerful resignation is that he is already adept in the philosophical practice of death, i.e., in the practice of the renunciation of the world in thought and in practice of living thoughtfully.

Should we regard Socrates as a pre-metaphysical and a pre-Platonic thinker? Heidegger is one of those contemporary philosophers whose work shows an actualization of Socrates' insight about the essential bond between death realization and philosophy.[13] Socrates' way of thinking is held in special esteem by Heidegger, as he remarks in his *What Is Called Thinking*:

> To be capable (of thinking) we must before all else incline toward what addresses itself to thought....This most thought-provoking thing turns away from us.... Once we are...drawn to what withdraws, we are drawing into what withdraws... whenever man is properly drawing that way, he is thinking...All through his life and right into his death Socrates did nothing else than place themselves into this draft, this current, and maintain himself in it. This is why he is the purest thinker of the west. This is why he wrote nothing.[14]

Heidegger calls all great philosophers after Socrates "fugitives" from this draft, for they let themselves be metaphysicians and system-builders. Socrates, however, through his relentless practice of death, became an adept thinker, who never

---

[12] Ibid., pp. 63c, 70b.

[13] See note 2.

[14] Martin Heidegger, *What Is Called Thinking*, trans. J. Glenn Gray (New York: Harper & Row, 1986), 17.

sacrificed "questions of thinking" for the sake of "answers of metaphysics." Nor did he sacrifice the "living a philosophy" to the "writing of philosophy." Heidegger's homage to Socrates seems to recognize all this.

Socrates was a pioneer among the expositors of death contemplation in the West. The existential merit and authenticity of death realization is also traced in the Vedanta literature worldview of the East. *Katha Upanishad* is one of the jewels of Vedanta literature known for its succinct description of and for its original response to human wonder about death. This commentary on the role of death in carving out a thoughtful and fulfilled life not only spells out the question concerning death but also provides us with Vedanta philosophy in a nutshell. It emphasizes that a living of death achieved through relentless practice of turning away from external sense-objects to internal thought-objects blesses one with an immortality in the here and now, which is thought to be the best gift of philosophy. The bond between death contemplation and philosophy is fully exposed in the *Katha Upanishad*.

In the *Katha Upanishad* the story of Naciketas, the young aspirant of *vidya* (ontological knowledge), begins with the illustrations of his being already adept in the practice of death and his personal commitment to an involvement in the philosophical quest. He was ready to seek philosophy all the way to the very House of death. Death, the teacher of us all who is even willing to teach us and inspire us to explore the meaning of existence "on our own," is the very guru whose instruction Naciketas seeks. *Katha Upanishad* reveals the gentle face of death. Yama, the god of death, who is shown as the kind host of philosophers, a giver of boons. The boon of knowing and practicing death is but the highest blessing sought by the wise. Accordingly, Naciketas insists:

> This thing whereon they doubt, O Death:
> What there is in the great passing-on—tell us that!
> This boon that has entered into the hidden—
> No other than that does Naciketas choose.[15]

As one whose detachment from the worldly and attachment with the philosophical is testified by his rejection of the temptations offered by Yama, Naciketas' main

---

[15.] Robert Ernest Hume, trans. *Katha Upanishad*, in *The Thirteen Principal Upanishads* (Oxford: Oxford University Press, 1931), 341–365, 1–29. Hume's translation with minor revisions will be used in several subsequent long quotations. Some translations are often my own.

concern is with the "boon that has entered into the hidden" (*gudham anupra-vista*), i.e., the obviously deep issue, one that provokes philosophical inquiry. Sankara explains that this boon that seems to concern the next World (*sampraye paralokavisya*) is in fact, a seeking of knowledge about *atman* and this subject is deep and hard to contemplate.[16]

If we take Naciketas' request literally as inquiring about the "great passing-on" we are perplexed with Yama's answer. Yama, For the most part, outlines what authentic and inauthentic existence in "this" world is like rather than painting a portrait of the hereafter. There is nothing comparable to Milton's descriptions of hell in *Paradise Lost* or Dante's details of Inferno, Purgatorio, and Paradise in *Divina Commedia* in Yama's instruction to Naciketas. Yama for the most part expounds on the *atman-jnana* (soul-knowledge) and its relevance to the authentic existence of man in "this life." There are some minimal references to karma and rebirth, but their clear-cut assertions do not appear before the fifth chapter of the Upanishad.

Yama's immediate response in the second chapter concerns man's ideal exis-tence on this earth and not the hereafter. He traces the distinction between good and the pleasant (*sreyas* and *preyas*) and the respective attitudes of the restrained and the thoughtless (*dhira* and *manda*). Presently he declares that "why so wide-apart and leading to different ends are *vidya* and *avidya*."[17] *Vidya* is not available to those who "fancy themselves as wise."[18] The passing-on is not apparent to the childish, those who think that "this is the only world, there is no other," i.e., Those totally absorbed in this-worldliness.[19] *Sampraye* (higher world) is meant at two levels, as hereafter as such and as a passing-on from *avidya* and *vidya*. Sankara elaborates that the way of achieving this stage (*prapti-prayojana*) and its specific means (*sadhana-visea*) are unavailable to the thoughtless (*avivekin*).[20]

Yama further states that this thought (*mati*) is not attained by the reasoning (*tarka*) alone. Only a guru who lives it can teach it to a student who deserves it.[21] Yama initiates this teaching by asking the accomplished student Naciketas whether he sees a reality "apart from *dharma* and *adharma* (moral and immoral), apart from

---

[16.] Motilal Jalan, trans. *Kathopanisad sanuvad sankarabhasya sahit* [Katha Upanishad with the Commentary of Sankara] (Gorakhpur, India: Gita Press, 1965), 48. All translations are my own.

[17.] Hume, *The Thirteen Principal Upanishads*, pp. 2–4.

[18.] Ibid., pp. 1–5.

[19.] Ibid., pp. 2–6.

[20.] Jalan, *Kathopanisad sanuvad sankarabhasya sahit*, p. 56.

[21.] Hume, *The Thirteen Principal Upanishads*, pp. 2–8, 9.

what is done and not done, apart from what has been and what shall be."[22] Is not Yama inquiring whether Naciketas is aware of the other-worldliness abiding in this-worldliness? That Being "desiring which they live the life of brahma-conduct (*brahmacaryam caranti*)" is denoted by the word "oum."[23]

> This knowing self is not born, nor does it die
> It has not come into being from anything,
> Nor anything came into being from it
> This unborn, eternal abiding and primeval
> Is not slain when body is slan.[24]

The knower of this *atman* is the desireless one (*akratu*), whose *buddhi*, in *Sankara's* word, has been "uplifted beyond visible and invisible external objects,"[25] that is, the practitioner of death contemplation who realizes the death of visible entities, as well as their invisible meanings and involvements, a realizer of the death of visible world and invisible worldliness. Conduct, living, practice, personal accomplishment, worthiness of knowing *atman* (*atman-jnani*), that amount to a practice of death, is time and again stressed by Yama:

> This atman cannot be obtained by the scriptural studies
> Nor by intellect, nor by much learning
> It is obtained by one whom it chooses...
> Not he who has not ceased from bad conduct
> Not the unrestrained, not the unmeditative
> Not one with unpacified mind
> Can attain it by intuition (*prajna*)[26]

One who cares for *atman* is inclined toward an other-worldliness and lives accordingly, not desiring this-worldliness and is unlike the one for whom "this is the only world, there is no other." He practices death for a higher and blissful life, achieves *sampraye* in the here and now. He or she is not an

---

[22.] Ibid., pp. 2–14.

[23.] Ibid., pp. 2–15.

[24.] Ibid., pp. 2–18, Translation mine.

[25.] Jalan, *Kathopanisad sanuvad sankarabhasya sahit*, p. 74.

[26.] Hume, *The Thirteen Principal Upanishads*, pp. 2–23, 24. Translation mine.

aggressive seeker. He or she waits for *atman* to reveal itself and only practices to be ready for and worthy of its illumination. The bond between "practice of death" and the "attainments of philosophy" is indeed precisely revealed by the *Katha Upanishad*.

The bhakti poet Kabir seems to sum up the insight of the *Katha Upanishad* in the following stanzas:

> Kabir, a rare one is he who dies while living
> Fearless, he dwells in the glory of Being
> and encounters Being whichever way he glances[27]
> Kabir, death that world is afraid of, brings me joy
> Supreme bliss one attains only upon dying[28]

In the *Vedanta* worldview, such a death, indeed, is the death of *moha* (attachment) with *maya* (illusionary worldliness). It is the same death of "matters bodily" that Socrates prescribed for the philosopher. Since death contemplation inspires contemplation as such and creates suitable conditions for philosophy to emerge, it should not be taken as leading to a standard outlook on reality. Socrates, Schopenhauer, Heidegger, the author of the *Katha Upanishad* and Kabir all realize the merit of death contemplation and expose it in their philosophical systems. But that does not make their systems entirely comparable in their contents. Whereas Socrates and the *Katha Upanishad* are both pioneers in exposing the role of death contemplation and do so in a remarkably similar way, Platonism and Vedanta continue to be distinct systems.

Just as Socrates upholds a constant effort on the part of the philosopher to free his or her thought and live "as far as possible" from "matters bodily," similarly Yama's instruction to Naciketas exposes the rewards of a renunciation of *maya* and *moha*. A picture is painted in both the *Phaedo* and the *Katha Upanishad* of contemplative life, and its merits fully exposed. The existential and ontological gains of the "practitioner of death" are outlined. Both these works expose the meaning of the kind of death that the contemplative man or woman constantly undergoes. It is not an embracing of actual death (i.e., suicide) but a realization of another life in this very life. Socrates describes it as "soul's dwelling in its own place

---

[27] *Salok Kabir Je Ke* [The Couplets of Kabir] from *The Adi Granth*, translation mine, *Sloka* 5.

[28] Ibid., *Sloka* 22.

alone, as in another life, so also in this."[29] *Katha Upanishad* calls it a passing-on (*sampraye*) not apparent to the childish who are driven by the assumption that "this is the only world, there is no other,"[30] that is, those absorbed in the world of *maya*. Both Socrates and the *Katha Upanishad* declare this matter is hard to understand, that is, Contemplation of death is easily misunderstood as an obsession with and seeking of actual death. Socrates in his response to Cebes remarks that "people have not (really) found out either in what sense the true philosopher is moribund and deserves death, or what matter of death he deserves."[31] The *Katha Upanishad* calls it the "boon that has entered into the hidden" that has to do with a passing-on (*sampraye*) from *avidya* (worldly knowledge) to *vidya* (philosophical knowledge).[32] Furthermore, both the *Phaedo* and the *Katha Upanishad* not only describe the character and preoccupation of a genuine philosopher but paint living portraits of the heroic death contemplators, Socrates and Naciketas.

The preceding exposition shows that the legends of Socrates and of Naciketas both shed light on the intimate connection between death contemplation and the wonderful preoccupation of philosophizing. Since genuine philosophizing must be done in a state of leisure, bodily and mental distractions, worldly anxieties, timely considerations, as well as fragmentary conceptual trappings, must be kept at Bay. A philosopher needs practice in living and in thought to seek the fundamentals of reality and to generalize about the nature of things. The death that the philosopher practices is the death of current and prevalent "answers" that constitute the horizon of accepted worldly meanings, since these answers fall short of being philosophical explanations. Death contemplation enables one to transcend ever-enticing worldliness, familiar patterns, and accepted metaphysical casts of thinking. It creates proper conditions for a fundamental, freer, purer thinking. It enables one to contemplate the "wholes" of life and fundamentals of reality unperturbed by *maya* and matters bodily.

---

[29.] Plato, *The Dialogues of Plato*, p. 67c.

[30.] Hume, *The Thirteen Principal Upanishads*, pp. 2–6.

[31.] Plato, *The Dialogues of Plato*, p. 646.

[32.] Hume, *The Thirteen Principal Upanishads*, pp. 1–29.

CHAPTER 13

# Simone Weil and Indian Thought

*Jacqueline Kumar*

Simone Weil, born in Paris, France, lived between 1909 and 1943. She was a distinguished scholar in philosophy, political theory, and social activism. Weil lived during World War II and steadfastly adhered to her values, which led to her death at thirty-four in a hospital, having refused most meals in solidarity with those fighting in the French resistance. Her life exemplifies the contrast between philosophers who write prolifically and those who live their philosophy. To truly grasp her contribution, we must understand her life.

Weil was deeply interested in various ideas and ways of thinking. Despite her primary focus on other intellectual pursuits, she was curious about other religions and philosophies, such as Hinduism. Little consideration has been given to her influence on the study of Hinduism. Therefore, it is crucial to highlight the significance of her thoughts on Hinduism. This interest in Indian ideas played a vital role in her broader journey to find truth and better understand life and human experiences. Weil's philosophy found greater expression in her life than in her writings. Essentially, she embodied her philosophy through experimental living.

This chapter is divided into two main sections. Firstly, I will delve into Simone Weil's life journey, focusing on her upbringing, education, and early experiences that shaped her deep empathy for others. I will explore how her observations of societal inequalities and her engagement in social activism contributed to her unique perspective on shared suffering and selflessness. Through her biography, we will understand the foundation for her philosophy and her commitment to embodying her beliefs. Lastly, I will explore Simone Weil's engagement with Indian philosophy, particularly, her study of the *Bhagavad-Gita* and its concepts of love/devotion, action, and knowledge. I will highlight how Weil's emphasis on attention, selflessness, and introspection aligns with the *Gita's* teachings. Although Simone Weil does not explicitly reference the three *yogas* in her writings, I argue that her philosophical inquiries are ethical practices closely aligned with the principles of *bhakti yoga* (love/devotions), *karma yoga* (action) and *jñāna yoga* (knowledge) as delineated in the *Bhagavad-Gita*. Additionally, I will discuss her exploration of the concept of *atman*, the (soul/self), which she viewed as the inner essence of the individual, considered eternal and beyond physical existence. This section will reveal how Weil's philosophy bridges Western and Eastern thought, offering insights into empathy and duty through a unique synthesis of perspectives.

## Simone Weil's Biography

Weil was born into a bourgeois, non-Orthodox Jewish family, situating her in the French middle-class milieu, dominated by petit bourgeois entrepreneurs and the merchant class.[1] Her father, a physician, held an agnostic stance. While her ancestors upheld Judaism, this belief had declined within her close family. Despite her outward appearance aligning with the common Jewish stereotype, she was raised with values that were inherently French—a fusion of Greek and secular Christian influence.[2]

At the tender age of six, Weil began to perceive societal incongruities, grappling with the issues of inequality. She chose to abstain from consuming sugar, recognizing that soldiers on the front lines were deprived of it.[3] Very early on, she developed an understanding of shared suffering and empathy.

Weil carried an overwhelming sense of guilt due to her birth into a privileged social standing, marked by stark class divisions. As she grew older, she even opted not to wear socks, recognizing that children of laborers were deprived of such basic essentials. Her elder sibling, Andre, who later gained eminence as a mathematician, significantly influenced her intellectual nourishment, inculcating scientific inquiry and literary exploration during her nascent years.[4]

Weil was an intellectually astute prodigy, astounding observers by reciting excerpts from the oeuvre of the 17th-century French dramatist Jean Racine at the age of six.[5] In 1928, Weil gained admission to a prestigious institution in France known for its exceptional philosophy programs, the École Normale

---

[1] Simone Weil, *Waiting for God* (New York: Harper Perennial, 2009), xv.

[2] Ibid., p. ix.

[3] Ibid., p. xv.

[4] Ibid., p. xvi.

[5] Ibid., p. 8.

Supérieure.[6] Securing a spot at this institution was an aspiration for aspiring philosophers, given the company of renowned thinkers like Jean-Paul Sartre and Michel Foucault. Simone Weil was among the fortunate ones to be admitted, emerging successfully among the eleven applicants in her class and notably being the sole woman accepted, which was a remarkable achievement. She finished first in the exam for "General Philosophy and Logic," surpassing feminist philosopher Simone de Beauvoir. However, Simone Weil never aspired to become a renowned philosopher. Instead, her priority was to experience life fully rather than seeking fame.[7]

After her stay at the École Normale Supérieure, from 1934 to 1936, Weil assumed an academic role at an all-girls secondary school in Le Puy.[8] In 1932, Weil engaged with labor unions, delving into the ideological divisions of socialism. Expanding her role as a social activist, Weil became involved in the Spanish Civil War, supporting the republican cause. While teaching at the secondary school, she demonstrated strong Marxist tendencies and immersed herself in the lives of the working class by laboring alongside them in factories.[9] During her time at the factories, she observed the extensive workload on the masses, their mental fatigue rendering them unable to contemplate, and the dehumanizing treatment they endured. While in Paris, her factory journal noted, "Time as an intolerable burden," indicating that her time at the factory felt like an unbearable weight.[10]

## Simone Weil and Indian Philosophy

In her work *The Notebooks of Simone Weil Volume 1*, she delves deeply into her reflections on various philosophical and religious concepts, including those from Indian philosophy. To her, the cultivation of religious life was not separate from her philosophical contributions her engagement with the concepts of *atman*

---

[6.] Ibid., p. xviii.

[7.] Ibid., p. xviii.

[8.] Ibid., p. xviii.

[9.] Ibid., p. xviii.

[10.] Simone Weil, *The Need for Roots: Prelude to a Declaration of Duties Towards Mankind*, trans. Arthur Wills (New York: Routledge, 1952).

(soul/self) and the *Gita* is particularly noteworthy.[11] As I have already noted, *atman,* in Indian philosophy, particularly Hinduism, refers to the inner self or soul. It is the essence of an individual considered eternal and beyond physical existence. She explored the concept of *atman* in the context of her own philosophical inquiries about the nature of self, the soul, and the divine. Her notebooks reveal a fascination with the idea that *atman* represents a deeper, spiritual truth that transcends individual ego and identity, similar to the Christian idea of seeking union with God. She sees *atman* as a key concept for understanding the human condition in the quest for spiritual liberation.

In this segment, I will discuss the fundamental concepts of Indian philosophy prior to delving into the relevance of the three *yogas* in the context of empathy and Simone Weil's perspective. In her literary piece "Waiting for God," she mentions engaging with the *Bhagavad-Gita.*[12] She perceived this revered text as resonating with Christian undertones and was convinced of its inherent religious truth. To gain a comprehensive understanding of the *Gita*, she undertook the study of Sanskrit, identifying parallels between its narratives and her personal experiences. As Weil Writes,

> In the spring of 1940, I read the *Bhagavad-Gita.* Strange to say it was in reading those marvelous words, words with such a Christian sound, put into the mouth of an incarnation of God, that I came to feel strongly that we owe an allegiance to religious truth which is quite different from the admiration we accord to a beautiful poem, it is something far more categorical.[13]

Weil expresses the impact that the *Bhagavad-Gita* has had on her just by reading it. She was enlightened by the words of the *Gita* though they are rooted in the Hindu tradition they can be compared to the spiritual depth of Christian teachings. When she mentions that we owe allegiance to "religious truth," she suggests that such truths demand a commitment beyond mere aesthetic appreciation, unlike a beautiful poem admired for his art. Religious truth transcends this, calling for a spiritual awakening that guides one's actions and way of living. Her interest in India seemed to be centered on the *Gita* and the *Upanishads.*

---

[11.] Simone Weil, *The Notebooks of Simone Weil*, trans. Arthur Wills (New York: G. P. Putnam's Sons, 1956), 19–20.

[12.] Simone Weil, *Waiting on God* (New York: Harper Perennial, 2009), 28.

[13.] Ibid., p. 28.

The *Bhagavad-Gita* is a 700-verse scripture that is part of the Indian epic *Mahābhārata*. The *Mahābhārata* is centered on a warrior, Arjuna, and his deity/ teacher Krishna. They discussed life's moral dilemmas on the battlefield. It offers profound insights into duty, spirituality, and paths to liberation, emphasizing selflessness and inner self-control.

In her writings on Cahiers, which were a collection of notebooks where she recorded her thoughts and reflections, Weil speaks about Arjuna and the importance of action.[14]

The first chapter of the *Bhagavad-Gita* describes how Arjuna is a renowned warrior. Arjuna's moral dilemma is based on the presence of his close relations and teachers on the opposite side that he has to battle with. The *Gita* depicts this symbolic battle which should not be taken literally, Gandhi said "the battle of Kruruk Shritta rages in every human heart."[15] The battle between good and bad, desirable and undesirable, assails every human heart which is the ground of ethics. We all face dilemmas between what to do and what not to do. The battle described in the *Gita* is symbolic of the basic moral and practical challenges that we face from moment to moment.

In the *Gita*, the three *yogas* are discussed. Lord Krishna expounds on the three *yogas*, namely, *bhakti* (love/devotion), *karma* (action), and *jnāna* (knowledge). The Sanskrit word *bhakti* is derived from the root word *bhaj*.[16] Its central tenet is to selflessly share one's love and devotion with fellow humans and God as demonstrated in the *Bhagavad-Gita*.[17] *Bhakti yoga* is concerned with the emotions/innovations of love and devotion, which are aimed toward caring and concern for others.

Similarly, the Sanskrit word *karma* stems from *kri*, which means "to do,"[18] pointing to the fact that our actions define who we are. The intensity of love and devotion is to be combined with *karma,* and it is in this sense that *karma* cannot be separated from *bhakti*.[19] *Bhakti* and *karma yoga* are interdependent and, to function successfully, they also require *jnāna yoga*.

[14.] Simone Weil, *Cahiers: Notebooks of Simone Weil*, trans. Arthur Wills (New York: Routledge, 1956).

[15.] Mahatma Gandhi, *The Bhagavad Gita According to Gandhi* (Berkeley, CA: North Atlantic Books, 2009).

[16.] R. Raj Singh, *Bhakti and Philosophy* (Lanham, MD: Lexington Books, 2006), 8.

[17.] Cf. Ibid., pp. 8–10.

[18.] Ibid., p. 12.

[19.] Ibid.

*Jnāna yoga* may be equated with inner knowledge, which includes the idea of knowing oneself. We attain wisdom by drawing on what we have experienced, and considered in this sense; *jnāna* or knowledge is best captured by appeal to abstract philosophical constructs such as "introspection," but mainly refers to knowledge of oneself through life experience.

Weil regarded the *Gita* as the most stimulating and thoughtful philosophical work by which she was greatly influenced. Her distinctive viewpoint intersects with these three *yogas*. In works like "Waiting on God" and "Gravity and Grace," she delves into the concept of "attention."[20] Weil's understanding of attention required a spiritual discipline that involved a profound and altruistic focus on reality both within oneself and the external world. Attention requires setting aside the ego and removing oneself from worldly attachments. This mirrors the selflessness and affection emphasized in *bhakti* yoga. We might compare this to Iris Murdoch's notion of "unselfing."[21] Murdoch gives the example of a mother-in-law who initially holds a negative opinion of her daughter-in-law, viewing her as unpolished and unintelligent. Through a process of careful attention, the mother-in-law begins to see the daughter-in-law more accurately, setting aside her ego and understanding the daughter-in-law as she truly is. Weil argues that genuine attention necessitates setting aside the ego, akin to the selflessness in the yogas.[22]

Furthermore, her analysis of actions aligns with *karma* yoga. She posits that conscientious, purposeful work can foster a deeper connection with the divine. This idea of action shaping our identity echoes the correlation among love, devotion, and *karma* in the *Gita*. Moreover, Weil's exploration of internal understanding and self-awareness parallels *jnāna* yoga's pursuit of knowledge.

## Conclusion

Simone Weil's journey teaches us that philosophy is not confined to the pages of books or the halls of academia; it is a lived experience that calls us to examine our personal beliefs and actions. This chapter has delved into two main sections: the first explored Weil's life journey, focusing on her upbringing, education, and early experiences that shaped her empathy and commitment to social activism.

---

[20.] Simone Weil, *Waiting on God* (New York: Harper Perennial, 2009), 57–58.

[21.] Iris Murdoch, *The Sovereignty of Good* (London: Routledge, 1970), 16–23.

[22.] Simone Weil, *The Notebooks of Simone Weil*, p. 206.

The second section examined her engagement with Indian philosophy, particularly the *Bhagavad-Gita*, highlighting how her thoughts align with the principles of *bhakti* yoga, *karma* yoga, and *jñāna* yoga.

Weil regarded philosophy as a lived experience, an inspiration to live a higher life. Her work is full of personal insights and lived enigmas of life. Simone Weil's philosophy challenges us to engage deeply with the world, to see beyond the surface of our daily lives, and confront the profound moral and spiritual questions that define our existence. She invites us to embrace the complexities of human suffering and solidarity, to recognize the interconnectedness of all beings, and to act with empathy and selflessness.

Weil's engagement with the *Bhagavad-Gita* and Indian philosophy reveals her quest for a universal truth that transcends cultural and religious boundaries. Her emphasis on attention, selflessness, and introspection resonates with the timeless wisdom of the *Gita*, reminding us that true understanding requires a synthesis of love, action, and knowledge.

# CHAPTER 14

# Simone Weil on the Teachings of the Buddha

*Jacqueline Kumar*

The Buddha (563–483 BCE) taught the irrefutable and universal reality that humanity and all other living creatures are affected by pain and suffering (*dukkhā*). He contributed to the philosophy by addressing these issues through the *Four Noble Truths*, motivated by his deep compassion (*karuna*) for all sentient beings. These truths are essential components of Buddhist doctrine and are revered by all Buddhists. Philosopher Simone Weil resonated deeply with the Buddha's teachings, finding a profound connection with his insights on suffering and compassion. In her book *Gravity and Grace*,[1] Weil discusses themes of detachment and the extinction of desire, drawing parallels to Buddhist teachings. She explores the concept of ending personal cravings and attachments, suggesting that true fulfillment comes from detaching our desires from specific outcomes and cultivating a state of pure, open-ended desire. Weil argues that by waiting in this state of detached openness, one can touch the "absolute good," resonating with the Buddhist practice of letting go of craving to attain enlightenment.[2]

This chapter explores the intersections between the Buddha's teachings and Simone Weil's philosophy, highlighting how both address the universal issues of suffering and the pursuit of spiritual enlightenment. By examining the Buddha's Four Noble Truths, the Dhammapada, and Weil's key concepts of *attention, affliction*, and *decreation*, this chapter demonstrates the convergence of Eastern and Western philosophical perspectives on the human condition. To achieve this, I first provide a brief account of the Buddha's life and teachings. Secondly, I explore the Buddha's *Four Noble Truths*: the truth of suffering, the truth of the cause of suffering, the truth of the end of suffering, and the truth of the path that leads to the end of suffering. Thirdly, I discuss some of the *Dhammapada* (a collection

---

[1] Simone Weil, *Gravity and Grace*, trans. Emma Crawford and Mario von der Ruhr (New York: Routledge, 2002), 13.

[2] Ibid., pp. xxi, 13.

of the Buddha's sayings), focusing on craving (*kāma-taṇhā*). I compare some of the teachings of the *Bhagavad-Gita* (song of the Lord) to the *Dhammapada* and argue that the former shows us how to deal with a life of suffering, whereas the latter does not. Lastly, I examine the work of Simone Weil and her connections to these themes, demonstrating how her ideas intersect with Buddhist philosophy, thereby providing a unique perspective on the universal struggle with suffering and the quest for spiritual enlightenment.

## The Buddha's Teachings

Siddhartha Gotama, known as The Blessed One or The Enlightened One (herein after referred to simply as the Buddha), was born into royalty. His father kept him confined to the palace, shielding him from life's hardships. Despite his sheltered upbringing, the young Buddha, even after marriage, wondered about life beyond the palace. His curiosity led him and a friend to venture outside, where they encountered a funeral procession, prompting the Buddha to question the reality of death. They also met an elderly man, leading him to ponder aging and suffering. A monk, explained that his life of seclusion allowed him to escape everyday suffering.[3]

These encounters caused the Buddha to question the realty of his life and the lives of others. Realizing that suffering was central to life, he sought a way to escape it. He abandoned his princely life to join monks who aimed to control mind's turmoil through fasting and meditation. However, the Buddha discovered that "self-mortification" alone did not calm the mind, leading to the discovery of the "middle path,"[4] which aimed to alleviate, worldwide suffering. According to the Buddha, pain and suffering are the cause of rebirth (*samsara*).[5]

Before delving deeper into the Buddha's central ideas, it is important to note that his thinking spawned several schools of Buddhism. Mahayana Buddhism, also known as the "Greater Vehicle," emphasizes living an ethical life and compassion for all sentient beings.[6] An earlier school, Hinayana Buddhism,[7] also known as

[3] Sarvepalli Radhakrishnan, *Indian Philosophy*, 2 vols. (London: George Allen & Unwin, 1923), 100.

[4] Ibid., p. 100.

[5] Bhikkhu Bodhi, trans. *The Middle Length Discourses of the Buddha: A Translation of the Majjhima Nikaya.* 2nd ed. (Boston: Wisdom Publications, 2001), MN 15, "Maha-Nidana Sutta: The Great Discourse on Origination."

[6] Santideva, *The Bodhicaryavatara*, Vol. 101, trans. Kate Crosby and Andrew Skilton (Toronto, ON: Oxford University Press, 1995), 43.

[7] Martine Batchelor, trans., *The Path of Compassion* (Walnut Creek, CA: AltaMira Press, 2004), 115–117.

the "Inferior Way,"[8] focuses on personal salvation. Despite different schools and goals, all Buddhist's adhere to precepts that are central to its philosophy/religion.

One of Buddhism's most important ideas, perhaps startling to the Western mind, is the concept of no-self. Buddhists hold that as conscious beings, we are a process of co-functioning. Consciousness is a combination of things working together. Unlike some Western thought that distinguishes between soul and body, Buddhists, combine the two through their understanding of consciousness. Consciousness must co-function with an object and therefore does not have an essence; neither are the soul and body distinct identities. This concept, known as dependent origination, leads to the idea of no-self.[9] Consequently, with no-self, or soul, Buddhists do not envision an afterlife, as many adherents of the Abrahamic religions do.

## The Four Noble Truths

The Buddha embraces the dilemma of suffering and remains silent regarding metaphysical questions, seeing them as futile and distracting from the eliminating pain and suffering (*dukkhā*). The Buddha argued that questions about theism or belief in God did not lead to edification.[10] To support his argument, the Buddha tells the story of a man who is shot by an arrow. Rather than asking about the shooter, the Buddha, living in the moment, advocates for removing the arrow to preserve the man's life.[11] It is our duty to attend to the man's pain rather than asking irrelevant questions like, "Who shot the arrow?" or "From which angle was it shot?" These questions do not alleviate the victim's suffering. Empty speculation leads to the continuation of *samsara* (the cycle of death and constant rebirth).[12] To escape this ongoing cycle, the Buddha formulated the *Four Noble Truths* to successfully tackle universal suffering.

The *First Noble Truth* highlights that pain, suffering (*dukkhā*) are encountered by all beings. The *Second Noble Truth* clarifies that *dukkhā*, has an origin. The

---

8. Paul Williams, in Santideva, *The Bodhicaryavatara*, trans. Kate Crosby and Andrew Skilton (Toronto, ON: Oxford University Press, 1995), xiii.

9. Walpola Rahula, *What the Buddha Taught*. Revised and expanded edition (New York: Grove Press, 1974), 25–26.

10. Ibid., pp. 25–27.

11. Ibid.

12. Ibid.

*Third Noble Truth* accentuates that there is a solution to the dilemma of *dukkhā*. Finally, the *Fourth Noble Truth* is a path that leads to the annihilation of *dukkhā*. This path is known as the *Noble Eightfold Path*.[13] I will explore on these four concepts throughout this chapter.

The *First Noble Truth* describes the pain and suffering which all sentient beings endure. The Buddha uses a series of examples to illustrate this: birth, old age, sickness, sorrow, dejection, despair, craving, and contact with unpleasant things. These emotions and experiences that all sentient beings share.[14] In addition to this list, ideas of imperfections, impermanence, and emptiness play a role in our existence. All these things are part of the continuous cycle of *samsara*.[15]

The *Second Noble Truth* deals with the causes of *dukkhā*. According to the Buddha, *dukkhā* has its origin in *Paticca-Samuppada* or *Dependent Origination*. This idea implies that nothing is independent of its origin.[16] *Paticca-Samuppada* means something depends on something else for its existence. The Buddha denies the existence of the *atman* (soul/self), insisting on the idea of no-self (*anatman*).[17] He taught that believing in the self leads to selfishness or self-centeredness, one of the central causes of *dukkhā*.

The Buddha divides the so-called self into the five *skandhas* or clusters: *rupa* (form), *sanna* (perception), *vedana* (sensation), *vijnana* (consciousness), *samskaras* (predispositions).[18] He states that these *skandhas* are transitory and subject to impermanence and constant change.[19] Therefore, the self is not a single entity but comprises different interacting aspects, making a unitary self impossible. In addition to the *skandhas*, *dukkhā* is also associated with *avidya* (lack of knowledge) and excessive cravings or *Tanha*.[20] Ignorance and desire are the driving force behind the perpetual cycle of rebirth (*samsara*) and *dukkhā*.[21]

---

[13] Radhakrishnan, *Indian Philosophy*.

[14] Karl Eugen Neumann, *The Life of Buddha: According to the Legends of Ancient India*, trans. Victor Arnold and Caroline Arnold (London: Routledge & Kegan Paul, 1957), 87.

[15] Rahula, *What the Buddha Taught*, p. 52.

[16] Ibid., pp. 52–53.

[17] Ibid., p. 53.

[18] Radhakrishnan, *Indian Philosophy*.

[19] Ibid.

[20] Ling Trevor, *The Buddha, Buddhist Civilization in India and Ceylon* (London: Temple Smith, 1973), 112.

[21] Rahula, *What the Buddha Taught*, p. 19.

*The Third Noble Truth* centers on cessation. To escape *dukkhā*, we must avoid craving (*tanha*). The banishment of craving (*tanha*) results in the demise of *dukkhā*.[22]

*The Forth Noble Truth*, also known as the *Middle Path*, is situated between excessive self-indulgence and self-deprivation, and is linked to the *Noble Eightfold Path*, which includes balanced views, intention, speech, action, livelihood, effort, mindfulness, and concentration.[23] Living a balanced life leads us to escape *dukkhā*.

Intentionality, or good intentions, is the foundation of the Eightfold Path. Living a life where we do not harm other sentient beings is a necessary component of a well-balanced path. This also requires moderation in speech and avoiding slander, gossip, and lying. Our words and deeds play an important role in being a good person. This also means never taking a life, stealing, or abusing sexual desires.

A well-balanced livelihood demands that we are law-abiding and engage in proper occupations. Moreover, we should not be pessimistic and always make the effort to engage in right thinking. When we do this, we will be mindful and aware of everything, and we will not fail in keeping our desires at bay. Our mindfulness and awareness will lead us to reject sensual cravings, doubt, and lust. Secondly, we will not engage in senseless, metaphysical musings. Thirdly, we will not be overcome by transitory emotions, which will also lead us into unnecessary desires or cravings. Finally, once we conquer our passions, we will be rid of those emotions that leave us entrapped in the cycle of *samsara*.[24]

In certain respects, Buddhism evokes parallels with Plato's portrayal of Socrates, particularly as presented in the Phaedo. Plato's Socrates, particularly as depicted in the *Phadeo*, shares profound parallels with Buddhist philosophy, evoking deep connections between their views on wisdom, the soul, and the nature of enlightenment. Here Socrates draws a distinction between the soul and the body, something that the Buddhist would never do. Plato, in noting the difference between the pure and not-so-pure soul, says that the latter has been ruined because of its attachment (*moha*) to bodily pleasures such as gluttony and lustfulness.[25] As a result, Socrates' tainted soul will return to another body and continue its earthly existence. The craving, or desiring soul will return to

---

[22] Ibid., p. 26.

[23] M. Ram Murty. *Indian Philosophy: An Introduction* (Peterborough, ON: Broadview Press, 2012), 102.

[24] Ibid.

[25] Plato. *The Last Days of Socrates*, trans. Hugh Tredennick and Harold Tarrant (London: Penguin Books, 1993), 150.

the body of "donkeys or other perverse animals."[26] Similarly, in Buddhism, the person who has lived a life of debauchery or an unbalanced life will not escape *samsara* and thus will not attain *"Nirvana"* (liberation).

## Dhammapada and the *Bhagavad-Gita*

The Dhammapada is a collection of the Buddha's teachings, whereas the *Bhagavad-Gita* also known as the *Gīta* (song) is a series of epic poems setting out religious and philosophical Hindu thought. The poems are allegorical illustrations on how to live one's life and what it means to be a human being. The Dhammapada mainly focuses on human existence in so far as it relates to the agony and pain of that existence. According to Ram Murty the Dhammapada does not provide a solution for our constant cravings and suffering other than to engage in the practice of meditation or *raja*. The *Gīta* (song) resolves this problem by suggesting we use our energies and focus on the four yogas; devotion/love (*bhakti*), action (*karma*), inner knowledge (*jnana*) and psychic control (*raja*). The yogas are co-dependent and their exercise will help us resolve the painfulness of everyday life, leading us escape the cycle of rebirth (*samsara*).[27]

*Bhakti* yoga stands for the principle that we love ourselves, our fellowmen and God. *Karma* yoga insists that we act on our love, be it for ourselves or other and to be just in our actions. *Jnana* yoga is the command to know oneself when engaged in our actions. We might also think of *jnana* as the voice of our conscience. *Raja* yoga involves the control of our minds and tells us not to get carried away with our attachments to others and material goods. It is in these respects that the *Gīta* (song) is more encompassing than Dhammapada as it considers the complex and diverse nature of humanity.

## Simone Weil on Indian Thought

Simone Weil (1909–1943), a French philosopher, engaged deeply with themes of suffering, compassion, and the human condition. Weil's intellectual journey

---

[26] Ibid., p. 151.

[27] Murty, *Indian Philosophy*, p. 100.

was marked by a profound engagement with diverse religious and philosophical traditions, including Buddhism.[28] Her work provides a bridge between Buddhist ideas and Western thought, offering a unique perspective on the universal struggle with suffering and the quest for spiritual enlightenment.

Central to Weil's philosophy is the concept of attention (*attente*), which resonates with the Buddhist practice of mindfulness. Weil's notion of attention is not merely a cognitive focus but a spiritual discipline.[29] It involves an openness and receptivity to the present moment and the needs of others. This focused, present-centered awareness transcends selfish desires and opens individuals to the suffering of others. In her view, attention is a form of prayer, a way to connect deeply with the world and with the divine.[30] This is similar to the Buddhist emphasis on mindfulness (*sati*) and compassion (*karuna*) as essential steps on the Eightfold Path.

Weil's notion of affliction (*malheur*) parallels the Buddhist concept of *dukkha*. She viewed affliction as a state that strips individuals of their personal identity and forces them to confront the void, much like the Buddhist understanding of emptiness (*sunyata*) and the transient nature of self. Affliction, according to Weil, is an unavoidable aspect of the human condition that can lead to a deeper understanding and connection with the divine. She argued that experiencing and understanding affliction can strip away illusions and false attachments, leading to spiritual growth and enlightenment.[31] This idea aligns closely with the Buddhist concept of facing and understanding suffering as a path to enlightenment.

Furthermore, Weil's idea of decreation aligns with the Buddhist notion of no-self (*anatman*). Decreation involves the unmaking of the self, a process of letting go of ego and personal desires to become an empty vessel for divine love. This echoes the Buddhist practice of relinquishing the illusion of a permanent self to attain enlightenment.[32] For Weil, decreation is a profound act of humility and self-surrender, where one aligns oneself with the divine will and recognizes one's limitations and dependencies. Similarly, in Buddhism, the concept of no-self involves a process of letting go of the ego and realizing the interconnectedness

---

28. Weil, *Gravity and Grace*, p. 107.

29. Ibid., p. xxv.

30. Ibid., pp. 116–117.

31. Ibid., p. 117.

32. Ibid., p. xxiv.

and impermanence of all things. Both perspectives advocate for a dissolution of the ego to attain a higher state of spiritual awareness.

Weil's thoughts on suffering and attention also intersect with the Buddhist path to end suffering. For Weil, attention is not just a mental exercise but a spiritual practice that requires a self-emptying process where one puts aside personal desires and distractions to fully engage with the present moment and the needs of others.[33] This concept is similar to the Buddhist practice of mindfulness, where one cultivates a focused awareness of the present, free from distractions and desires. Both Weil and the Buddha emphasize that this mindful, compassionate attention to the present is crucial for spiritual growth and the alleviation of suffering.

Moreover, Weil's critique of society's emphasis on power and success over compassion and humility reflects the Buddhist critique of material craving and attachment. Both Weil and the Buddha advocate for a life that prioritizes spiritual development and ethical behavior over worldly achievements and materialism.[34] Weil was particularly critical of the ways in which society's pursuit of power and material success leads to the oppression and suffering of others. She believed that true justice and compassion require a radical reorientation of values, away from self-centered pursuits and toward a selfless dedication to the well-being of others. This mirrors the Buddhist teaching that material cravings and attachments are the root causes of suffering and must be overcome to achieve true enlightenment.

In her work *Waiting for God*, Weil delves deeply into the nature of affliction in the human condition. She describes affliction as a state that crushes the soul and body, leading to a profound sense of loss and emptiness.[35] This experience, according to Weil, can lead to a deeper understanding and connection with the divine, as it strips away illusions and false attachments. This idea is parallel to the Buddhist concept of facing and understanding suffering as a path to enlightenment. Weil emphasizes that true attention involves a form of self-emptying, where one puts aside personal desires and distractions to fully engage with the present moment and the needs of others. This concept is similar to the Buddhist

---

[33] Simone Weil, *Waiting for God*, trans. Emma Craufurd (New York: Harper & Row, 1951).

[34] Ibid., p. 6.

[35] Ibid., pp. 117–118.

practice of mindfulness, where one cultivates a focused awareness of the present, free from distractions and desires.

Weil's writings often explore the tension between human suffering and the search for meaning and transcendence. She believed that by embracing and understanding our suffering, we could transcend our individual egos and connect with a higher reality.[36] This process of decreation, or self-emptying, is akin to the Buddhist practice of meditation, where one learns to detach from the ego and recognize the interconnectedness of all life. Weil's profound sense of compassion and her commitment to social justice also reflect the Buddhist ideal of compassion for all sentient beings.

In conclusion, Simone Weil's philosophical and spiritual reflections offer a profound resonance with Buddhist teachings. Both traditions emphasize the importance of compassion, the need to transcend the ego, and the necessity of facing and understanding suffering as a path to spiritual enlightenment. Weil's concept of attention as a form of prayer, her understanding of affliction, and her idea of decreation provide a unique and valuable perspective that bridges Western and Eastern philosophies. Through her engagement with these themes, Weil enriches our understanding of the universal human quest for meaning and the alleviation of suffering.

## Conclusion

In this chapter, I have discussed the early life of the Buddha and his path to the Four Noble Truths: the suffering of sentient beings, its causes, how to end suffering, and the path to that ending. The Buddha's teachings emphasize the importance of living in the present moment and avoiding metaphysical speculation, as illustrated by the story of the man shot with an arrow. The Buddha argued that we should focus on alleviating immediate suffering rather than engaging in abstract questions about its cause.

I also highlighted the distinction between the Western concept of the separation of soul and body and the Buddhist idea of no-self (anatman). While Western thought, as seen in Plato's philosophy, often posits the existence of a distinct, eternal soul, Buddhism rejects this notion, viewing the self as an impermanent aggregation of

---

[36.] Weil, *Gravity and Grace*, pp. 32–33.

different elements. Despite these differences, there are notable parallels between Buddhism and the teachings of Socrates, particularly in their concern with ethical living and the human struggle against common failings such as lust, gluttony, and greed.

Furthermore, I compared the Dhammapada and the *Bhagavad-Gita*, two foundational texts in Buddhism and Hinduism, respectively. While the Dhammapada focuses primarily on meditation and the alleviation of suffering through mindfulness, the *Bhagavad-Gita* offers a more comprehensive approach to overcoming suffering through the practice of four yogas: devotion (bhakti), action (karma), knowledge (jnana), and meditation (raja). The *Gīta's* inclusive approach addresses the complex and diverse nature of human existence more thoroughly than the Dhammapada.

Finally, I examined Simone Weil's engagement with Buddhist thought, particularly her concepts of attention, affliction, and decreation. Weil's philosophy resonates deeply with Buddhist teachings on mindfulness, suffering, and the dissolution of the ego. Her idea of attention as a spiritual discipline that involves openness to the present moment and the needs of others parallels the Buddhist practice of mindfulness. Weil's notion of affliction, akin to the Buddhist concept of dukkha, highlights suffering as a pathway to spiritual growth and enlightenment. Moreover, her idea of decreation, or the unmaking of the self, aligns with the Buddhist rejection of a permanent self and the emphasis on interconnectedness and impermanence.

Weil's critique of society's emphasis on power and material success over compassion and humility further reflects Buddhist values. Both traditions advocate for a life centered on spiritual development and ethical behavior, rejecting the pursuit of worldly achievements and materialism as sources of suffering.

In conclusion, the teachings of the Buddha and the philosophy of Simone Weil offer profound insights into the human condition, emphasizing the universal struggle with suffering and the quest for spiritual enlightenment. By exploring the intersections between these Eastern and Western perspectives, we gain a richer understanding of the ways in which different philosophical traditions address the challenges of human existence. Through this comparative study, we see how the Buddha's path to ending suffering through mindfulness and ethical living resonates with Weil's call for compassionate attention and the relinquishment of ego. Together, these teachings provide valuable guidance for anyone seeking to navigate the complexities of life with wisdom and compassion.

# BIBLIOGRAPHY

Aggawal, Purushotam. *Kabir: Sakhi Aur Sabad.* National Book Trust, 2015.

Aurobindo, Sri. *The Synthesis of Yoga, Part Four: "The Yoga of Self-Perfection," Chapter 24, "The Supramental Sense."* Sri Aurobindo Ashram, 1999.

Aurobindo, Sri. *The Life Divine.* Lotus Press, 1920.

Aurobindo, Sri. *The Collected Works of Sri Aurobindo.* Vols. 26, 84. Aurobindo Ashram, 1972.

Aurobindo, Sri. *The Essential Aurobindo.* Edited by Robert A. McDermott. Lindisfarne Books, 2001.

Banerjea, P. *Early Indian Religions.* Vikas Publishing.

Batchelor, Martine, trans., *The Path of Compassion.* AltaMira Press, 2004.

Bhandarkar, R. G. *Vaisnavism, Saivism and Minor Religious Systems.* K. J. Trubner, 1913.

Bhikkhu, Bodhi, trans., *The Middle Length Discourses of the Buddha: A Translation of the Majjhima Nikaya.* 2nd ed. Wisdom Publications, 2009.

Bikkhu, Nanajivako. *Studies in Comparative Philosophy.* Lakehouse Publishers, 1983.

Bloom, Paul. *Against Empathy: A Case for Rational Compassion.* HarperCollins, 2016.

Bowles, Chester. "Gandhi as I Understood Him." In *Gandhian Thought and Contemporary Society*, edited by J. S. Mathur. 1974.

Cartwright, David E. "Schopenhauer on Suffering, Death, Guilt and the Consolation of Metaphysics." In *Schopenhauer: New Essays in Honour of His 200th Birthday*, edited by Eric von der Luft. Edwin Mellen Press, 1988.

Coplan, Amy, and Peter Goldie. *Empathy: Philosophical and Psychological Perspectives*. Oxford University Press, 2011.

Dhavamony, M. *Love of God According to Saiva Siddhanta*. Oxford University Press, 1971.

Divedi, Hazari Prasad. *Kabir*. Sahitya Sarovar, 1942.

Fox, Michael. "Schopenhauer on Death, Suicide and Self-Renunciation." In *Schopenhauer: His Philosophical Achievement*, edited by Michael Fox. Barnes & Noble Books, 1980.

Gandhi, M. K. "What Is Truth." In *Navjivan*, November 20, 1921. In *The Moral and Political Writings of Mahatama Gandhi*, vol. 2, edited by Raghavan Iyer. Clarendon Press, 1986.

Gandhi, M. K. "War or Peace." In *Young India*, May 20, 1926. In *The Moral and Political Writings of Mahatama Gandhi*, vol. 2, edited by Raghavan Iyer. Clarendon Press, 1986.

Gandhi, M. K. "A Complex Problem." In *Young India*, May 9, 1929. In *The Moral and Political Writings of Mahatama Gandhi*, vol. II, edited by Raghavan Iyer. Clarendon Press, 1986.

Gandhi, M. K. *The Moral and Political Writings of Mahatma Gandhi*. Vol. 2. Edited by Raghavan Iyer. Oxford University Press, 1986.

Gandhi, M. K. *The Moral and Political Writings of Mahatma Gandhi*. Vol. II. Edited by Raghavan Iyer. Clarendon Press, 1986.

Gandhi, M. K. *Yeravada Mandir*, 1935. In *All Men Are Brothers*, edited by Krishna Kriplani. Continuum, 1987.

Gandhi, M. K. *Harijan*, May 16, 1936. In *All Men Are Brothers*, edited by Krishna Kriplani. Continuum, 1987.

Gandhi, M. K. *Harijan*, March 28, 1939. In *All Men Are Brothers*, edited by Krishna Kriplani. Continuum, 1987.

Gandhi, M. K. *Harijan*, February 22, 1942. In *All Men Are Brothers*, edited by Krishna Kriplani. Continuum, 1987.

Gandhi, M. K. *From Yeravada Mandir*. Navajivan Publishing House, 1945.

Gandhi, M. K. "Speech at Meeting in Laussane." In *The Moral and Political Writings of Mahatama Gandhi*, vol. 2, edited by Raghavan Iyer. Clarendon Press, 1986.

Gandhi, M. K. *All Men Are Brothers*. Edited by Krishna Kriplani. Continuum, 1987.

Gandhi, M. K. *The Bhagavad Gita According to Gandhi*. North Atlantic Books, 2009.

Garver, Newton. "What Violence Is." In *Philosophical Issues*, edited by James Rachels and Frank Tillman. Harper & Row, 1972.

Gokhale, G. "Bhakti in Early Buddhism." In *Tradition and Modernity in Bhakti Movements*, edited by J. Lele. E. J. Brill, 1991.

Goyal, S. R. *A Religious History of India*, vol. I. Kusumanjali, 1984.

Halbfass, Wilhelm. *India and Europe: An Essay in Understanding*. State University of New York Press, 1988.

Hegel, Georg Wilhelm Friedrich. *Lectures on the Philosophy of World History*. Cambridge University Press, 1975.

Heidegger, Martin. *An Introduction to Metaphysics*. Translated by Ralph Manheim. Yale University Press, 1959.

Heidegger, Martin. "Letter on Humanism." Translated by Edgar Lohner. In *Philosophy in the Twentieth Century*, vol. 3, edited by William Barret and Henry D. Aikin. Random House, 1962a.

Heidegger, Martin. "Plato's Doctrine of Truth." Translated by John Barlow. In *Philosophy in the Twentieth Century*, vol. 3, edited by William Barrett and Henry Aiken. Random House, 1962b.

Heidegger, Martin. *Being and Time*. Translated by J. Macquarrie and E. Robinson. Harper & Row, 1962c.

Heidegger, Martin. *What Is Called Thinking*. Translated by F. E. Wrick and J. G. Gray. Harper & Row, 1968.

Heidegger, Martin. "The Thinker as Poet." In *Poetry, Language, Thought*, translated by Albert Hofstadter. Harper & Row, 1975.

Heidegger, Martin. "The Question Concerning Technology." Translated by William Lovitt. In *The Question Concerning Technology*. Harper & Row, 1977.

Hume, David. *A Treatise of Human Nature*. Edited by David Fate Norton and Mary J. Norton. Clarendon Press, 2011.

Hume, Robert Ernest, trans., Katha Upanishad. In *The Thirteen Principal Upanishads*, edited by Robert Ernest Hume. Oxford University Press, 1931.

Kalupahana, David J., trans., *Nagarjuna: Mulamadhyamaka-karika*, XV.7. State University of New York Press, 1986.

Kennedy, Paul. "The Worst of Times?" Review of Niall Ferguson's *The War of the World*. Penguin, 2006.

Lanzoni, Susan. "A Short History of Empathy." The Reader's Digest: *The Atlantic*, October 15, 2015.

Ling, Trevor. *The Buddha, Buddhist Civilization in India and Ceylon*. Temple Smith, 1973.

Macnicol, Nicol. *Indian Theism*. Munshilal Banarsidas, 1915.

Murdoch, Iris. *The Sovereignty of Good*. Routledge, 1970.

Murty, Maruti Ram. *Indian Philosophy: An Introduction*. Broadview Press, 2013.

Neumann, Karl Eugen. *The Life of Buddha: According to the Legends of Ancient India*. Translated by V. A. and C. B. Arnold. Routledge & Kegan Paul, 1957.

Nicholls, Moira. "The Influences of Eastern Thought on Schopenhauer's Doctrine of the Thing-in-itself." In *The Cambridge Companion to Schopenhauer*, edited by Janaway. Cambridge University Press, 1999.

Nietzsche, Friedrich. *Beyond Good and Evil*. Translated by Helen Zimmern. George Allen & Unwin, 1967.

Patra, Sanjeev. "Technologies- Boon or Bane for the Sadhaks of Integral Yoga." Savitri, Kireet Joshi Books, 2018.

Plato. *Phaedo*. Translated by Benjamin Jowett. In *The Dialogues of Plato*. Encyclopaedia Britannica, 1952.

Plato. *The Last Days of Socrates*. Translated by Hugh Tredennick and Harold Tarrant. Penguin Books, 1993.

Prinz, Jesse. "Against Empathy." *Southern Journal of Philosophy* 49, no. 1 (2011): 214-233.

Radhakrishnan, Sarvepalli. *Indian Philosophy*. 2 vols. George Allen & Unwin, 1923.

Radhakrishnan, S., and Charles A. Moore. *A Source Book in Indian Philosophy*. Princeton University Press, 1989.

Rahula, Walpola. *What the Buddha Taught*. Revised and expanded edition. Grove Press, 1974.

Raj, R. Singh. "Bhakti as the Essence and Measure of Art." In *Frontiers of Trans-Culturality in Contemporary Aesthetics*, edited by G. Marchiani and R. Milani. Trauben, 2001.

Schopenhauer, Arthur. *The World as Will and Representation*. Translated by E. F. J. Payne. Dover Publications, 1969.

Sen, Amartya. *Identity and Violence*. Penguin Books, 2006.

Singh, B. J. *Sant Kabir*. Waris Shah Foundation, 2006.

Singh, R. Raj. "Gandhi and His Original Ontological Contemplation." In *Mahatama Gandhi: 125 Years*, edited by B. R. Nanda. Wiley Eastern, 1995.

Singh, R. Raj. *Bhakti and Philosophy*. Lexington Books, 2006.

Tagore, Rabindranath. *Angel of Surplus*. Visva-Bharti, 1978.

*The Adi Granth*. Translated by Ernest Trumpp. W. H. Allen, 1877.

The Buddha. *Majjhima-nikava*. In *Buddhism in Translations*. Translated by H. C. Warren. Harvard University Press, 1953.

The Buddha "Anguttara-nikaya." In *Buddhism in Translations,* translated by H. C. Warren. Harvard University Press, 1953.

The Buddha. *The Samyutta-nikaya.* In *A Sourcebook of Indian Philosophy*, edited by S. Radhakrishnan and C. A. Moore. Princeton University Press, 1973.

Warder, A. K. *Indian Buddhism.* Motilal Banarsidass Publishers, 1970.

Weil, Simone. *The Need for Roots: Prelude to a Declaration of Duties Towards Mankind.* Weil, Simone. *Waiting for God.* Translated by Emma Craufurd. Harper & Row, 1971.

Weil, Simone. *Cahiers: Notebooks of Simone Weil.* Translated by Arthur Wills. Routledge, 1956a.

Weil, Simone. *The Notebooks of Simone Weil.* Translated by Arthur Wills. G. P. Putnam's Sons, 1956b.

Weil, Simone. *Gravity and Grace.* Translated by Emma Crawford and Mario von der Ruhr. Routledge, 2002.

Weil, Simone. *Waiting for God.* Harper Perennial, 2009.

Williams, Paul. In *The Bodhicaryavatara*, translated by Kate Crosby and Andrew Skilton. Oxford University Press, 1995.